Problem Gods:

In Search of a Meaningful Deity

James J. Garber

Bäuu Institute and Press

1 2 3 4 5 6 7 8 9 10

Library of Congress Cataloging-in-Publication Data

Garber, James

Problem Gods: In Search of a Meaningful Deity /
by James Garber.
p. cm.
Includes bibliographic references and index.
ISBN 978-1-936955-05-3 (paperback : alk. paper)
1. Religion. 2. Philosophy 3. Theology

The paper in this book meets the guidelines for permanence and durability of the Committee on Production Guidelines for Book Longevity of the Council on Library Resources, Inc.

ACKNOWLEDGEMENTS

As always, I wish to thank my wife Rachel, for all the help and encouragement she has given me in the preparation of this book.

Also thanks to our daughters Ann and Clare for troubleshooting Microsoft Word whenever I was computer befuddled. Thanks, also, to Naomi Lichtenberg my PhD professor and advisor who provided constructive comments on several topics used in this book.

I want also to thank my theology professor Gerald Fitzgerald for his patience and assistance over the course of my master's in theology program.

DEDICATION

To Rachel and all our grandchildren: Jake, Ray, Angela, Hannah, Ava, Tshepo and Emmanuel.

TABLE OF CONTENTS

PREFACE

No one knows when the idea of God first emerged. As *Homo sapiens* evolved they undoubtedly began asking questions about the mysterious world that surrounded them. How did the world begin, who made it and what kept it going? All the joys and sorrows to which we humans are subjected cry out for a source. Someone or something had to be responsible for the world's wonders and woes. We know that the Sun has been adored as a divinity. The Moon, planets and stars have all been viewed as 'higher powers'. People believed these 'divine beings' offered answers for the myriad of persistent questions that have ravished our reason from time immemorial. Even today's religions provide answers that are frequently linked to nature. At some point the human mind reached beyond nature for explanations, Aristotle posited a soul and the unmoved mover. The supernatural realm was born and God, who was at first much like us humans, eventually evolved into a transcendental being that was above and beyond nature and us mere mortals.

As our knowledge of the Universe expanded so did our idea of God. This book attempts to use the current level of scientific knowledge to redefine God in keeping with our much more sophisticated understanding of the world around us. This process of making God equal to the awareness we have of our world is nothing new. The more we have come to know about nature, the greater is our concept of God. Each age has had a God defined by the level of human learning. As our understanding of the Universe progresses, will our image of God follow suit? This has indeed been the history of God. What is written here is one person's attempt to update God, to make our notion of the deity conform to modern science and our conception of the marvelous world in which we find ourselves. As a consequence, this modern God should be more worthy of our adoration, more marvelous, meaningful and reasonable. This 'higher power' ought to heighten our spiritual sensibilities but also provide a stimulus to search more energetically for a better understanding of nature. I believe that if we define a better God, our world will be a better place in which to live.

PART I: PROBLEM GODS

CHAPTER 1

IN THE BEGINNING

What is a Catholic Jew doing writing a book like this?[1] I was destined to be a Catholic even before being conceived. My mother was Catholic, and my father Jewish. There were about six or eight Jews in my hometown and my father was, I think, the only unmarried Jew among them. In those days, in order for my Catholic mother to marry my non-Catholic father and remain in the good graces of the Church, it was mandatory that my father sign a paper before their nuptials, promising to raise any children arising from this union as Roman Catholic. In due course, two sons were born under the terms of this agreement. The first was my brother Bob, who came into this world a tad early–two months 'early', though physiologically full term. I arrived on schedule, as predicted by our family practitioner, Dr. John Butzer.[2] The fact that my father ended up marrying my mother probably related to the 'conceptual haste' that characterized their relationship i.e. they 'had to get married'. Nonetheless, my father was a good man, a loving father and for the most part a good husband. Without doubt, my father kept his nuptial promises to raise Bob and me Catholic. I have only been in a Jewish synagogue four times, all for funerals or Bar Mitzvahs. In retrospect it would have been enlightening if my father had broken his promise on occasion to give us a taste of Judaism, or even taken us to the synagogue the two weekends a year he went there for Yom Kippur and Rosh Hashanah.

There was one minor problem when I was baptized. My parents wanted to name me James Jay Garber–the Jay having been the name of one

---

1   I am aware that unless my mother were Jewish I am not considered a Jew. However, studies show that Jews tend to have a relatively 'pure' Hebrew genome so, if nothing else, I'm a 50% ethnic Jew. My Y chromosome is 100% from my father. The female 'Jewish' mitochondrial DNA is not generally 'pure' whereas the male 'Jewish' Y chromosome is. In addition, 'Jewishness' up to about 200 B.C.E. was based on paternal inheritance. See *Before the Dawn* by Nicolas Wade.

2   Dr. John Butzer was kindly and sanguine–the perfect picture of a general practitioner–a physician esteemed in the community and one that I tried to emulate during my medical career.

of my father's relatives possibly his brother. It seemed a small concession to make since my father, having married a gentile, was never to see any of his relatives again. His marriage to a German Catholic was a breech of Jewish custom and my father, as a result, was considered dead to his family. The pastor, a forceful Jesuit, who baptized me, claimed Jay was not a Christian name and told my parents I had to be christened James Jacob after my grandfather, a tavern owner (and former chief of police). And so I became James Jacob Garber, at least on my baptismal certificate. It mattered little that James, Jay and Jacob are all etymological equivalents. I never used Jacob, although we gave our son David, Jacob as his middle name.

This middle name issue has always been a sore point with my wife, Rachel, who was never given a middle name. She claims her family was 'too poor' to afford one! I had three middle names, including my confirmation name, John. She remains envious over this unjust situation to the present day. She views James Jay Jacob John Garber as just too narcissistic.

Bob, my brother, and I both spent thirteen years in the Catholic parish schools and Bob four years at Catholic colleges. I managed only three years at a Catholic institution of higher learning, the University of St. Thomas, because (as I tell my incredulous adult children) in those days, if you were 'really smart', you could get into medical school after just three years of undergraduate studies.

Catholic grade and high schools were punctuated by daily classes in religion. We studied the old Baltimore Catechism all through grade school. In eighth grade I even entered the regional catechetical contest–having been 'volunteered' by my eighth grade teacher, Sister Mary Madeline. I lost in the first round to a smart young man who later earned his doctorate in sacred theology and became an honest-to-God theologian. He also beat me out academically in high school. He was valedictorian and I was salutatorian–not that I've ever been bitter about this!

In high school, we continued to study religion on a daily basis. I was elected treasurer of the Sodality–a movement devoted to the veneration of the Virgin Mary. We were supposed to meditate on the attributes of Mary for fifteen minutes every day–something I was never able to do–my meditations in those pubescent days didn't center on Mary but other young virgins I knew.

I can't remember ever questioning any of the tenets of the Catholic Church until many years later. Bob and I frequently argued with great intensity over theological issues, now long forgotten but no heretical views were voiced by either of us.

The greatest religious crisis I endured during my teens related to the time I was refused absolution in the confessional for being 'impure with myself". Fr. DeMuth asked me if I had ever confessed this sin before (after all I was a teenage boy of fifteen or so). When I said, "Yes", he proclaimed that I was obviously not penitent for this sin of the flesh and summarily ejected me from the confessional. This was a great blow to my hopes for sainthood not to mention the embarrassment when I had to tell Fr.Youngren, moments later what had happened. He said nothing demeaning, absolved me and I went off reassured for the moment, knowing that if I were to die then and there, Hell would not be my eternal destination. I still occasionally think of kindly Fr. Youngren, he was my favorite priest after that. In spite of this near excommunication, I would have been considered a 'good Catholic' for many years thereafter. I continued to go to church regularly for the next 50 years or so. I discontinued confessing my 'sins', however, around age 40–it just didn't seem necessary any more.

For over 35 years I was physician to Catholic clergy who were in treatment for chemical dependency, mostly alcoholism, at Guest House, where our family went to Mass weekly. The men at Guest House included seminarians, deacons, priests, monsignors, bishops and an occasional archbishop, I never saw a cardinal. This was a favorite part of my practice, in general, these clergy were good men though early on we saw several pedophiles. However, in time it became evident that these men were more pedophiles than alcoholics and untreatable.

My religious views changed only gradually over many years. Rachel and I married in 1962 and children began appearing on a yearly basis. We then decided it would be morally acceptable if Rachel took oral contraceptives, which she did for three years. We then had two more children and she agreed to have a tubal ligation. Both of these decisions (the oral contraceptives and tubal ligation) were contrary to Church teaching. However, it seemed prudent to limit the number of children mostly to provide emotionally and physically for our five children and give us respite as parents.

Seeing patients on a daily basis with their many problems–some physical but almost always mixed with psychological issues that needed attention–it was evident that making a medical diagnosis was not the most important thing I could do for my patients. Mostly they needed to be listened to about their problems. Religion was often very important to them. Sometimes they felt abandoned by God and their church. Catholics, especially young Catholics, were faced with reproductive issues for which the Church offered little help. In the 1980's, my wife and I did graduate studies in counseling. Later I taught listening skills for a local university. The more involved in counseling I became, the more evident it was that people with issues needed an empathic ear more than solutions for their problems. They didn't need to be told what to do; rather they sought sincere understanding by a fellow human. Telling them what they should or should not do by the church or its minister/priest/rabbi helped little. They were alone with their issues. Many were mad, sad or scared. Comfort not confrontation was the necessary remedy. They yearned for a humanistic healer not a dogmatic doctor or clergywo/man. This growing awareness began to overshadow the religious dogma that had been injected into my psyche by the nuns and priests of my youth. These religious and clergy were most important to me and were influential in many ways. Their efforts were almost always well-intentioned (though I wasn't so sure about Fr. DeMuth, who kicked me out of the confessional) and I'm thankful for their care and concern. For the most part they were very good people and I'm grateful to them for all they did for me. But the fact is, that our world is ever changing and new ideas–theological and secular–are necessary to cope with the evolving environment in which we find ourselves.

Over time Rachel and I gradually noticed that attending Mass didn't meet our spiritual needs. The homilies seemed less pertinent in our daily lives. The Vatican appeared to be less and less attuned to the spiritual and psychological needs of the majority of the Catholics we knew. We had been members of the Christian Family Movement (CFM) in the sixties and even then most of our friends showed signs of religious rebelliousness. The Catholic Church became more and more divided–conservatives versus liberals–and we drifted to the religious left. Five or so years ago, we stopped going to Mass. However, we maintained a belief in God and a sense of spirituality. Rachel listens to "Speaking of Faith"[3] each Sunday and I have begun a religious odyssey in an attempt to find a God that is meaningful and rational–a God I can believe in and with whom I can feel comfortable. In all honesty, the Catholic Church no longer seems credible. Having studied church history while following the various issues the Catholic Church has faced in recent years, it seems they have been and continue to be an isolated behemoth that lives to protect its position and power and has lost the message that Christ articulated so well in the short time he was on Earth. His was a message of true love. He loved sinners and the sick. He taught only one theological doctrine–love God and neighbor. The Catholic Church is not alone in its obsessive interest in theological trivia. In this regard, it and other religious traditions have often forgotten the needs of the faithful. The Inquisition was not the only Church institution to kill 'heretics'. Calvin was responsible for the death of Michael Servetus because he did not believe in the Trinity. Isaac Newton hid all his religious writings (he was also a Unitarian) for fear the same would happen to him. Religion has been criticized by many theologians

---

3	Tippett, K. 2007, *Speaking of Faith* (London: Viking). Her program is now called *On Being*.

and lay people over the last two millennia. Writers such as Richard Dawkins,[4] Sam Harris[5] and Christopher Hitchens[6] are well known today for their anti-religious polemics. The fact remains, however, that religion and spirituality have a role to play in the lives of the majority of people worldwide. Religion with all its failings should not be thrown out like the baby with the bath water. Rather religion as with everything else on Earth must change in order to survive.

I've always liked philosophy and I maintained an interest in it long after leaving the confines of St. Thomas. Continuing to take philosophy courses, I found that philosophy began to have new meaning for me. There was no one 'right' philosophical system. I took a year of metaphysics in college. This consisted of reading Aristotle's *Metaphysics* and Thomas Aquinas' *Commentary on the Metaphysics*. Our professor, R. A. Kocourik, translated the *Commentary* from Latin to English as he lectured, a feat by which I am still impressed. Many years later, I enrolled in a metaphysics class at the University of Minnesota (the nuns had told me this was an atheistic stronghold–a remonstration I chose to ignore). We read Robert Nozick[7] and studied logical linguistics. You wouldn't have known the two metaphysics courses were remotely related. What had been so obvious in college now became confused and disorienting. For the second metaphysics course I wrote a paper on the concept of identity, based on current neuroscience. My professor liked it but the paper was soundly criticized and rejected for publication by a philosophy journal to which it was submitted. I was crushed but also enlightened by the experience.

I came to believe that philosophy was of more use as a history of humankind's attempt to understand the world and *Homo sapiens* rather than an effort to define 'truth'. It is not an exact science. Philosophy is also involved in a search for God or some cosmic force that could help us in pursuing self and Universe.

Ignorance is sometimes a great motivator. Unfortunately, ignorance can also be a place to hide for some. We shall see how the love of ignorance enters into the search for a rational, meaningful God.

In due course, I found myself in a graduate program in astronomy.

---

4   Dawkins, R. 2008, *The God Delusion* (New York: Mainer Books).

5   Harris, Sam, 2006, *Letter to a Christian Nation* (New York: Alfred A. Knopf).

6   Hitchens, C. 2007, *God is Not Great* (New York: Hachette Book Group).

7   Nozick, R. 1981, *Philosophical Explanations* (Cambridge, MA.: Bellican, Harvard University Press).

I'm truly an inveterate learner.[8] Astronomy had been a long time interest and this seemed a good way to pass a few years of academic time. Astronomy also helped me in my search for a sensible definition of God. Not only was the immensity and endless marvels of the heavens mind expanding but in addition relativity and quantum physics seemed to raise and sometimes answer a host of questions about both the macrocosm (the Universe) and the microcosm (we humans). Newton and Laplace gave us a deterministic world. Quantum theory gave us back a world in which God did indeed play dice. In spite of Einstein's protests, God was after all, a gambling God. This was a 'good news, bad news' trade off. Relativity took away absolutes but quantum mechanics gave us back free will. Ethicists generally love absolutes. The rules for an ethical life are a lot easier to follow if we have moral absolutes. But if there are absolutes, the world is deterministic and free will is out. With uncertainty (Heisenberg's Uncertainty Principle) free will is in but the rules of right and wrong are much more complex and difficult to define–they vary depending on the time, place and circumstances in which a moral decision is made. This was heresy 500 years ago and many theologians still think it is high religious treason today.

Philosophy and astrophysics seemed to be (for me at least) a valuable but 'odd couple' in my attempt to understand humans and the heavens and, indeed, in making sense of the divine. Thus, it is with this background that I begin my journey to find the theological Holy Grail: Who is God and what is IT all about? What follows is an analysis of the gods of history and the monotheistic God of Judaism, Christianity and Islam. We have had many hundreds of gods[9] but they can be reduced to a handful of divine types. These divine types will be listed, analyzed and their deficiencies catalogued. Some aspects of past and present religions will also be discussed for the benefits they offer and the deficiencies they contain. We will also look at what science, especially relativity and quantum theory, can tell us about God and finally propose a Neo-Naturalistic definition of God with ITs pluses and minuses. Neo-Naturalism will be explained fully later but for the moment suffice it to say that this is a system that is based on the mysterious Universe in which we live rather than the Bible, tradition or a system of supernatural beings. It could be labeled a natural theology.

---

8   Inveterate means to persist but also has the connotation of growing old. I can relate to both. I now have two bachelor degrees, three master's (counseling, astronomy and theology), a PhD in humanities and my MD. I may do a master's in art history if I live long enough.

9   Jordan, M. 1993, *Encyclopedia of Gods: Over 2,500 Deities of the World* (New York: Facts On File Inc.).

After I had completed this book, for all intents and purposes, based on my prior studies, it was my always-perceptive wife Rachel, who said to me one day, "As long as you are writing a book on theology, you ought to know something about theology"! As a consequence I've spent the last eighteen months getting a master's degree in theology. In fact, I have just finished the final exam of my final course, The Problem of Evil. I'm now revamping this book and think it will be better for the theology I've so recently studied.

CHAPTER 2

GOD AND PROBLEM GODS

Whether a parent or not you know about the problem child, Dennis the Menace, who is forever getting into trouble, causing problems at home, school or the super market. For theologians the God of Theism is a problem child or, more accurately IT is a problem God just like Dennis only on a bigger scale. Maybe IT should be labeled 'Dennis the Problem Deity'. The traditional definition of God involves an endless array of inconsistencies and contradictions. In addition to the doctrinal difficulties, so long associated with the gods of history, there are the legal, social and political problems, including oppression, persecutions and wars carried out in the name of these gods. The ancient gods were horrific problems for the Greeks. They were forever squabbling among themselves. The ten-year long Trojan War of Homer's *Iliad* was, in part, over which Olympic goddess was the most beautiful. Of course, Helen had no small part in Troy's troubles. These gods continually bothered humans. Zeus was a womanizer of the worst sort. He makes Tiger Woods look like a rank amateur rake. The gods were given to blowing ships off course, marooning sailors on far-away islands, turning them into pigs and harassing them in a host of other ways. Just looking at Medusa's head could turn one to stone. They were jealous, ornery and oversexed.

The monotheistic God of the Old Testament (OT) assumed some of these same unsavory qualities. The New Testament (NT) God was somewhat better. IT became less like we emotionally fickle humans (less anthropomorphic) and developed more metaphysical characteristics. The NT God, as interpreted by Thomas Aquinas, was almighty i.e. omnipotent and could accomplish anything including creating the Universe out of nothing (*ex nihilo*). The Greek gods hadn't created everything; they just organized what chaotic soup was around. They ordered the Earth and the heavens and created men and women. Often they played favorites for sexual or other reasons. But the NT God was not only all-powerful (omnipotent) but IT was also all-knowing (omniscient) eternal, having no beginning and no end. IT was infinite i.e. unbounded and unlimited in all respects. The NT God was also all-perfect and all-good. This is the classic metaphysical

God of Theism. But this NT God also was in many ways anthropomorphic because IT had human qualities like feelings such as love. This NT God is also personal and providential, that is, IT knows all our wants and needs and responds to our prayers (sometimes) when we ask God for some favor. The theistic God is capable of anything and everything. IT can do the big things like creating this vast Universe of ours and at the same time helps us find our lost car keys. In this chapter, we shall deal with Dennis the Problem Deity, the ultimate doctrinal problem child. Thus, the theistic God, the God of traditional religion is both anthropomorphic and metaphysical. IT is part human and part divine. IT can do all the little things like love each one of us like a father (or mother) and all the big things like creating everything with a single divine word. The theistic God is an all-purpose God.

We all believe in a higher power. The only separation between a theist and an atheist is how s/he defines that power. We all (save a few psychotics) know that there is something greater than we are. For many it is a theistic God as classically defined by the three monotheistic religions of Judaism, Christianity and Islam. For the atheist this higher power is the material Universe. And, of course, whether one is willing to use the term God or simply 'Nature' in referring to this power, it matters little; there is still some kind of higher power all of us must accept. Everyone knows instinctively that s/he is not the biggest and best 'being' in the Universe. As the kindly priest in the movie, *Rudy,* says, "I know two things for sure; there is a God and I am not he". The atheist might say, "I know there is a higher power and I am not IT.

The label 'higher power' is open-ended and only implies that there is something greater than any human being. Most would agree that there is something, someone or some force 'out there' or 'in here' that we don't entirely comprehend. There are a number of ways that this 'entity' has been defined. We shall begin by looking at the various divine types but first let us deal with a housekeeping issue that came up briefly in the last chapter.

IT

Throughout this book when using a pronoun in referring to God, I shall use the impersonal pronoun, IT. Hopefully this will not be too disconcerting for the reader. I intend no disrespect to God or those who prefer the masculine pronoun he or He. We know so little about God and to assign a gender to IT is presumptuous and certainly chauvinistic. IT is gender neutral and I use upper case letters to emphasize the special nature of God or the higher power. IT may stand for Ill-defined *Theos* (Greek for the divine being), Illustrious *Theos,* Infinite *Theos* or Ineffable *Theos.* There is any number of epithets one might devise. This pronoun at least takes us out of the age-old stereotypical image of God. IT is neither anthropomorphic, creative nor any of the other depictions of God that have been applied to IT over the centuries. This pronoun leaves open the definition of God–a definition that is to be developed as we proceed. One of the other problems with our 'Problem God' is the very word God. Use this word with an atheist and the conversation is over, it presses too many negative buttons. The word immediately raises the specter of the theist's traditional divine being. It is likely that as long as one uses the label, 'God', no meaningful theological dialogue will follow between a theist, a deist and an agnostic or atheist. It is difficult to find an acceptable verbal compromise and for better or worse, I shall very often use 'God', 'gods' or IT when referring to the higher power I am trying to define in this book.

THE ANTHROPOMORPHIC GOD

The Anthropomorphic God (AG) is the most problematic of all the problem gods. IT has been responsible for most of the theological battles waged over the past two millennia. It is hard to get away from a humanoid God. Feuerbach (1804-1872) expressed it this way:

> We cannot conceive of God otherwise than by contributing to Him without limit all the real qualities that we find in ourselves.[1]

Even Paul Davies, a well-respected writer on science and religion, speaks of *The Mind of God*.[2] I had thought the original title of this book might be, "Does God Have a Mind?" This would have emphasized the idea that we are in love with the anthropomorphic image of God. Many of us are emotionally tied to a loving, fatherly deity that always takes care of us. We find comfort in the image of someone to whom we can go for love and solace when nobody else seems interested in us.

The fact is that there are areas of the brain that light up when we 'feel the presence of God". There is a 'warm and fuzzy' feeling associated with the idea of God. Mystics, monks and nuns feel close to God when they pray or meditate,[3]. Such religious experiences allow humans to feel comforted and they have a sense that they are no longer alone. The fact is that the majority of humans 'experience' God in this way sometime during their lives. Does this prove there is a 'real' God 'out there' some place? No, but this sense of

---

1   Feuerbach, L. 1989, *The Essence of Christianity* (Buffalo, NY: Prometheus) p. 40.

2   Davies, P. 1993, *The Mind of God* (NewYork: Simon & Schuster).

3   Newberg, A. 2007, *God and the Brain* (Louisville, CO: Sounds True).

God speaks to a deep-seated human need that helps support many people psychologically and/or spiritually. We will discuss the concept of spirituality later.

There are a number of difficulties that emerge when analyzing the AG. For one thing, God cannot be anthropomorphic; IT cannot have a mind like ours. God as supernatural and immaterial, as defined by the theists cannot have humanoid characteristics. God has traditionally been anthropomorphic, because this is what we, as humans, have wanted IT to be. We want to be God-like. A God made in our image and likeness (rather than the other way around as the Bible says)[4]. This is human egoism in its ultimate form. If we are like God, we are, as a consequence, greater, more perfect and more intelligent than we actually are. We must be a cut above all lower animals. If we were cattle we would see God as 'bovino-morphic; if dogs, as canino-morphic and so on. The AG is a comfortable concept. The AG is not only easy to grasp but is emotionally appealing.

Unfortunately, the AG creates more problems than IT solves. The AG, without any metaphysical qualities lacks the where-with-all to create the Universe and keep it in existence. It's a big job to do all the things the classic theistic God must do. If God were simply an AG, IT could not fill the job description required of IT. To do all the things we demand of God requires that IT be omnipotent, omniscient, perfectly good, infinite and eternal. But as we will see next, the AG, as typified in the Greek polytheistic pantheon can't cut the divine mustard.

One of the reasons we as humans favor an AG is because all we know, all we can conceive of, is anthropomorphic. We, of course, are aware of lower forms of life but to have a bovino-morphic God would be illogical. Humans are the highest form of life with which we are familiar. Obviously we seek after a God that is great and good and a human template of God is the best we can intuitively manage. In order to come any where near to a deity that is rational and workable within the framework of our known Universe, we must, as they say today, look outside the box i.e. the anthropomorphic box.

THE METAPHYSICAL GOD

Metaphysics has always been a bit of a mystery. When Aristotle's students first penned his lectures into book form, they didn't know what to call the subject that Aristotle covered after his *Physics*, so they called it 'after physics' or using the Greek, *Metaphysics*. When discussing a Metaphysical

---

4   Genesis, 1:26.

God (MG) one might expect a lot of abstruse, abstract verbiage and this is just what we find.[5]

The MG is important in understanding the monotheistic God of Judaism, Christianity and Islam. Monotheism emerged during the millennium before Christ. The God of the Jews is a hybrid–part anthropomorphic and part metaphysical. As part metaphysical, IT is also transcendent, that is, above and beyond the world of human experience. More will be said about the Transcendent God (TG) later.

Metaphysics, with its many rational but non-empirical concepts, is considered by many to be outdated as a field of philosophy. Logical Positivists believe that the only knowable things are those that are empirically verifiable by the five senses. The positivists from August Comte (1798-1857) onward, saw science as the only way to determine 'truth'. Comte was not the first to deny the validity of metaphysics. Both David Hume (1718 -1776) and Immanuel Kant (1724-1804) had questioned metaphysical notions. Their 'radical', even heretical, beliefs about the MG were 'children of the Enlightenment'. Some authors, such as J. F. Hurst (1834-1903), called these philosophers "Rationalists" insisting that they relied too heavily on reason and natural theology.[6]

The MG is characterized by a series of abstract concepts. IT is infinite having no limits or boundaries in space or time. In fact, the MG cannot exist in space or time. Only material beings live in the world of space-time.[7] Supernatural beings, such as the traditional God of monotheism, cannot be so confined. For one thing, the MG, as supernatural (above and beyond nature) is entirely immaterial. IT 'resides' in the supernatural, non-material realm. The very idea that God 'resides' anywhere is an anthropomorphism that cannot apply to the MG. IT is non-spatial and non-temporal, God is nowhere! The idea of God being in Heaven, that is, somewhere 'out there' in the sky, is a contradiction of terms. The concept of God existing 'anywhere' is an oxymoron. The MG and the idea of position in space are mutually exclusive. Further, the theistic God (see below) has to be infinite, for IT is by definition, not limited in any way. God has to be bigger, greater and stronger than anything else in the Universe–our Universe and any other universes there may be. Additionally, the MG must be all-perfect, all-good, all-powerful (omnipotent), all-knowing (omniscient), eternal, omnipresent

---

5   Metaphysical thought is that which is based on speculative and abstract reasoning. It is characterized as highly abstract, theoretical, abstruse and immaterial in nature.

6   Hurst, J. F. 2010, *History of Rationalism; Embracing a Survey of the Present State of Theology* (Charleston, SC: Forgotten Books). First published in the early nineteenth century.

7   Space-time is a concept that was developed within Einstein's Special Theory of Relativity in 1905. Our Universe is four-dimensional with width, breadth, depth and time.

(everywhere) and as mentioned earlier, infinite. If God were anything less than this, IT would not be God, at least not a MG or theistic God. Metaphysical qualities are not easy to define and are essentially incomprehensible. Some metaphysical terms seem, at first glance, to be everyday, commonplace concepts that many know and accept without question. However, with further consideration these concepts are counterintuitive. With common usage they assume a certain familiarity that prompts an 'Oh, yah, I know what that means' response but, in fact, when pressed, most would not be able to explain infinity or any other metaphysical abstractions.

The notion of infinity is a good example of a metaphysical concept that tests our imagination and intellect. The concept of infinity has a long history. Aristotle did not believe there was such a thing as infinity. Centuries later the story is told of Rabbi Akiva (c. 50-125 C.E.) who, along with three other rabbis contemplated, among other things, the idea of infinity.[8] One rabbi died, one lost his faith and one ended up psychotic. Only Rabbi Akiva came through unscathed.

George Cantor (1845-1918) was the most successful mathematician of infinity. Even he, however, spent much of his life in an asylum for the insane. One of the ideas that may have driven him mad involved what he called 'set theory'. He reasoned that the set of numbers, 1, 2, 3...ad infinitum is the same size, or equivalent to the set of all *even* numbers, 2, 4, 6...ad infinitum. Both sets of numbers are infinite and exactly equivalent. He demonstrated this mathematically but how can this be? The set of all even numbers should be half the size of all whole numbers! Similarly, we cannot imagine infinite space, time or kumquats. In fact I can't imagine even one kumquat, having never seen one.[9] Infinity is a little like a kumquat; if you've never seen infinity you can't envision it. No one has ever seen infinity so it is an unimaginable concept.[10] Trying to comprehend such conundrums is mind-boggling. Metaphysics may mean one thing to one philosopher and something else to another as we have already seen–Aristotelian metaphysics and the analytic philosopher's view of this subject differ substantially.

Another aspect of the MG is that it cannot be influenced, affected, contacted or moved in any way by any being. IT is immutable, that is, unchangeable. If IT could be impacted by any outside object or force, IT

---

8   Aczel, A. D. 2001, *The Mystery of the Aleph: Mathematics, the Kabbalah, and the Search for Infinity* (New York: Packet Books) p. 26.
9   Kumquat: Any of several trees or shrubs of the genus, *Fortunella*, having a small, edible, orange-like fruit.
10   Mathematicians can work with infinity. For example, $\infty/0$ = indeterminate, whereas $0/\infty=0$. ∞ is the symbol for infinity. To truly understand either of these equations is admittedly difficult.

would not be the one and only infinite MG. As defined, there can be only one MG. To be influenced in any way, would imply limitations; something not allowed in an infinite entity. IT would be less than a MG. IT would be limited, confined, restrained or in some way restricted—none of these is possible without destroying the MG's divine integrity.

Any anthropomorphic characteristics applied to the MG are logically impossible for the same reasons. Either God is God or IT is simply another mythological character out of Ovid's *Metamorphosis*.

All this means that the MG cannot be a benevolent, providential, merciful (or for that matter angry, vengeful or jealous) deity. Either IT is an aloof, distant, unemotional, 'hands-off' God or IT is less than perfect, less than omnipotent and omniscient. Note that all these epithets are anthropomorphisms. Even labeling God as a 'being' is considered by some philosophers and theologians as inappropriate. 'Being' is an ontological concept (relating to the nature of being itself). Since all our knowledge of things is based strictly on sense perception, God, as a spirit is insensible and cannot be known through the five senses. Some sects such as the Gnostics or thinkers such as the nineteenth century theologian, Schleiermacher (1768-1834), believed we have an innate intuition of God. If it is true, however, that all knowledge comes through our five senses, then, we cannot know the MG. Also, even if we have an intuition of God, how is this intuition presented to our imagination since we are limited to knowledge based on the five senses? We might be able to 'feel' God as the mystics claim but we cannot imagine God, describe IT or communicate the notion of God to a fellow human being. In the final analysis, knowledge of God, even if *a priori* and not derived from the senses cannot be communicated to anyone else. We cannot talk about God because all communication is through the senses. Also, since God is insensible, none of ITs characteristics is communicable– we are unable to talk about insensible ideas. Metaphysical terms, as we have seen, are meaningless unless converted into anthropomorphisms. But anthropomorphisms are not applicable to the MG as discussed above.

We are four-dimensional creatures–living in space-time. This is the only world we know–the only context within which we can operate. Since the MG is not a space-time entity, we cannot know IT. However, God must be metaphysical in order to do the fantastic things we expect of IT. Nonetheless, as metaphysical, God is unknowable by humans. Anything we posit about the MG is pure unverifiable speculation.

On the other hand, God needs to be anthropomorphic in order to fulfill our psychological needs to be loved and cared for. We all require some kind of security blanket or teddy bear. This warm and fuzzy God has to be an AG in order for us to sin, gain Heaven or go to Hell. A MG is totally deterministic. ITs world would run like a precision clock. Free will, chance and probability are, thus, impossible with the MG. The God-man, Christ, who died on the cross to save us all, is anthropomorphic by necessity. Christ had to be fully human to fill his job description. This is why traditional religions need, indeed, demand a hybrid God–both anthropomorphic and metaphysical, even though this God is illogical, irrational and for many intellectually unacceptable.

If I am to believe in a God at all, IT has to make sense and not just fulfill human needs and wants, As a AG/MG hybrid, God is replete with contradictions. This God is infinite and limited, all-perfect and yet flawed, personal and providential while utterly divorced from all ITs creations. The God with which many of us were raised and believe in is an AG/MG hybrid– at one and the same time connected to us and totally divorced from all of us. We shall look at this God next.

THE THEIST'S ALL-PURPOSE GOD

The classic AG/MG is the God of Theism. For the theist the higher power is eternal, exists within our time and space, has created all things and keeps everything in existence at every moment. This God watches over all creatures with fatherly care. IT is personal and providential. IT is personally interested and involved in our every thought and deed and is willing to intervene on our behalf, if requested to do so by prayer or sacrifice. For many theists, IT made Heaven and Earth in six days and, like any hard-working artisan, rested on the seventh day. The theist's God is often depicted as a fatherly figure with a long, white beard, sitting on a throne, scepter in hand and surrounded by humanoid angels. IT has many of the feelings and behaviors of humans. In addition to being like humans, IT also possesses many abstract qualities that transcend humankind. This partially MG is all-powerful (omnipotent), all-knowing (omniscient), infinite, perfectly good and eternal, having always existed and will exist forever into the future. This God is a logical disaster, full of inconsistencies and contradictions. IT's like Santa Claus. There's no way that Santa Claus can possibly get down all those chimneys throughout the world in one night. And what about the houses that have no chimneys! Likewise there is no being that can do all we ask of God. Thus, the AG/MG is all-purpose. IT can do everything we humans would like it to do. Unfortunately, such a God fails the test of reason. IT meets all our emotional needs but does so only by logical contradictions that make IT an impossible being. The theist will say that God can do anything even internally irrational acts. On the other hand, God as defined must be unequivocally rational and consistent otherwise IT is logically flawed–something God cannot be. God by definition is utterly perfect!

THE DEIST'S STARTER GOD

The deist's God is a Creative God (CG) who has made everything including the physical laws that keep the Universe running smoothly. This system allows God, once having made everything from nothing, to sit back and take it easy ever thereafter.[11] The physical laws take care of things once the Universe has been created. The CG is not necessarily anthropomorphic and since this God has a 'hands-off' policy (forgive this anthropomorphism, they are very hard to avoid), the CG is neither fatherly nor providential and in the deist's system we humans most likely don't have free will to guide our moral behaviors because natural laws determine all that happens to us and the rest of the Universe. The issue of morality will be discussed more fully later on.

According to the deist the concept and proof of this God can be arrived at by reason and the evidence of Nature. Natural Theology is a valid discipline for the deist. Our experience of nature allows us to prove the reality of God. This CG was a consequence of the Enlightenment when science first began to ferret out the mysteries of the Universe following the work of Copernicus, Galileo, Newton and others. The CG is mostly metaphysical, nonetheless, IT is the universal creative force and as such performs some initial 'hands-on' work in setting up Nature and its laws. IT is still problematic, however. In order for the CG to act as the ultimate creator IT has to be omnipotent, omniscient, infinite and eternal. This means it is essentially metaphysical. On the other hand, IT is a 'hands-on' creator so it must be in this respect anthropomorphic. Again, God cannot be infinite and interactive. The latter requires boundaries, which in turn preclude being infinite. An infinite being cannot have boundaries–no boundaries, no interactions with other beings. As discussed earlier the MG and AG are mutually and logically exclusive.

SOME OTHER PROBLEM GODS

We have seen the AG and MG, the former is much like us humans with all our failure and foibles: IT loves, hates, becomes angry, is prone to vindictiveness, jealousies and other humanoid imperfections. Here my wife would say, "That's why IT's considered male". The MG is far from human. IT

11   Note that whenever God rests on Sunday or lives forever into the future or sits back and just watches things as they go merrily along, all these are temporal anthropomorphisms and cannot logically apply to a MG.

is, as we have seen, infinite, eternal, etc. In other words, IT is the ultimate being with no defects. The theist's God is a hybrid of the AG and MG. There are other variations on these divine types that have been devised over the centuries.

The Gnostics, an early Christian sect, believed that the higher power was a Transcendental God (TG), that is, a power totally beyond the spiritual or physical reach of humans. IT was outside the world in which humans live, the TG did not create the Universe, live within it or contact any of the beings on Earth or anywhere else. The TG worked only through intermediaries–for some Gnostics this was Sophia or some other lesser divinity. It was she who created the world and maintained it. She was responsible for all evil in the world. Obviously God couldn't be tagged as the source of evil–IT is perfectly good. This avoided the uncomfortable issue of directly attributing evil to God; this is the so-called 'Problem of Evil'. All interactions with the TG are through Sophia, a kind of Platonic demiurge or in today's terminology a 'super' archangel. She acted as an intermediary between God and us humans relaying prayers to God and, in turn, passing any gifts to us that the TG granted as a result of our prayers. The Gnostic God was not totally transcendent, however, for there was said to be a 'bit' of God, the '*gnosis*', present within each of us that provides an intuitive sense of God and ITs spiritual truth. It was through this *gnosis* that one could 'know' this TG even though by definition this should not be possible. There are those who claim to be Gnostics even today, although the sect for the most part died out around the third century C.E. Considered to be a type of heterodox (heretical) Christianity, the various brands of Gnosticism were replaced over time by orthodox (true) Christianity.

Plato (427-347 B.C.E.) introduced the idea of divine intermediates. It was he who proposed that the stars and planets were divine beings that did God's bidding, allowing IT to remain truly transcendent. Plato posited Forms or Ideas such as the Good, Justice, Beauty and the like, that were the only true or 'real' objects in our world. These Forms existed 'out there' someplace but were more 'real' than physical objects of our material world. Everything in our world was only a flawed copy of these Forms. Everything known by sense perception is merely a shadowy replica of a 'real' Form. So what we know as good, just or beautiful is but an incomplete representation of its Form. As a result, sense perception is capable of providing only an incomplete and imperfect image of reality. The five senses are not to be trusted. Only reason can yield truth through awareness of the Forms.

In the Christian era, Platonism evolved into Neo-Platonism, through the writings of Plotinus (205-270 C.E.) its founder. Later Augustine of Hippo (354-430 C.E.) applied Neo-Platonism to Christian theology. The divine stars and planets, according to Augustine, were angels that acted as intermediate messengers for God (angel is from the Greek for messenger). Throughout this theological transition, the Christian God maintained a certain transcendence along with ITs anthropomorphic features. IT was both a TG and an AG. As such, the idea of God became the oxymoron that influences theology even today.

The MG is much like the TG but is not always totally disconnected from creation. The two are difficult to separate except logically. Nonetheless, many of the logical inconsistencies that apply to the MG also apply to the TG.

THE FICKLE POLYTHEISTIC GODS

Polytheism was one of the earliest forms of religion. E. B. Tylor and J. G. Frazer in the last century suggested that Animism was the first, primitive religion.[12] Animists believe that individual spirits inhabit all natural objects, such as trees, rivers, the wind and, of course, humans. Thus providing a 'vital principle' that makes all creatures 'function', as the name implies, 'spirits' animate all of nature. The seas, as one example, are alive and might cause humans much grief, or if so inclined provide safe passage to far-away lands. The seas later on in Greek mythology were under the control of Poseidon or Neptune. Thus, it was that in time a pantheon of gods came to populate the mythological, religious world of the Sumerians, Babylonians, ancient Egyptians, Greeks and Romans along with Hindus past and present. The Polytheistic Gods (PolG) were heir to the animists' spirits but fully anthropomorphic, functioning as humans do, only they were bigger and better than humans.

The various PolG performed a variety of tasks. Besides Poseidon and Pluto there was Hades who ruled over the underworld–the Greek version of Hell. Apollo was the Sun god and drove his sun chariot through the sky each day. He was also god of medicine and music. His son was Asclepius, better know to us as the god of medicine. Demeter managed the crops, Hermes (Mercury) was messenger for the Olympian gods. Aphrodite (Venus) was, of course, goddess of love, Diana was the goddess of the hunt and so on.

Christianity adopted some of this polytheism in the angels and saints who have been assigned certain earthly tasks. There are guardian angels that watch over each individual human. Angels administered to Christ in the desert after he fasted for forty days (Matt 4:11; Mark1: 13). Archangel Gabriel was the messenger that informed Mary she would be the mother of Christ

---

12   Pals, D. L. 1996, *Seven Theories of Religion* (New York: Oxford University Press) pp. 16-53.

(Luke 1:26-38). And of course, the persons of the Trinity have certain tasks as Creator, Savior and Sanctifier. Mary has a variety of roles and reaches nearly divine status though she is not considered to be a god or demigod. Similarly the angels and saints are not divine in Christian theology. I was never sure whether angels were male or female. As a teenager I wanted my personal guardian angel to be a very glamorous female. Polytheism is still around in Christianity in one form or another depending on how one interprets the status of saints, angels or the Trinity. The Roman Church denies that these are polytheistic in any sense.

The problem with Polytheism is that these gods are fully AG's and suffer from the same logical defects that have been discussed earlier. They may be bigger and better than humans but they may also be jealous, vindictive, fickle or immoral as are we humans. Obviously, as the ultimate anthropomorphs they are not capable of all the deeds required of a universal higher power. They are bigger and better but not nearly enough to accomplish what the job demands.

THE MYSTICAL GOD

Our next deity is the mystic's God (MysG), which is ill-defined with no discernable features. The MysG can only be experienced; IT cannot be described or defined. The MysG communicates with the mystic through an individual, personal and mysterious process known only to the mystic and is entirely ineffable, that is, words cannot describe IT. This God can only be felt. Mystics speak of feeling the presence of God during the mystical state. In a way, the MysG is the most believable deity though not one that can be explained to anyone else, save possibly another mystic. IT is personal and individual, ITs ineffability is its major drawback. This ineffability is also its greatest strength, for some theologians believe the only 'proof' for the existence of God is found in this divine mystical experience. The mystic simply 'knows' there is a God because IT is present during the mystical state. IT is real and united with the mystic at these times. There is no question of God's existence, a mystic will tell you; IT is as real to them, if not more so, than anything one can experience through the five senses. Many fundamentalists will feel this same awareness of God. God is present with them as truly as any sense experience can be.

Gnosticism, with its *gnosis* within each person, prefigured the MysG. In the nineteenth century Schleiermacher posited an internal intuition of God that was similar to the *gnosis*[13]. As we shall see later in more detail, there are areas of the brain that are active when feeling the presence of God.

---

13   Cross, G, 1911, *The Theology of Schleiermacher* (Kindle Books).

The MysG is second only to the AG in its impact on monotheistic religions, past and present. All three monotheisms have mystical sects–Kabbalah for the Jews, Christian mystics and Islamic Sufis.

THE PROBLEM WITH PROBLEM GODS

In order for God to do all the things we require, especially of the theistic God, IT has to be able to do anything and everything. God's duties require that IT be able to create our vast Universe out of nothing and keep it going. The MG manages every aspect of the Universe from subatomic particles to huge, energetic swirling galaxies. IT has to know our every thought and deed. IT must be aware of our comings and goings along with those of every creature in the Universe from the lowliest bacterium to the most complex self-conscious human. And there are trillions of living and non-living creations on our small planet alone. This task is indeed gargantuan, no wonder God had to rest on the seventh day. This is, of course, one of these unfortunate anthropomorphisms that we humans slip into so easily when speaking of God. Having created this unimaginably huge and complex Universe, God can, of course, never rest, at least according to the theists. IT has to be acting every moment to keep everything in existence. If IT were not active continuously, the Universe would suddenly disappear. So all these tasks make it necessary that God be metaphysical. These qualities are, however, purely speculative features of God–we cannot comprehend any of them and they are not empirically verifiable. As metaphysical and transcendent, God is unknowable through empirical science and defies reason.

The theist's God is full of contradictions. IT is spiritual and not material yet has created and maintains the entire physical Universe. This God cannot be material yet is everywhere in space and time. By their very nature, spirits do not exist in space or time. God is inextricably bound to the spiritual realm yet we want IT to be mysteriously capable of acting in and on material things. But how can a spirit be interactive with matter? Their very nature precludes such connections. This is the essential problem of the mind–body dichotomy that to this day is unexplained. How can the spiritual, which is beyond space and time, connect with matter that resides entirely within a four-dimensional, temporal domain (space-time)? Further, how can the infinite coexist with the finite? The infinite leaves no 'room' for the finite. How can a Transcendental God be immanent yet totally aloof while comforting us and drying our tears? The two domains cannot hold hands; the spirit has no hands, the material has hands but cannot touch a spirit. There is an unbridgeable abyss between these two worlds. One can know the MG only through reason and revelation yet both of these have failed us so often when it comes to knowing God.[14] In sum, the theist's God is magical but not truly meaningful. IT offers solutions but no explanations. If God is rational, so too must be ITs Universe. Nature though complex and often quizzical, offers the promise of being knowable. We have so many perfectly good scientific answers to what were total enigmas just a century ago. Every day we learn more about our world, and we need to define a God that is consistent with the rational workings of the world. We can do better than just settling for a magical God.

THE AGNOSTIC'S GOD

The agnostic's God (AgG) is more difficult to talk about because the agnostic doesn't know what to believe about God. Does IT really exist and if so, what is ITs nature? Is IT anthropomorphic, metaphysical, hands-on or hands-off, providential, creative or does IT simply watch an uncreated, eternal world move merrily along an uncharted path? Did IT give us free will, what happens to us after we die, is the Universe simply a physical machine as the atheistic materialists claim? These are all unanswered questions for the agnostic. Of course, the agnostic can ignore all these issues and live in the here and now, oblivious to any spiritual or religious concerns. Even if willing to ignore all these puzzling questions the agnostic knows in his or her heart that there has to be something in this vast Universe more powerful than s/he. What that power is, remains for the agnostic unknowable. Who is to say s/he isn't right, at least for the agnostic there are no contradictions. The Universe may be all there is. Their higher power, as for the atheist, may be the Universe itself and nothing more. With all the religious debates and unanswered and unanswerable theological questions maybe the best way is to do as the agnostic does and simply move on to disciplines in which there are resolvable issues.

THE ATHEIST'S GOD

And then there is the atheist's higher power; this God is no God (NG). As we have seen, all the Gods so far are impossible concepts. The NG is still a Problem God, however, for when one speaks of God, this conjures up an image that is too biblical, anthropomorphic, providential, creative or metaphysical. For the atheist the NG is the vast Universe, there is matter and physical laws and nothing more. Why not make the material Universe the end-all and be-all of existence? Do we really need anything more? Why

---

14   Op. cit. Ehrman, B. D. 2005.

not simply use an updated version of Democritus' 'atoms' to explain the world? Democritus (c. 460-c.370 B.C.E.) was a Greek natural philosopher–one of the first atomists. He believed the world was composed of an infinite number of atoms that moved ceaselessly through the 'void', that is, the empty space between atoms. For the atomists, there were only atoms of varying shapes that moved randomly in a vacuum. The world was mechanistic and deterministic. No one had made the void or the atoms. Matter, for the atomists, was uncreated, in constant motion and eternal. There need be nothing more to explain the Universe.

Dialectical materialism is the description that was applied to Atheism by Karl Marx.[15] (1818-1883). For him, this construct applied not only to his view of the world as a whole but specifically to economic forces in society. In Marx's system, two opposing or contradictory forces (the proletariat and bourgeoisie) meet head-on, culminating in a communistic, atheistic society. The world was a Hegelian dialectic with a thesis, antithesis and synthesis. In Marx's view the workers and capitalists are the thesis and antithesis; Communism is its synthesis. At bottom, our world can only be understood through reason and the five senses. The spirit or supernatural play no role in Marx's scheme. The only reality is matter and its laws. His was the ultimate atheistic, materialistic worldview. But even this NG is a Problem God for IT leaves unanswered the question of creation and the end-times. How did the world begin and how will it end? And what is to become of us humans? Are we doomed to a beginning and an end and nothing more? Indeed, what's the purpose of humankind? On the other hand, since it is impossible to prove an immaterial, spiritual realm and we have only Scripture and reason upon which to base the existence of God; isn't it just as reasonable to make the material Universe the uncreated, eternal force behind all things? If the theist's God is uncreated, why not skip one step in the order of things and make the Universe uncreated? Many would consider this view a reasonable one.

Some theologians prefer the term 'naturalism', rather than materialism when speaking of a NG system. This terminology avoids any question of a supernatural domain. Naturalism is the system that claims all phenomena can be explained in terms of natural causes and laws. This definition allows a more flexible worldview and sidesteps the more rigid, deterministic and negative connotations often associated with the term materialism. The classic Communist was a dialectical materialist. Naturalism stays away from the pejorative term, materialism.

---

15   This is the logical process especially associated with Hegel in which one arrives at truth by stating a thesis, developing an opposing antithesis, then combining and resolving them into a coherent synthesis.

Naturalism, in light of relativity and quantum theory can be expanded to a system I choose to call Neo-Naturalism, which allows a broader, more inclusive philosophy and theology of the Universe. This concept helps to bridge the gulf between science and religion by utilizing twentieth century physics. Neo-Naturalism can not only provide a better understanding of the Universe and us humans but it also clarifies the concept of a higher power. Using the Neo-Naturalistic view, one may be able to incorporate social, psychological and spiritual elements that are usually associated only with traditional religions into a scheme that may hopefully answer some as yet unanswered questions while allowing us to redefine God in a way that is more meaningful and rational. I call this approach Neo-Naturalism because the 'new' sciences of evolution and modern physics provide tools with which we may elevate natural theology to a higher level, making the notions of God less magical and more meaningful. In any event, Atheism though rational, fails to meet the emotional and psychological needs of many, ignoring the evident desire of most humans for more than just *logos*. *Mythos* still remains part of human nature–a part the atheist either demeans or ignores.

THE PANTHEISTIC GOD

Pantheism claims that God and the Universe are one. Baruch Spinoza (1632-1677) is the best-known pantheistic philosopher. In brief, if one can do his system justice in a truncated presentation such as this, Spinoza believed the material and spiritual realms were but two (of infinite many) aspects of the Pantheistic God (PanG). He called these aspects of God, 'attributes'. The material and spiritual are the only two attributes humans know though God is infinite and IT has infinite attributes. This is a clever way of getting around the 'mind-body' problem with which so many philosophers and theologians have struggled over the centuries. The corporeal and spiritual worlds are simply different ways of viewing God. Spinoza chooses not to provide a definitive view of God but rather offers this scheme as one solution to the God problem. This is a solution that contains aspects or attributes of the higher power that are currently and, may be eternally, beyond the reach of both the human intellect and scientific investigations. This results from our necessarily limited view of the Universe, bound as we are to this four-dimensional, sense perceptual world. Humans are considered 'modes' of God. All creatures, including humans, are thus classified as divine modes of God. These modal aspects of God would be considered the different ways that God exists. We then, according to Spinoza, are elements of God's being. On the other hand the material and spiritual attributes of God would be the ways in which IT exists. These attributes might be likened to the various dimensions of God's being.

The problem with pantheism is that it raises questions of individuality–how are we distinct from God? There are also questions of individual free will. How can we be free if we are just divine elements or modes? How can humans perform immoral acts? If we are part of God and IT is perfectly good, is it possible that we can choose to do evil, i.e. sin? If God is omnipotent, omniscient, etc why are we not similarly so constituted? In solving the mind-body question, we then face multiple other problems related to human individuality.

An allied concept associated with the PanG is the Panentheistic God (PanenG). Whereas the PanG is co-existent with the Universe, the PanenG includes the Universe but encompasses much more. God exists beyond ITs creations. What this means is problematic. Bound as we are to space and time and since God is not so limited, just how or where does IT exist outside the Universe? Certainly, God cannot be limited by space and time as we are. However, if one of God's attributes is material then IT should reside in some way in space and time. Nonetheless, having the spiritual attribute, this 'part' of God must reside outside of space and time. If God does exist outside of the material world just 'where' is this existence? Can God be within the material world and simultaneously found in the spiritual realm? Can we carve God up into infinite attributes as Spinoza suggests? If God is simple and undivided as most theologians claim, how can IT have infinite attributes some of which are mutually exclusive such as the spiritual and material domains? These are all mind-boggling questions. Indeed, they represent more logical conundrums.

HUMANISM

In dealing with religions or for that matter, non-religions, such as Agnosticism and Atheism, it is necessary to say a word about Humanism. This philosophical, social and ethical system is thought of by some as nonreligious or even atheistic. I don't think either of these labels necessarily applies to Humanism, though many Christians would balk at calling humanists, religious. They are often referred to as Secular Humanists. It is true that humanists need not espouse any religious sentiments or even a belief in God but the label does not exclude either being Christian or living a moral life. Humanism is a system of thought that centers on humans and their values, needs and capacities. As Protagoras said many centuries ago in

Plato's dialogue of the same name: "Man is the measure of all things."[16] Values and morals all stem from the nature of humankind; religion and God are not the only source of ethical standards. We need only look to our selves and other humans for guidance in how to behave, although the Bible, other sacred texts, tradition, reason and experience may also help develop moral norms. How we treat our neighbor can be determined solely by common sense and common agreement among our peers. There are many philosophers who hold this view including Darwinists such as sociobiologists and evolutionary psychologists.[17]

Humanism goes back to the Greeks. Jesus Christ, if one can rely on the Gospels, was a humanist as were many men and women of the Renaissance and Enlightenment. Erasmus was a Christian humanist.[18] Christ was not a theologian, He offered few ethical rules other than love of God and neighbor (Matthew 7:12). He willingly embraced tax collectors, harlots, adulterers, lepers, paralytics, grieving parents, widows and the poor. Jesus excluded no one and put people above the Jewish law .He was a humanist in the fullest sense of this term.

Many theists, deists, agnostics and atheists are humanists; humanism excludes no one. John Sponge's book, *Jesus for the Non-Religious* makes a strong case for the universality of Christ's Humanism.[19] Islam includes Christ among its prophets. Many Jews are comfortable with Christ's message. If one chooses to ignore or deny the divinity of Christ (as Spong and others do) his message still stands as a modern moral paradigm. The point is that humanists don't need traditional religion or even a God to support their social and moral philosophies. On the other hand, Humanism doesn't preclude any theological belief system–depending on how one defines the higher power or Santayana's 'cosmic force'.[20]

WHAT'S AHEAD?

In the following chapters we shall discuss many questions modern science has raised that are beyond our intuitive imagination and the realm

---

16   Plato, 1927, Plato Selections, *Protagoras* (New York: Scribner and Sons) p. 309.

17   These systems hold that natural selection has resulted in societal norms that are partly determined by DNA.

18   Huizinga, J. 1957, *Erasmus and the Age of Reformation* (New York: Harper & Row).

19   Spong, J. S. 2008, *Jesus for the Non-Religious* (San Francisco: HarperOne).

20   Santayana, G. 1982, *Reason in Religion* (New York: Dover). Santayana (1863-1952) was a naturalistic philosopher who maintained a sense of religion as found in Christianity in spite of views that might be considered irreligious. He saw the Bible and religious beliefs as poetic myths that teach us about the human condition.

of daily experience. In the last century, however, mathematics and physics have revealed puzzling realities in which, I believe, we can find a rational, believable deity. It is in these mystifying regions of our world that the divine cosmic force is to be found. All previous images of God, as profound and awe-inspiring as they have been, pale in comparison to the view of God that modern science brings to us. All our current ideas of God fall hopelessly short of the concept of God that we are now only beginning to grasp in light of modern astronomy, Einstein's theories of Relativity and the concepts quantum mechanics brings to us. Physicists have struggled unsuccessfully for a 100 years to find a unified theory of everything.[21] The difficulties they face, the many options offered including the concepts of symmetry, super-symmetry and string theory, only point to the immensity of the problem and monumental mysteries that face us in our quest to find the "real" God–a God that is no longer one of the Problem Gods.

The goal of this book is to offer a new view of the God problem–a view that moves beyond the AG and all the other gods of myth and religion. We have to look past human egoism and emotional needs in order to accept what is possible in a rational higher power, even if this God doesn't meet all our psychological, philosophical and/or religious needs. All of us were told at one time or another by our parents that we cannot have everything we want. This is the case with a meaningful and rational God. We have to be humble and accepting of what is possible in a God. There is a humongous world out there, full of unknowns and unknowables. We must shed the personal chains that prevent us from embracing a new vision of the Universe and a new view of the divine. We can no longer fall into the trap of thinking about a cosmic force as some humanoid. IT isn't anything like humans. IT can't be like us and at the same time be rational and believable. We are not made in God's image and likeness, rather we have made God in our image and likeness. Nonetheless, we have the capacity to find a much better divinity. Just how much better remains to be seen. But in the meantime, if we can rise above our provincialism and longstanding concept of God as just another human, only bigger and better, we will find a much more satisfying God than we have ever known before–a God that does justice to God and not to us humans. We are not the center of the Universe. This newly defined God must not be a God that makes us think better of ourselves; that boosts our ego or satisfies some human Darwinian need for survival or security. It is time to admit that we are not the ultimate creation of God. Rather, we need to see God and us in a more realistic context. God is truly beyond our comprehension currently and if we continue to see IT through human eyes alone and not as IT really is, we are doomed to never know God even in the

---

21   Smolin, L. 2006, *The Trouble with Physics* (New York: Houghton Mifflin).

limited way humans can. We cannot use our four-dimensional, Euclidian world as a prism to view God. Relativity, quantum theory, mathematics, astronomy and biology along with reason are some of the tools with which we can find God. We must look beyond the myths of antiquity and medieval theology in order to have any hope of finding the 'real' God.

The Bible is a great book but it cannot unlock the mysteries of our world. We can still consider ourselves a significant part of the Universe but not the only significant aspect of the cosmos. This may be humbling but it is also liberating and expanding. We may still worship God and this newly defined God will be more worthy of worship than ever before. This is a marvelous world and whatever the force(s) behind it, the world remains a majestic phenomenon.

This idea of a new kind of God obviously will not go down well with traditional religious. And it is not my intent to change the way the majority of people view their God. There is a need for most people to have an AG that they can talk to, find solace in and with whom they may connect as a friend or father. But an expanded view of God as offered in this book is intended to define a God that fits with our current understanding of the Universe. In the end, this is a God that can satisfy the needs of many, including scientists and atheists. If one chooses to call this Neo-Natural God atheistic, so be it. But for me this God is more realistic, rational, and palatable and in the long run more satisfying. I'm a mere human being with many wants and needs, many of which will never be fulfilled. If my very existence ends when my worldly life ceases, that's OK. I've enjoyed life, my family, friends, career and hobbies. It has been a good run. Everything, even stars are born, live and die. Humility demands I find the real world and make the best of it, the same applies to my concept of God.

Finally, I do not intend to prove that there is a God. I don't think this is possible but I hope to offer enough scientific data along with adequate analyses of these data to at least suggest the possibility of a cosmic or higher power that meets both the intellectual and psychological needs of a thinking, feeling human being. We all know, in one way or another, that there is something out there greater than we–call IT God or what you will. What follows is one person's search for that something, this is my theological odyssey.

PART II

RELIGION: THE GOOD, THE BAD AND THE UNBELIEVABLE

CHAPTER 3

RELIGION: THE GOOD

Religion has been around a very long time. There is archeological evidence that primitive hominids possessed a sense of religion.[1] Certainly religion was 'alive and well' when language first developed (around 55,000 years ago).[2] The Sumerians had a well-developed polytheism as early as 4000 B.C.E.[3] The Egyptians, Babylonians, Assyrians, Greeks and Romans all accepted a polytheistic pantheon and mythology. Much of what went into the making of monotheism grew out of these earlier religions. The so-called 'pagan' religions provided a mythology that was incorporated into Judaism, Christianity and Islam.[4] The roots of religion have spread deep into all cultures and what we experience as religion today stems in large part from past, even, primitive beliefs.[5] There are vestiges of Tylor and Frazer's Animism even in the Jesuit writer, Teillard de Chardin (1881-1955) when he speaks of:

> Some sort of psyche [soul] is in every corpuscle even in those... whose complexity is of such a low or modest order as to render it imperceptible.[6]

---

1   Lewis-W. D. 2002, *The Mind in the Cave: Consciousness and the Origin of Art* (New York: Thames & Hudson).
2   Wade, N. 2007, *Before the Dawn: Recovering the Lost History of Our Ancestors* (New York: Penguin).
3   Kramer, S. N. 1959, *History Begins at Sumer* (Garden City, NY: Doubleday).
4   Carpenter, E. 1996, *The Origins of Pagan and Christian Beliefs* (London: Senage Random House).
5   Lowie, R. H. 1952, *Primitive Religion* (New York: Liveright).
6   De Chardin, T. 1950, *The Phenomenon of Man*, trans. B. Wall (New York: Harper & Row). pp. 301-2.

In other words, every being even primitive unicellular organisms has some vital principle that enlivens it–call it a soul or psyche if you wish. Although de Chardin considered himself an orthodox Catholic, as noted in *The Phenomenon of Man*, he couldn't help slipping into this little bit of heretical Animism.

Some writers, such as de Chardin consider evolution to be active in all sociological and religious developments.[7] Because myths, religious or otherwise, provide a means to communicate social norms, as well as an understanding of one's world, they promote a better, more harmonious society. This gives a selective advantage to the society imbued with myth-making. It is easy to see how the Bible provides moral standards as well as explanations of how the Universe began and what is responsible for all of the mind-boggling marvels that astronomers have discovered billions of kilometers from Earth and billions of years in the past.[8] The Universe is full of never-ending marvels and mysteries; new ones are found every day. Similar marvels are evident in the microscopic world.

THE BIBLE, QUR'AN AND OTHER SACRED WRITINGS

For over 2000 years the Bible has been a source for answers to questions that have puzzled humankind since the dawn of history. We, as humans, have sought answers to all the mysteries that surround us and the Bible has offered solutions to many questions. Most of what is in Genesis is errant but, nonetheless, it has satisfied the psychological, if not intellectual needs for billions of people, past and present.

The Bible has also established standards by which we may live in order to achieve a harmonious society. The Bible demands punishment for those who break the rules and offers rewards for those who comply with social norms. It tells us how to live. It speaks of faith, trust, loyalty, hard work and charity toward our neighbor. All of these guidelines make for a better world in which to live; one in which we are more likely to prosper.

---

7   Op cit. De Chardin, T. 1965,.

8   When we look into the sky we see light rays that have been traveling for billions of years in order to reach Earth so we are, in fact, looking into the past. Currently the Universe is estimated to be 13.7 billion years old and we could potentially see to within 300,000 years of the Big Bang. Cosmic microwave background radiation that represents remnants of the Big Bang is now being intensively studied.

PSYCHOLOGICAL BENEFITS OF RELIGION

The biblical myths not only offer answers and provide standards of conduct but they give us a sense of control, offer solace, security, a feeling that we are worthy beings and, more importantly, that we are 'right' and that God is on our side. Religion tells us that we are the 'chosen people' and God will protect and provide for us. Religions have told kings they have a divine right to rule. Some presidents of the United States claim God has spoken to them and what they proclaim, therefore, is the will of God. These psychologically fulfilling ideas are found in all religious myths and beliefs. Indeed, they are a strong cohesive force that helps to bind society and its members together. Any threat to this societal 'glue' could easily be viewed as threatening the very underpinnings of society and the welfare of all its members. Such perceived threats to one's belief system have fostered active, even violent, resistance to those posing such apparent or real threats. Anyone not holding to the accepted societal norms is seen as an outsider, an enemy of accepted mores and a destructive force within society. In their view, the very foundations of society are under attack by 'nonbelievers'. It is little wonder that murder, terrorism, such as on 9/11, assaults on abortion clinics, churches, mosques and synagogues, as well as assassinations have become commonplace in all parts of the world. Religion meets some very basic human needs or it wouldn't ferment such fierce folly.

William James (1842-1910) divides religion into two parts: personal and institutional.[9] The various types of religious i.e. spiritual experiences are personal and the institutional aspects of religion deal with theological tenets, church hierarchy, buildings, rules of membership and the like. In James' view it is the personal aspects of religion that are important. He believes the value of religion is found in the feelings that religion promotes. The primary benefits of religion are to be found in its psychological and spiritual effects. Theology, as such, is of less value according to James. The latter is what occupies the minds of theologians but adds little to the lives of individual Christians.

Although James wrote the *Varieties* in 1902, based on anecdotal observations, much of what he claimed has been verified by recent studies.[10] Argyle in *Psychology and Religion*, points out that:

> Religion is a very important part of human life and experience and psychologists have something to learn from it.

---

9   James, W. 1902, *Varieties of Religious Experience* (New York: Modern Library) Lecture II.
10   Argyle, M. 2005, *Psychology and Religion* (London: Rutledge) p. ix.

He goes on to say, "altruism…is affected by religious and other ideas in people's heads". Religion is not the sole source of altruism certainly but it plays a role in creating beneficial interpersonal relationships. Argyle also notes, "that finding a possible psychological origin for a belief does not imply that the belief is false". And, of course, the converse is also true; it doesn't prove the validity of any religious tenet. That a religious experience is beneficial is sufficient in and of itself. Since we are, as Thomas Aquinas says, 'rational animals', our cognition is not the only aspect of our humanity that must be attended to; our emotional life needs to be taken care of as well and religion can play a role in fulfilling these 'animal' i.e. emotional, needs.

This may be the major criticism one can level against the Neo-Atheists such as Dawkins, Harris and Hutchins.[11] It might be convenient if we could function unemotionally like Star Trek's, Spock but such is not the case. Emotions have survival benefits for all higher animals including humans.

Children early on, if offered the opportunity, attach themselves intellectually and emotionally to religion. Belief systems of necessity must be easily grasped in order to provide explanations for which children continually yearn. We see this with Santa and the Easter Bunny. Later on, older children find these 'fairy tales' unsatisfactory. Our desire for simple explanations may fail us as we become more sophisticated. More intellectually rewarding answers are needed. Many older people attend church less often, for a variety of reasons. Often they simply don't have a need for communal services. In recent years church attendance in Europe and America has dwindled. Nonetheless, religion or more precisely spirituality plays a very important role in the lives of many people to one degree or another.

Americans and Europeans are less 'religious' than even 50 years ago. Some studies find church attendance rates of 20% for Catholics and 10% for Protestants. About 12% of Americans are atheists. When Americans are asked how important religion is in their lives about 60% say religion is very important, 25% say not very and 15% report that religion is of no importance. These figures have not changed much over the past ten years, even with the apparent 'surge' in religious conservatism. It may be that people have become more polarized in their beliefs so that the far right and far left are stronger than previously. The perception in this country is that religion is losing its influence–with about 55% believing this to be the case. About 5-10% of Europeans attend church. In a local Catholic church, it is evident from watching the congregation file up to the front of the church for the

11   Haugtht, J. F. 2008, *God and the New Atheism*, (Louisville, KY: Westminster John Know Press).

Eucharist that four out of five are elderly and that within ten or twenty years the overall numbers will be significantly depleted. In a local 'megachurch', on the other hand, the majority are young people with children.

Church attendance is motivated by both social and personal factors. Some go to church because they think it is expected of them, however, a significant percentage attends because they have a religious experience of the type William James writes. This is an emotionally satisfying event for them. Prayer is largely done for psychological or, if you will, spiritual reasons–the person feels connected to or loved by God or believes s/he is helping the people for whom they are praying. Religious attitudes are to some extent genetically influenced. Truett et al. found, using identical twin studies, that 16% of religious tendencies are inborn.[12]

The fact remains that church attendance has fallen dramatically in Europe and in America over the past 50 years or so. In England this trend was noted in the early twentieth century. Third World countries remain more religious than the developed areas of the world.

Certain fundamental groups often tenaciously hold religious doctrines. Many men and women prefer to be married and baptize their children in church and in the end be prayed over and buried from a church, even if they never set foot inside a church otherwise. Religion plays a major role in their spiritual, emotional and social lives. A significant number of my patients admit to a strong spiritual sense or feeling, though they rarely enter a church, synagogue or mosque. Nearly 90% of Americans expresses a belief in God. God's role in our lives may have changed but there still seems to be a place for some sort of spiritual or God experience.

Table 3.1. gives the top sixteen triggers of religious experiences. It is evident that not all such triggers are religious in nature and consequently these might better be labeled spiritual experiences. Nonetheless, they point to the pervasiveness of some kind of feeling that is beyond the purely rational side of human nature.

Forty-five percent of Americans believe in the Genesis version of creation and this figure has held stable from 1982 to 2004.[13] Religion and certainly spiritual experiences are not going away anytime soon in spite of the prognostications of Marx, Schopenhauer and Nietzsche. And though Dawkins sees no reason for God or religion today, it does meet some basic human needs. It is good for something and I don't say this glibly. Religion has been an important part of society, culture, the psyche and our corporeal wellbeing for as long as *Homo sapiens* have been around. It has played a role

---

12   Ibid. Quoting Truest et al. 1992, *Social Teachings of the Christian Churches* (London: Allen & Unwind). Kindle Edition) location 477.
13   Gallop Poll.

also in economics and politics for too long to simply dismiss as outmoded, passé or meaningless. Dawkins very correctly shows religion is a flawed system in its many forms but it remains with us. It provides comfort, solace, community, symbolism and for the moment fills the many gaps in our understanding of the world. It also helps allay fear.

Table 3.1: Triggers of Religious Experience[14]

Listening to music	49%
Prayer	48%
Beauties of nature	45%
Moments of quiet reflection	42%
Attending church services	41%
Listening to sermon	40%
Watching little children	35%
Reading the Bible	31%
Being alone in church	30%
Reading a poem or novel	21%
Childbirth	20%
Sexual love making	18%
Your own creative work	17%
Looking at a painting	15%
Physical exercise	1%
Drugs	0%

Karen Armstrong, in *The Battle for God*, asserts that Fundamentalism is fired by fear and this may, in part, explain its popularity. The world has been and continues to be a fearsome place in many ways. Every age has had its stressors, personal or institutional. Religion seems to assuage this 'fear and trembling', to use Kierkegaard's phrase. For him, however, dread was all pervasive–dread of both good and evil–indeed, fear was pathological for Kierkegaard.[15] All of us have fears and these can be relieved by religion with its many ways for lessening anxiety through prayer, liturgy, socialization, theological doctrine, counseling, community support as well as physical and economic assistance. It is well known that prayer and meditation lowers blood pressure, slows the pulse and reduce sweating–all signs of a peaceful mood.

---

14   Op. cit. Argyle, M. 2005, p. 61.
15   Kierkegaard, S. 1973, *The Concept of Dread*, trans. W. Lowry (Princeton, NJ: Princeton University Press).

Institutional religion offers moral guidance and direction. Even the black-and-white (absolute) moral rules of religion make it easy for many to live life in perceived safety. The Ten Commandments are straightforward and for many leave no doubt as to what should be permissible or prohibited. These are easy rules to understand and where there is ambiguity, one need only read the Bible or consult a priest, minister, rabbi or other religious clergywo/man and the answers to life's problems are often given in a clear and concise way. Indeed, this system works for the majority of people worldwide. I heard a psychiatrist one time say that guilt, not love, makes the world go round. Catholics and Lutherans are noted for their excess of guilt so I am told, this may or may not be true. Certainly my Catholicism provided ample guilt as far as I was concerned. Every time I 'sinned" guilt flooded over me like a waterfall. But this can be beneficial, if not excessive. Children learn from their guilt and shame to behave in more productive ways. Obviously, if our superego is totally derived from guilt and shame, this is destructive. However, these emotions play a role in personality development and religion can foster this process in a variety of ways. Religions reinforce ethical norms and parental example. Religion-based standards can help build ego strength through a kind and caring affect and positive reinforcement. A child that feels good about him/herself is more mature, humane and less prone to destructive risk taking behaviors and is better able to learn and grow both academically and socially. They are also less often given to criminal behavior.[16]

Religion is neither necessary nor sufficient in the building of the ego and superego but it can contribute to their development. Unless there is self-love there cannot be love of others. Those who are insecure for whatever reason, find it hard to accept people as they are and often insist that other people believe as they believe, live as they live and conform to their social mores. Anyone outside his or her 'clan' is treated as a lesser being. Some of the most caring people that treated me well and helped me feel good about myself were priests and nuns. Good Fr. Youngren, whom I've mentioned before, often stayed up till after midnights in order to keep the gym open for pick-up basketball games. He quietly read his Breviary while we ran around the basketball court. His efforts unfortunately failed to make me a skilled basketball player. The one time I tried out for the varsity team, our coach, Bill Steiner, kindly suggested that I not bother to buy a new pair of tennis shoes that year. After a few moments I figured out this meant I hadn't made the team. My parents though religious, were only moderately so and while never very demonstrative with their love always let us know that we were

---

16   Op. cit. Argyle, M. 2005, p. 218.

doing OK even at times when we failed to fully live up to local religious or societal norms.

I never felt a hint of any misconduct on the part of the priests that mentored me. In fact, Fr. Earl Burns, our pastor, bailed me out once when I got in trouble with the nuns as a result of behaviors in school that were certainly worthy of firm reprimands. I loved to make trouble and I look back warmly on the religious that educated me all the way through college even though I was not always a model young man. They were good people and very tolerant of my shenanigans.

Religion can bring a host of healthy influences to the faithful. Religious liturgy is full of pomp and symbolism in the Roman Catholic, Jewish and Eastern Orthodox churches and provide a sense of well-being for those in attendance. I remember the feeling I had while at a Russian Orthodox service in Leningrad before the USSR broke up–it was a religious oasis in the heart of Marxist atheism. More recently we attended a vespers service at Notre Dame in Paris that was most spiritually moving. There is something comforting, uplifting and joyous about the liturgy. It seems to fill a real human need. Some call this a spiritual experience, though as will be discussed later, I am not sure what this means. For several years after losing confidence in many of the tenets of institutional religion, I continued to call myself a 'liturgical Catholic' because the ritual of Mass still stirred me–whether this was spiritual or simply a learned psychological response, the liturgy meant something special to me.

Part of religion's value lies in its symbolism. Joseph Campbell has stressed the utility of symbolism as found in myths from all over the world and from every historical period.[17] Campbell quotes Thomas Merton as having said that symbols provide an experience that most clearly and fully expresses religious beliefs and practice. Further, Merton says that the symbolism of the various religions fosters a commonality more real than any abstract formulation of official church doctrine. Merton claims:

> Symbolism awakens our consciousness to a new awareness of the inner meaning of life and of reality itself.

As a picture is worth a 1000 words, so too a symbol is an ineffable expression of thoughts, intuitions, feelings and yearnings that bring meaning to our lives.

Symbolism is found in all religions. Christ on the cross (or just the cross itself for Protestants) stirs the heart in many ways. This symbol is evidence of God's mercy and love in sending his son to die for the sins of all

---

17   Campbell, J. 1972, *Myths to Live By* (New York: Penguin) pp. 256-7.

humans. It is a sign of redemption and the key to everlasting life. The cross tells many that God truly cares for them and that Christ was willing to give the ultimate gift in order to save our souls. How comforting this image is for many Christians.

Early on, the crucifixion was a source of shame for Christians. It was a symbol of Christ's defeat. Later, Christ was portrayed in the Eastern Church as not showing anguish on the cross. This was a sign that he had conquered the cross. In the Middle Ages, he was the suffering, dying Christ but now was seen as the glorious savior who had given his life to benefit all sinners. Thus, the shame of crucifixion was transformed symbolically into the Christ who had overcome all the sins of the world. We sinners were now assured of redemption. There was nothing to fear–Heaven was guaranteed. No matter what this earthly 'veil of tears' brings, we will have our blissful reward–truly a symbol of hope.

Paul Tillich saw miracle stories as symbols or as he labels them, "sign-events" that though "absurd", nonetheless provide religious revelatory value.[18] He even suggested the greater their absurdity, the greater their value. Indeed, miracles speak to the power of God–a God that can suspend the laws of nature in order to help the saintly and in so doing, stir us to give glory to God as a kindly father. As children and even as adults, each of us, at one time or another, has wished we could manage our world magically. And though we may not be so gifted, one can believe anything is possible in God. This is a comforting thought; God can give us the strength we as human do not possess. Whether any of the above is true or not, is of little consequence, the positive psychological and spiritual benefits they produce are what count.

The Roman Catholic and Eastern Orthodox Churches use the sacraments to symbolize God's grace working in our lives. The Baltimore Catechism tells us that a sacrament is an external sign instituted by Christ to give grace.[19] The sacraments are religious symbols that in the Roman Church indicate the granting of grace at seven important milestones in one's life. Baptism not only symbolizes the purification of the soul, removing all traces of Original Sin but it also celebrates initiation into a community that provides recognition, care and comfort as well as social membership and status among his or her peers–it provides a sense of belonging. The sacrament of the Eucharist symbolizes the presence of Christ the God-man within our faith community who saves us from sin. The Eucharist likewise symbolizes

---

18   Tillich, P. 1951, *Systematic Theology*, Vol. I (Chicago: University of Chicago Press) p. 115.
19   Baltimore Catechism No. 2, 1977, (Rockford, IL: Tan Books) p. 27. This definition is unchanged from the catechism I used in 1948 when in the regional Catechetical Contest.

our participation in his divine nature when we consume the host.[20] This emphasizes the special nature of humankind as having status above all other created beings except the angels. Certainly our ego may receive a boost from this imagery. Catholics sometimes call the sacrament 'Communion' as symbolic of our union with the divine Christ. Also, recently in Paris at Saint Denis church we stumbled on to a First Holy Communion ceremony. It reminded us of the sense of belonging and maturity these young people experience as part of this symbolic milestone. The sacrament of Penance relieves us of all sins, guilt and punishment for up to a lifetime of misdeeds helping to banish guilt and shame. Confirmation reaffirms our status as an adult member of the faith community and marks the passage into adulthood as a full member of the church. The sacraments of Marriage and Holy Orders sanction these special vocations before God and the community. The Sacrament of the Sick provides comfort to the sick and dying at the end of life.

All these symbols strengthen our position in a special society; provide support, as well as a sense of belonging, security and status– all psychologically necessary aspects of being human. Indeed, there are Darwinian features to religion that help us survive as an individual within society as a whole. All these important milestone's in life may be recognized by other than religious means, however, religion has for centuries been the main method by which western society has marked and celebrated these various life events.

All religious groups have charitable functions whether within or outside the parish, synagogue or mosque that help the poor, sick, mentally ill or those with marital, family or grief issues. These are concerns we all face at one time or another. Missionaries abroad do more than proselytize for their particular belief system. There are many kind and caring ministers, priests, nuns, rabbis, monks and lay people involved in such work. These are concerned people that perform untold numbers of good, altruistic acts. My wife tells the story of one Christmas when her family had no money for presents and her sister and she were told that Santa had had an accident and there would be no presents. On Christmas morning they woke to a room full of dolls and other gifts all from the priests and nuns of her parish. There are charitable agencies such as Catholic Charities, Lutheran Social Services and many more such religious, helping organizations. I've known priests that have worked in Korea, Africa, Japan, South American, South Dakota and

---

20   This symbolism applies whether one believes in the Catholic view of transubstantiation (bread and wine become the body and blood of Christ), the Lutheran consubstantiation (bread and wine coexist with the body and blood) or the Reformed view that the bread and wine are only symbols of Christ's body and blood.

Wyoming, not only spreading the faith but also helping people in need. You can tell they love their flocks.

The institutional church has been much maligned and, as we shall see in the next chapter, many times for good reason but the process of institutionalization is not all bad. For the early Christians, it was a necessity. Without organization and standing in the community their sect could not have survived. Constantine, in 312 C.E. brought recognition, as well as political and economic stability to the Christian Church. He allowed it to grow and prosper. In a real sense the Church took over many of the functions of the Roman Empire as it gradually disintegrated during the early centuries of the first millennium C.E. For much of Western Europe it remained the only social and economic resource until Charlemagne brought some semblance of a centralized royal power in the latter part of the Dark Ages. Even then the Pope continued to crown the Holy Roman Emperor (with few exceptions) and helped impose times of peace on the all-too-frequently fighting and fragmented medieval nobility.

The institutional Church was able to build impressive religious edifices that have been criticized for the toll they took on the poor; nonetheless, these were centers of safety and community. Even criminals were offered respite within their walls. Sometimes only an institution can provide the many necessities that make a civilization grow. Art, architecture, preservation of learning, education, law and medicine (primitive as it was) were all fostered by the Church. We are told that Irish monks saved civilization.[21] However, it was Islam that preserved the works of Aristotle for the West. Arabic philosophers and physicians like Averroes and Avicenna contributed in a significant way to western culture. When Rome had dwindled to a mere 30,000 souls in the late Roman period, it was the Church that held its diminished political and economic structure together.[22]

And as much as one may criticize the Roman Church for its oppression of men of science such as Roger Bacon and Galileo Galilei, the fact remains that much science has been quietly carried out by wo/men of the Church over the centuries. By 1611, two years after Galileo described the moons of Jupiter, the Jesuits had reported their first telescopic observations. The Vatican Observatory still exists at Castel Gondalfo, the summer residence of the Pope with its main observatory on Mt. Graham two hours east of Tucson, Arizona. They have a house in Tucson, near the University of Arizona that is owned by the Pope and provides living quarters for the Jesuits who spend their time observing the skies and carrying out theoretical astrophysical

21   Cahill, T. 1996, *How the Irish Saved Civilization* (New York: Anchor Books).
22   Duggen, C. 1994, *A Concise History of Italy* (Cambridge Concise Histories) (Cambridge, UK: Cambridge University Press).

research. The Jesuits are noted for their institutions of higher learning both in the United States and abroad. There are Jesuit universities all over America including Fordham, Marquette, St. Louis University, Creighton and the several Loyolas in Chicago, New Orleans and Los Angeles among others. They are not the only religious order to be involved in education, turning out men and women with business, law, medical, teaching, engineering and a host of other degrees. Many Protestant universities are also well known, for example both Harvard and Princeton began as seminaries.

Not all priests are as conservative as the Vatican would like you to believe. Having worked with priests for 35 years, I know the majority is very concerned about the needs of their parishioners. Some of them hold surprising views on birth control, gay rights, divorce and, yes, even abortion! There are many humanists among the clergy. Certainly this is not the case with the hierarchy–they are carefully selected to follow traditional dogma but among those working clergy who deal daily with troubled people, these men and women often have an empathic view of those in need.

We have heard much about the many misdeeds perpetrated by religions, past and present but one must not ignore the good they have done over the centuries. We will deal with religious failings in the next chapter but it is important to see the full spectrum of religious activities before condemning religion wholesale. Religion fills many needs and it, as an institution is not about to go away anytime soon–my guess is that unless the basic nature of *Homo sapiens* changes dramatically, religion will be with us for a long time to come with all its blessing and blunders. Let us not forget that it is the institutional church that keeps the gym open late at night so some energetic high schoolers can play basketball and allows a few kindly nuns to make Christmas happen for a poor girl who yearns for a baby doll from Santa.

CHAPTER 4

RELIGION: THE BAD

THE EARLY CHURCH

Many early Church doctrinal decisions have come about as a result of political and economic influences along with chance scriptural transcription errors or intentional alterations made by individual scribes as a result of his personal theological biases.[1] The many inconsistencies in Scripture suggest that even if the Bible were initially divinely inspired either God has changed ITs 'mind' or the Bible is not currently infallible. Biblical content, including its stories and morals seem to represent more the myths and mores of the day than the workings of an omniscient, infallible God that dictated Scripture to the early prophets and apostles. We now know that the authors of the Gospels and many other books of the OT and NT are not as they were once thought to be. As useful as the Bible is as a literary, metaphorical, moral or philosophical document, it is not a reliable source of scientific or historical information. Though Genesis tells us that the Universe was made in six days, one has to give credence to the geological, physical and biological evidence that tell us, without question, that our Earth is some 4.6 billion years old and it, along with all its inhabitants, past and present, have and still are evolving over time. The Earth was not created in the year 4004 B.C.E on Saturday, October 22 at 8 a.m. as Bishop James Usher asserts.

The early Church had a name recognition problem, they were little known, poorly understood and even less well defined. Was this just a modern form of Judaism as Christ seems to have intended it to be? Should all male Christians be circumcised? Must Christians follow Jewish dietary laws?[2] And who was this Christ fellow? What was his status and how were Christians supposed to relate to him? Who was to be their leader after Christ died? Was the Church to be run from Constantinople or Rome? What was

[1] Op. cit. Ehrman, B. D. 2005.
[2] The Passagians were a heretical group that believed Jewish law was to be followed by all Christians. They were finally condemned in 1184 by Pope Lucius III. It was this pope that issued the decretal, A*d abolendum,* that some consider the charter for the Inquisition.

the message by which his followers were to live? Was there only one God, as the Jews believed or were there more, as the Greeks and Romans maintained? And what was the exact nature of this one God? Were there three persons in the one God? Was Christ divine? Was Mary a virgin and was she the mother of God? There were many issues that needed to be sorted out in the first several centuries of Christian history. Somehow the Church needed to be unified and authority centralized. Its theology had to be formulated and defined or else this new religion would lack consistency and cohesiveness. It needed to be crystallized into a lucid whole or shatter into many pieces. This would be the only way Christians could develop an identity with distinctive characteristics that set it apart from other religious communities. Something had to provide the institutional 'glue' that would hold them together.

It was important from the outset that there was one religion, one theology and one liturgy and, most importantly, that it should be one ultimate entity just as the Roman Empire had been. Fragmentation must not destroy this nascent group of believers.[3] They had to be one in Christ. All had to love and care for his or her brother and sister Christians.

In contrast to Judaism, women initially played a prominent role in early Christianity. Mary, Christ's mother, was held in high esteem and Mary Magdalene was a full member of the apostolic community of Christ and appears to have been seen as equal to the other disciples. There is some evidence that she was not a 'fallen woman' and in fact, was a person of some means and that this appellation was not used until much later when the Church had become male dominated. There were other woman apostles. Prisca, Junia, Julia, and Nereus' sister are included among the apostles (Romans 16:3-12). Paul praises Junia (or Juntas) as "prominent among the apostles". Paul also mentions Mary and Persis as apostles. Some theologians understand the name to be that of a woman, suggesting that Paul recognized female apostles in the early Church. Over time women were relegated to lesser roles and this persists today in the Catholic Church, Eastern Orthodoxy and some Protestant sects.

Chauvinism runs rampant in the Vatican and sexual issues generally are viewed as anathema i.e. heterodox or heretical. The use of oral contraceptives to prevent conception was formally forbidden by Paul VI in *Humanae vitae*. Contraception other than by Natural Family Planning[4]

---

3   Evans, G. R. 2003, *A Brief History of Heresy* (Oxford, UK: Blackwell).

4   Natural family planning (NaPro Technology) is a system of birth control by limiting intercourse to non-ovulatory portions of the menstrual cycle based on the characteristics of the woman's vaginal secretions.

(NaPro) is prohibited and condoms had been proscribed even if they might save thousands of lives by preventing HIV infections in Africa.[5]

It took several centuries to unify Christianity. A number of heresies surfaced in the first four centuries of its history. Marcion of Sinope (died c. 160) taught that there were two gods, one 'bad' as represented in the Jewish Bible (OT) and one 'good' as found in the NT. As a consequence, he rejected the OT and wrote an abbreviated version of the NT. The Gnostics believed that a piece of God (*gnosis*) resided within each person and provided individual enlightenment, thus reducing the authority of and the need for an ecclesiastical hierarchy.[6] The Manicheans also believed in a good and a bad god, each of which sought to overcome the other. This seemed a good way to explain the presence of evil in the world. How could a good God tolerate evil in ITs creation and creatures?

The nature of God became a major point of contention among early Christians. Was Christ divine and if so, what was his status vis-à-vis God, the Father? Were there really three Gods rather than one? These two issues were sorted out in the fourth century at the Councils of Nicaea (325) and Constantinople (381), largely based on political considerations. These issues were only the tip of the theological iceberg.

Over time, more and more doctrinal disputes came to light. These all needed discussions, clarification and disposition as to whether they were orthodox or heterodox (true or false) beliefs. As the number of theologians multiplied, it seemed they all needed to be busy working on spiritual issues of one sort or another in order to establish their value as theologians. Some, such as Arius (c. 256-336), who taught that Christ was not fully divine, fell afoul of Church authorities as a result of his views. There were theological strongholds in Antioch and Alexandria and they held two opposing positions. Antioch denied the value of Socrates and his philosophical progeny whereas Alexandria favored the inclusion of Greek philosophy in their theology. In Antioch they asked, "What does Athens have to do with Jerusalem?" In other words, Greek philosophy and Christian theology were distinct disciplines. Several important Church fathers such as Origen (c. 185-c. 254) and Tertullian (c. 160-c. 230) were condemned for their views even though they were very influential in the early Church. Origen opposed a literal interpretation of the Scriptures, a view now generally accepted by many modern Scripture scholars.

---

5   Benedict XVI recently rescinded this prohibition so long as the intent was to prevent HIV infections and not conception.

6   Rudolph, K. 1977, *Gnosis: The Nature and History of Gnosticism*, Trans. R. M. Wilson (San Francisco: Harper).

Much heterodoxy was weeded out by the fifth century and heretical tenets were few and far between until the High Middle Ages. Obviously, the Church was not one, united institution in its beginning in spite of later claims of infallibility.

THE MEDIEVAL CHURCH

Thomas Aquinas (1225-1274) ran into difficulties early on because of his attempt to Christianize Aristotle but subsequently, by sheer force of intellect, convinced Church authorities of his orthodoxy. The bishop of Paris nonetheless, condemned Aristotle's views in 1272, two year before Thomas' death. Theological doctrines seemed to expand logarithmically over time. The more complicated their theology the better it seemed. Scholasticism, which grew out of Thomas' teachings, became the 'gold' theological standard until the Enlightenment. It was the ultimate 'hair-splitting' theology and has been criticized as being too rational and unrealistic. Voltaire's, *Candide* is the classic satire of Scholasticism.[7]

Over the centuries, the Eastern Church viewed their regional patriarchs at Athens, Alexandria, Antioch, Constantinople, etc. as more or less equal, while in the West, Rome gradually asserted its hegemony. There were disputes over the authority of the pope versus that of the Church councils however in the end the pope won out. The Western Church grew up under the Roman emperors and assumed a top-down hierarchy as the Roman emperors had. This continues to the present time in the Catholic Church.

By the tenth or eleventh centuries, a new 'corporate personality' came to characterize the hierarchy–an ever-increasing, indiscriminate use of power along with blatant moral and political depravity. The Church had become so powerful that their only rival was the Holy Roman Emperor (who was neither holy nor Roman), of whom the best known is Charlemagne (c. 742-814). The pope and emperor struggled to assert their authority and this continued until Italy was united under Victor Emmanuel II in the last half of the nineteenth century. The Papal States were dissolved in 1870. In the twelfth century the power of the Church, as is so often the case with any over-developed institution, showed signs of unbridled corruption. An early example of this was that of Pope John XII (papacy 955-964). He was the illegitimate son of Alberic II, ruler of Rome from 932-954. Although it was against Church law, dating back to a decretal by Pope Symmachus, in 499, Alberic extracted a promise from the leading citizens of Rome that, upon the death of the reigning pope, Agapitus, Alberic's son, Octavian, would

---

7   Voltaire, 1966, *Candide* (New York: Norton & Company).

be elected pope. John XII was only18 when he ascended to the throne. He was little interested in spiritual matters and lived a debauched life style. Some claim he turned the Vatican into a brothel. In spite of this, he was not without administrative abilities. He attempted monastic reform and through an alliance with Otto I of Germany (936-973) he was able to expand the Papal States to nearly two-thirds of present day Italy, invoking the Donations of Pepin and Charlemagne[8] (both of whom had given land to the Church earlier) as a basis for expanding the Papal Sates. For this, Otto I was crowned Holy Roman Emperor. John was involved in many political intrigues but lived only nine years after being elected pope and is said to have suffered a stroke while in the arms of a married noblewoman, dying a week later.

In defense of the political and military activities of many popes, as noted elsewhere, it must be mentioned that the Middle Ages were unsettled times. Rome was often threatened and at one point its population was only 30,000 compared to the one million during the zenith of the empire. The pope was the only guardian of Rome for long stretches and the unstable economy and political situations required that the pope assume several roles not considered appropriate for the Vicar of Christ today. Nonetheless, the pope's autocratic rule, coupled with an opulent, frequently immoral life style had their effect on the faithful and their attitude toward the hierarchy of the Roman Church.

Following the initial heresies of the early Church, heterodoxy became less of a problem for the Holy See. Except for the growing rift between East and West that finally culminated in a complete schism in 1054, there were few heresies of significance. However, in the eleventh century there was a resurgence of heretical thought. In 1022, a group surfaced in Orleans, France that believed in *gnosis*, the spirit of God within each person that allowed him or her full understanding of the Scriptures. This *gnosis*–'knowledge' or 'illumination'–made the Church, its sacraments and the Vatican's interpretation of Christ's message superfluous. Even creation by God, the Father, was denied. A group of heretical clergy, canons (unordained clergy) and nuns were burned alive while trapped in a building. A few who recanted were spared this fate. This heresy was a throwback to the Gnostics of the second century. No heretic had been so treated since Priscillian of Avila in 383. How much of a role Church corruption played in the origins of the heresy is uncertain but the *gnosis* allowed these heretical souls to shed the yolk of the hierarchy and worship God without interference from Church authorities that had lost all popular respect.

---

8   The Donation of Constantine was an eighth century forgery and the so-called Donation of Charlemagne was in part based on this forgery.

About the same time, Tanchelm of Antwerp fostered a heresy that was the direct result of Church corruption among its priests and bishops. Tanchelm was on the fringe mentally, believing he was God. He married a statue of the Virgin Mary, claiming the Church had become a brothel. Indeed, the celibate priest at the time was the exception. Tanchelm rejected transubstantiation, that is, the belief that the Eucharist was the real body and blood of Christ and no longer bread and wine. He saw the clergy as immoral and thus incapable of administering the sacraments validly. Donatism, a fifth century heresy, denounced by Augustine of Hippo, had held this same view. The point here is that the Church was felt to need radical reform and Tanchelm was one of the first to openly voice this view.

Arnold of Brescia (c. 1100-1155) is probably the best known of early reformers. Benedict of Nursia (480-547), the founder of the Benedictine Order and Bernard of Clairvaux (1090-1153) worked their reforms from within the Church. Arnold had begun in the same manner, trying to spread his message while still in the good graces of the Church. He wished to reform the clergy, whom he saw as wealthy, secular, simoniacal (hungry for church offices, property and wealth) and unchaste. Having tried local reforms, it seemed to him that other measures were called for. He preached poverty, a return to Christ's unworldly ways and chastity for the clergy. He sought true radical Church reform. This was too much for the hierarchy to swallow. Pope Innocent II failed to support Arnold and in 1139, he was condemned and forced to leave Italy. Making his way to Paris, he studied under Peter of Abelard (1079-1142), also a theological reformer. Arnold's attacks on the clergy, included sanctions against Bernard of Clairvaux, which led to a further condemnation at the Synod of Sans in 1141. Subsequently, Pope Eugenius III brought him to Rome to keep a closer eye on him. Soon Arnold, after witnessing the depravity of the hierarchy first hand, extended his criticisms to the Pope himself. He developed a Donatistic mind-set and with the help of the people and nobles managed to have the Pope expelled from Rome for a time but in the end all was for naught and he was burned at the stake.

The times were difficult and political and secular involvements by the clergy seemed necessary in order for the Church to survive. Nonetheless, instead of working reforms from within the Church the hierarchy attempted to maintain unity through brute force. How much of this related to their personal needs to continue in power and bolster the institutional Church rather than seek relief for the poor and underprivileged is uncertain. Undoubtedly, there were elements of institutional decay evident from at least the tenth century. Immorality and secularization of the Church continued to the Reformation and beyond.

THE CRUSADES

The Crusades represent a challenge to theologians and Church historians alike. In 1095, Pope Urban II convened the Council of Claremont, considered by most to have marked the beginning of the Crusader Age.[9] The Council itself was to deal with 'routine' issue, such as, church reform, lay investiture,[10] simony and the King of France's adulterous ways. Fighting among feudal lords had been an escalating problem and the 'Peace of God' (periods of amnesty during feudal wars) was to be discussed. There was only one issue relating to 'crusades'. This involved the conditions under which a knight fighting for Christ was to merit a spiritual reward. On the 105th day of the Council, Urban gave a speech dealing with suppression in the Levant of Christian churches by the Seljuk dynasty [11]. The pope spoke of churches and holy places having been defiled and destroyed. By redirecting the war-like tendencies of European nobles, Urban thought local conflicts could be avoided and peace brought to Christendom. An added benefit was the acquisition of land for second-born noble sons, who by the rule of primogenitor, were deprived of land by which they could maintain themselves and their families. These 'lords without lands' were always looking for property and power, which often led to fratricide, producing widows and orphans along with continuing hostilities. Even churches and abbeys were not invisible to the greedy eyes of the nobility. With attentions diverted eastward the Peace of God would be easier to enforce thus reducing much family feuding. Famine and poverty would also lessen as a result of a more stable agricultural economy. The response to Urban's call to arms was enthusiastic and widespread and resulted in the First Crusade, which was the most successful of all the Crusades. By 1099, Jerusalem had been occupied and this was to hold for nearly one hundred years. Unfortunately, the crusaders turned out to be less than truly Christian. Upon entering Jerusalem a veritable bloodbath ensued with few Muslims, Jews or resident Christians surviving. Though the overt reason given for invading the Middle East was religious in character, there were many unspoken agendas at play including economic and political prospects for the invaders. The crosses

---

9   Mayer, H. E. 1988, *The Crusades*, 2nd Edit. (New York: Oxford University Press) p. 8.

10   Lay investiture involved the appointment of bishops, archbishops and other hierarchy by civil authorities such as kings and emperors rather than by the pope.

11   The Seljuk was a Turkish dynasty that ruled over central and western Asia from the 11th to the 13th century.

embroidered on their clothes failed to soften their military zeal and brutal treatment of the inhabitants of the Holy Land.

The most unchristian crusade was the Fourth. In 1198, Innocent III was elected pope. He was an ambitious man and one of his priorities was to launch a crusade in order to recapture Jerusalem, which had been taken back by the Muslims in 1187. Innocent believed that the pope was superior in authority to mere secular kings. After all, the pope was Christ's representative on Earth; the king was only a secular ruler. It was Innocent's idea that he, as pope, should organize and supervise the crusade he spawned in 1198. He courted the maritime city-states, especially Venice, whose ships and money were needed to carry out his plan. One of the preachers who marketed this crusade was Fulk of Neuilly, a true reformer who emphasized Christ-like poverty. As a result of Innocent's stance, the kings were portrayed as unworthy of leading the crusade. This viewpoint may have been in part responsible for the ill-fated Children's Crusade of 1212. This totally unrealistic venture resulted in the deaths of several thousand children.

The Fourth Crusade and its ultimate outcome are still debated by scholars. The crusaders were to invade Egypt in order to gain a foothold in the Middle East before moving on to take Jerusalem. Serendipity stifled this plan, however. A shortage of funds forced them to bargain with the Doge of Venice, Enrick Dandolo (1192-1205). He was to supply transportation and food for 4,500 knights plus their squires and foot soldiers, totaling 33,500 men. In order to persuade the Doge to lower the fee he was charging, they agreed to invade Zara, a Christian city on the Dalmatian coast that the King of Hungary had taken from the Venetians in 1186. Obviously, it was politically and economically advantageous for the Doge to recapture this Christian city–no religious fervor was involved in his motivations. He had, in fact, insisted on the same payment for the ships and supplies even though the number of troops that were to be deployed had dwindled form 35,000 to 11,000. Dandolo was to make a nice profit plus reclaim Zara without lifting a finger. Innocent III was opposed to the whole scheme and excommunicated everyone involved in it. Later, he gave the French and Germans a reprieve but not the Venetians. The Pope was so intent on launching the crusade that he set aside principles in favor of expediency, thus, joining the conspiracy to take Zara with the anticipated slaughter of many Christians. This was, indeed, an unholy, holy war.

The Fourth Crusade was to be tainted by subsequent political events. Isaac II was the King of Byzantium, however, his ambitious brother, Alexius III, dethroned and blinded him. Isaac's son Alexius IV, sought to take back the throne for his father. There followed a complex series of alliances involving Irene, the sister of Isaac who was the wife of Philip of Swabia as well as other nobles, abbots and even Innocent III. All of these machinations were purely political in nature. Adding spice to this whole military meal was the knowledge that Constantinople was in possession of great wealth, not a small part of which consisted of precious religious relics. Additionally, Alexius IV offered to reunite the Eastern Orthodox Church with Rome. They had been at odds with the West since 1054 and the schism persists to the present day. The invasion of Constantinople followed the bloodbath at Zara, with a slaughter rivaling that of Jerusalem over a hundred years earlier. The prized four horses or Quadriga, part of the Constantinople booty, remain in St. Mark's Cathedral, Venice, to this day. Mostly Christians were slaughtered at Constantinople during the three days of destruction that followed. The Fourth Crusade never captured Jerusalem, its original target. For the next several decades, Christians fought Christians over lands that are now part of Greece and Asia Minor–all territories having little or no religious value.

The Albigensian Crusade from 1209 to 1229 was not directed at gaining control over Jerusalem either. The Albigensians were a heretical offshoot of the Cathars that preached an aesthetic life, reform of corrupt Catholic clergy and separation from the Roman Church. Even though considered heretics they, as with similar heretical movements of the time, were intent on reform of the Church. As with several other crusades, there were secular aspects to this 'Holy War' as well. The sect was centered near Toulouse, France and protected by Raymond VI. The Capetian monarchy had its eye on southern France and especially the region of Languedoc and it was land acquisition rather than reconciliation of heretics that fueled this Crusade. Once more these wars resulted in the loss of many Christian lives. One may explain away much of the brutality of the Crusades by the mores of the times but, as most would agree, Christ was not a militant man eschewing such behaviors in word and work.

THE INQUISITION

The Inquisition is often cited as one of the Church's most extreme and excessive uses of its authority and power. It has been suggested that Inquisitional methods date to Roman times.[12] It was Pope Lucius III, in 1184, with the promulgation of *Ad adolemdam* that the first hint of more severe handling of heretics first came to the fore. The extent of punishment adopted thereafter was based, in part, on the perceived similarity between heresy and high treason. Also, John's gospel is quoted as saying:

---

12   Blötzer, J. Catholic Encyclopedia: Inquisition.

If anyone abide not in me, he shall be cast forth as a branch and shall wither, and they shall gather him up, and cast him into the fire and be burned. (John 15:6)

On the other hand, Christ also said:

I have not come to destroy but to fulfill. (Matt. 5:17).

From the time of Constantine and the Nicene Creed (325) the Church came to see itself as, "a society perfect and sovereign" based on 'pure and authentic revelation'. Christian doctrine, it was believed, must be maintained at any cost.[13] Blötzer states that the Inquisition "is a phase in the growth of ecclesiastical legislation, whose distinctive traits can be fully understood only by a careful study of the conditions amid which it grew up." In the OT Blötzer notes that punishments were harsher than those Christ generally proposed, so that excommunication replaced death in the early Church and that the infamy of the Inquisition came only with the Middle Ages and its plethora of heretics. Heterodoxy the Church maintained required stern suppression in order to save human souls and to promote harmony in society. If thieves, who steal only material goods, are judged deserving of death at the stake, should not heretics who steal men's souls, be punished in like manner for this much more heinous crime? The Church in word, if not in deed, proclaimed mercy for all unbelievers preferring recantation and reunion rather than the rack or stake. It was more important to seek the return of the wayward to the fold than condemnation to eternal Hell fire. Nonetheless, this in practice was not always the case.

By the fifth century, a compact between Church and State was arranged whereby the former could enlist the latter in carrying out civil punishment for religious offenses. Augustine of Hippo initially fostered persuasion in dealing with heretics although later he favored force.[14] Pope Leo I, in 447, while suppressing the Priscillianists for their lax attitude toward the institution of marriage, civil laws and general decadence, sanctioned the death penalty for these heretics. The shedding of blood for such offenses became a civil affair. In other words, the Church preferred not to be the executioner in these cases. The hierarchy apparently wished not to bloody its hands after passing sentence. At least in word, if not in deed, the Church continued to view the death sentence as incompatible with Christ's teachings. As we have already seen, the eleventh century saw an increase in the number of heretical groups and the Church felt the need to suppress

---

13   Ibid.
14   Ibid.

these unorthodox sects. Lucius III, having laid the groundwork for an accelerated effort to control heterodoxy, used Frederick II's (1194-1250) civil authority to implement these penalties. Frederick was the first to institute laws sanctioning the death penalty for heresy and these were used by popes after Innocent IV to strengthen the authority of ecclesiastical inquisitors for the next several centuries. A body of theological opinion emerged during the Middle Ages in support of more severe penalties for heretics. Thomas Aquinas was among those who considered heresy a capital offense.[15]

There were Inquisitions in Rome, the Netherlands, Portugal, Germany and France. The Spanish Inquisition, however, is considered by many to have been the most brutal of inquisitional courts. It is not entirely clear why King Ferdinand fostered this extreme form of the tribunal. Durant suggests that the king may have thought this helped maintain control over his subjects.[16] Though confiscation of property was one of the penalties levied against heretics, financial gain was probably not his primary motivation. The Spanish Inquisition was directed primarily at Christianized Jews (*conversos*) who secretly practiced the faith of their fathers. Life-long Catholics were not immune to the inquisitor's suspicious eyes, however. In Spain only the sovereign could overrule the Supreme Inquisitor. This cleric, often a Dominican friar, made his own rules and Durant believes that the accused was assumed to be guilty before entering court. Often the 'heretic' was not allowed access to his or her accusers or even the charges against him or her. No counsel was allowed and the 'trial' might be over in a day or less.

There are differing views of inquisitional history. In the sixteenth century there were the Catholic and Protestant histories of the Inquisition. Some refer to these as the 'White' and 'Black' histories. In 1571, Pope Pius V set up a commission to provide an *apologia* against the Protestant version (Magdeburg Centuries) of the Tribunal's history. Caesar Baronius took on the task and several volumes of the Roman response were published as the *Annals Ecclesiastic*. In essence, Baronius asserted that the Church had never deviated from Christ's teachings.[17] Luis de Pàrama, who had been the inquisitor in Sicily from 1584 to 1605, wrote a history strictly devoted to the Inquisition and not as part of a general Church history, as earlier writers had done. It was one of the Inquisition's 'White' histories.[18] He began with creation of Adam and Eve and their expulsion from the Garden of Eden as

15   Aquinas, T. *Summa Theologiae*, II-III:113.
16   Op. cit. Durant, W. 1956, p. 209.
17   Peters, E. 1988 *Inquisition* (Berkeley, CA: University of California Press) p. 265.
18   There were three volumes in all. The first carried the lengthy title of *The Origin and Development of the Office of the Holy Inquisition and on its Dignity and Truthfulness*. The last volume was published in 1598.

a prototype of the Inquisition and God as the first and greatest Inquisitor. God's 'excommunication' of Adam and Eve was a just and legal act by the Supreme Judge just as were the punishments of the medieval inquisitors. Pàrama goes on to depict Christ, John the Baptist and all the apostles as inquisitorial archetypes. The bishops of the Church, as successors to Christ and the apostles, inherited inquisitorial powers. Dominic, founder of the Dominicans, was portrayed as the first Inquisitor General. The mendicant orders (Franciscans and Dominicans) were especially involved as inquisitors, though Jesuits, later on, performed this function as well. Pàrama's history can be best described, from the Catholic viewpoint, as a 'triumphant ' picture of truth over falsity. The Roman Church saw this 'holy office' as having saved the souls of many misguided men and women while at the same time, preserving the peace and harmony of society as a whole.

The Venetian Inquisition is considered by many to have been the most humane form of this tribunal. Even some Protestants looked with favor on this edition of the Inquisition. It was from Venice that the first 'Black' Catholic history of the Inquisition came. Paolo Sarpi, (1552-1623) describes the workings of this tribunal in a republican City-State, whose relations with Rome were often acrimonious, in a more favorable light. The hierarchy of Venice was subservient to civic authority in contrast to other parts of Europe and, thus, the handling of heretics was more moderate. Sarpi was a Servite friar and consulting theologian to the Republic of Venice after 1606 and he attempted to analyze the rift that separated Catholics and Reformers. In 1606, a dispute between Venice and Pope Paul V resulted in a papal interdiction[19] against Venice. As the theologian for Venice, Sarpi wrote a series of treatises in response to Rome's interdiction. One of these was, *On the Office of the Inquisition* (1615). This work emphasized 'due process' in tribunal proceedings and maintained the autonomy of the Venetian Senate in such matters. He openly criticized the suppression of harmless dissenters and noted the ineffectiveness of such measures in other countries, which resulted in heightened resentment by other principalities. While condemning inquisitional practices, he also noted injustices perpetrated by Calvin in the Michael Servetus case. Servetus as mentioned earlier, was a Spanish theologian and physician who fled his homeland to avoid the Inquisition only to be burned at the stake in Geneva for his views on the Trinity. Calvin supported Servetus' murder .

---

19   An interdiction by the pope limited church activities in the area under interdiction. It may include a city, region or an entire country. The clergy in these areas was forbidden to administer most sacraments and was unable to perform Christian burials. No Masses were allowed. The congregations were most adversely affected by interdiction, the clergy less so.

Sarpi asserted that the Apostles never sanctioned the death penalty and advised only reprimands and expulsion for those holding deviant theological views. He also disparaged some of the pronouncements of the Council of Trent (1545-1563), which had formulated the Vatican's major counter-Reformation strategies. All these opinions earned Sarpi considerable favor in other countries and further hostility from Rome. In all this, Sarpi was pushing the Venetian political agenda while at the same time providing an alternate historical vision of the Inquisition.

However one approaches this topic today, whether from the more guarded Catholic stance or the more critical viewpoint of some modern historians, the fact remains that the historical Christ (and this is often difficult to define) did not judge the sinners of the NT harshly. The woman caught in adultery (John 8:1-11) and the woman at the well (John 4:1-42) was treated mercifully. The ten lepers, despised by all, were healed (Luke 17:11-19) and Christ invited Levi the despised tax collector to join him (Luke 5:27-32). He forgave his torturers (Luke 23:32-35) and the thief crucified beside him on the cross (Luke 23:39-43). The woman who was a sinner (presumably a prostitute) was treated humanely (Luke 7:37-39) and he made Mary Magdalene one of his apostles. By the sixth century the Roman Church had considered her a woman of ill-repute, though this label is denied by some scholars today. Christ was not a militant man. His was a gospel of forgiveness, acceptance and peace. To dismiss the actions of the Inquisition as culturally acceptable at the time is to forget the new covenant of love that Christ had proclaimed—a lapse of memory evident in the Church of the Middle Ages.

Charles Kimball, in his book, *When Religion Becomes Evil,* defines five signs of a declining religious institution.[20] These include (1) claims of being the only religion to possess the 'truth'; (2) requiring its adherents to show blind obedience to the authority of this institution; (3) a Machiavellian approach to maintaining power at any cost; (4) pursuing holy wars; and (5) establishing the 'ideal' time for many events. These features are evident in the medieval Church, Reformation Churches and of course in certain Islamic and Christian sects today. Fundamentalism whether Jewish, Catholic, Protestant or Islamic, past and present, has succumbed to these five failings. It is part of being human. We all love power, authority, riches, control over others, being 'right' and forcing our ideas on others. These all make us feel good, superior and secure. Along with these manifestations of religious decline there are also a variety of unethical behaviors including greed, pride, arrogance, promiscuity and lying to cover their immorality and

---

20   Kimball, C. 2002, *When Religion Become Evil: Five Warning Signs* (San Francisco, CA: Harper).

other failings. We are all familiar with the list of 'sins' 'holy people' are prone to commit, most notably today those of tele-evangelists and Catholic clergy.

THE RENAISSANCE

Beginning with Dante Alighieri (1265-1321) in the early Renaissance, the Church came under more sophisticated gunfire. In the *Divine Comedy*, Dante leveled both subtle and blatant attacks on the Church and its clergy. At one point, Dante portrays the Church as a chariot beset by Islamic heretics and the French King as holding its reigns symbolizing the control the French had over the pope during the Avignon papacy.[21] Phillip the Fair of France induced Pope Clement V to move the Holy See to Avignon, France in 1309. Clement V and his predecessor, Boniface VIII were politically corrupt. Dante characterizes the Church as a military institution having grafted a sword onto the crosier–the shepherd's crook symbolizing Christ, the loving caretaker of his flock. Recall that Christ was a pacifist in the NT but during Constantine's reign he became a militant figure (with little or no support from Scripture) in order to suit the image of the Roman emperor. Though Dante places none of the popes or kings in the lower levels of Hell, they are adequately represented in the other regions of Satan's sanctuary.

Boccaccio (1313-1375) in the *Decameron* tells the story of a Christian, Giannotto, who continually urges his good Jewish friend, Abraham, to convert to the 'true faith'.[22] Finally, Abraham agrees to consider baptism but beforehand, he wishes to see Rome, the center of Catholicism. His friend, with great trepidation, awaits Abraham's return from Rome the city that is also the hub of clerical hedonism. Abraham returns ready to be baptized. Astonished, his friend inquires into the reason for his decision. Abraham responds that the one, true God must most assuredly guide an institution that can withstand such corruption for so many centuries!

Similarly, Geoffrey Chaucer (c. 1340-1400), in his satirical way, portrays many of the clergy as less than holy.[23] In the *Summoner's Tale*, as one example, he tells of a friar who is avaricious and gluttonous, seeking monetary rewards for prayers never offered for his benefactors. In the *Canon's Yeoman's Tale*, Chaucer tells of a canon[24] who dupes a fellow clergyman into thinking he has the power to turn base metals into pure silver. In this scam

---

21   Dante Alighieri, 1950, *The Divine Comedy, Purgatorio* (New York: Random House, Modern Library), Canto XXXII.

22   Boccaccio, G. *Decameron* (New York: W. W. Norton), Second tale of the first day.

23   Chaucer, G. *The Canterbury Tales*, trans. N. Coghill (London: Penguin).

24   A canon is an unordained clergyman, bound by vows and generally involved in the administration of a cathedral.

the priest is swindled out of a sizable sum of money. There are a number of such priestly portrayals in Dante, Boccaccio and Chaucer. Many stories tell of clerical immorality–mostly sexual in nature. All three of these poets wrote in the vernacular making their exposés of the clergy, nobles, common folk and physicians available to a wider audience. It was evident that the Church was under siege and this state of affairs was not to go away. With the death of Chaucer and the dawn of the fifteenth century, things were only to get worse for the Church.

JOHN WYCLIFFE

John Wycliffe (c. 1320-1384), an Oxford scholar, advocated for the clergy's return to the plain, unworldly, humble apostolic way of life as Christ himself had preached. Wycliffe also railed against civil and political activities in which the clergy had become involved. He diminished the authority of the Church, sponsored an English translation of the Bible and denied the doctrine of transubstantiation. He spoke of an invisible light within each of the faithful, rather than the visible light from the institutional Church; a notion reminiscent of the Gnostic's *gnosis*. He was removed from his post at Oxford and condemned by the Council at Blackfriars in 1382, two years before his death. Wycliffe wished to reform the Church and not to defy it, however, this was not to be. He was spared a heretic's death and died of natural causes.

Clerical immorality and corruption was nothing new in the Renaissance but the outflow of cash from the local churches to the Papal coffers had become an increasing problem for England and other Western European governments. In England, the Parliament was pressured by its clerical members–bishops and abbots–to provide funds for Rome. Ecclesiastical land holdings were significant and reduced the flow of taxes into public coffers. Particularly irritating, at the time, was the Avignon Papacy. English wealth was supporting a Church controlled by the French, the perennial foe of England. And, of course, ecclesiastical earnings were tax exempt. Some of Wycliffe's polemics related to the issue of Church affluence.[25] Among the English nobility John of Gaunt was especially concerned with these matters and it was his protection that largely allowed Wycliffe to avoid the gallows. This was not the case with John Hus as we shall see next.

A group of followers, the Lollards, persisted for a time after Wycliffe's death. Wycliffe is considered one of the early reformers that paved the way for the Reformation that was to come crashing down upon the Roman Church in the following centuries.

25   Durant, W. 1957, *The Reformation* (New York: Simon & Schuster), pp. 30-31.

JOHN HUS

John Hus (c. 1372-1415) is perhaps the most tragic of early Renaissance reformers. He was a sincere, devout and honest man who, without malice, wished to guide wayward clergy and laity to a Christ-like spiritual life. In 1388, a number of Bohemian students received scholarships to study in England. On their return, they brought back copies of John Wycliffe's writings. In 1391, the reform Bethlehem Church, was established in Prague and Hus was living there as a seminarian. He completed his Master of Arts in 1396 and was ordained in 1401. He preached at the Bethlehem Church and soon became the most famous homilist in all of Prague. He practiced what he preached– an austere and holy life. The Eucharist at the time was limited to distribution at Mass of the host only. Probably this practice had developed out of convenience but was viewed by many as diminishing the status of the lay people. Following Wycliffe, Hus began giving out Communion under both species–a practice not reinstituted in the Catholic Church until after Vatican II in the 1960's. In 1403, the University of Prague banned Wycliffe's writings, with Hus dissenting.[26] For his persistent reformist views, Hus was ultimately excommunicated. The Archbishop demanded that all of Wycliffe's writings be surrendered. Hus and others complied, and all manuscripts were burned. Hus appealed to Pope John XXIII (later declared a false pope)[27] who called Hus before the Papal Court–an offer Hus wisely refused.

In 1411, Pope John, looking to fund a crusade, announced a new indulgence, which was considered by many to be simony, pure and simple– the selling of salvation for papal profit–a policy that was to be opposed by Martin Luther some 96 years later. Following this, Hus preached against indulgences and also questioned the doctrine of Purgatory.[28] He then called the Pope a money-grubber and the anti-Christ. Three youths who supported Hus' views were beheaded. Further sanctions were levied against Hus by the Pope and he went into seclusion for two years. Hus continued to attack the Church for simony, as well as the clergy for charging fees for baptisms

---

26   Ibid, p. 163.

27   This is why we had a second Pope John XXIII in the 20th century.

28   Purgatory as a theological concept was not fully developed until the twelfth century. The Scriptural basis used to support the doctrine of Purgatory comes from "The Bosom of Abraham" mentioned in the NT. In the Bible, the expression "the Bosom of Abraham" is found only in Luke's Gospel (16:22-23). It occurs in the parable of the Rich Man and Lazarus, the imagery of which is plainly drawn from the popular representation of the unseen world of the dead that was current in Christ's time. According to the Jewish conceptions of that day, the souls of the dead were gathered into a general tarrying-place the *Sheol* of OT literature, and *Hades* (Hell) of the NT writings (Luke 16:22-23);

and the other sacraments. He adopted a Donatist's view of corrupt clergy, claiming they could not validly administer the sacraments. He accepted Wycliffe's idea regarding predestination. Denouncing the worldliness of the Church, he denied papal authority and held that Christ, not the pope was its head. He believed, as alleged recently, that Pope John VIII was actually Pope Joan who gave birth to a child while pope. All of these pronouncements were most unsettling for the Church. As a result, in 1415, John Hus, having been guaranteed safe passage, foolishly went to the Council of Constance in order to defend himself, only to be put in chains and in short order burned at the stake. This Council was to end the Great Schism, a series of anti-popes that had plagued the papacy beginning in 1378. At one point there were three claimants to the papal throne.

Wycliffe and Hus were only two of many reformers that surfaced in the fourteenth and following centuries. They were, however, not fringe characters as some had been earlier. Rather, they were well-educated theologians who sought honest reforms from within the Church. Unholy behaviors on the part of both common clergy and high ecclesiastics had prompted their actions. How much they influenced Luther, Henry VIII, Calvin and other reformers is disputed but whatever their role in the Reformation, they fostered a religious sentiment that was to grow into a tsunami-sized wave of social, cultural and clerical change.

ERASMUS

Desiderius Erasmus (c. 1466-1536) was a Dutch Augustinian monk who did not like monastic life and spent most of his active years outside monastery walls.[29] In 1492, he was ordained a priest well versed in Latin and Greek literature. He became a 'literary citizen' of both Rome and Athens, reading Plato, Euripides, Epicurus as well as Cicero and Seneca. Although always Catholic, he is one of the most famous Reformation humanists. Lorenzo Valla, a contemporary Italian humanist had proved that the so-called Donation of Constantine[30] was a forgery at about the same time that errors in Jerome's *Vulgate*, which was a Latin translation of the Bible based on Hebrew and Greek texts, were discovered. The *Vulgate* had been the 'gold standard' of Scriptural documents since the late fourth century. All Scriptural translations up to the sixteenth century were based on the *Vulgate*. Discrepancies in such important, long-accepted documents whetted

---

29   Op. cit. Durant, W. 1957, pp. 271-2.
30   The Donation of Constantine was an eighth century forgery that claimed most of Western Europe had been granted to the Roman Church by the fourth century emperor. It provided the basis for the Church's claim to their secular power and property.

Erasmus' appetite for more such discoveries. He attempted to reconcile ancient Greek Epicurean philosophy with Christian theology–an unsettling idea at the time. This philosophical system was long considered hedonistic and thus immoral, although a critical reading of Epicurus does not support this view. There were also questions lurking in Erasmus' mind regarding the doctrines of transubstantiation[31] and the Trinity. He was especially smitten by Christ's humanistic message.

England was agreeable to Erasmus and it was here that he met Thomas More (1478-1535). While living with More, he wrote, in a matter of days, *The Praise of Folly*. The Latin title is *Encomium Moraine* from which our word 'moron' is derived, implied absurdity, ignorance, stupidity as well as, simplicity. All of human behavior is predicated on folly, mindless attraction to women, addiction to opulence, foolishness of marriage by both men and women, the latter paying for its questionable joys by the pains of childbirth and motherhood. These are all human follies. Erasmus cynically maintains that humans would be appalled if they thought for only a moment about the evident idiocy of these behaviors. Wisdom is likewise foolishness, for it only brings sorrow and grief. It is fortunate, he asserts, that the majority of the world ignores science and philosophy thus saving itself from all sorts of grief. Philosophy only "confounds the confused and darkens the obscure". Metaphysical babbling produces nothing but wind, he proclaims. Physicians are described as impostors and theologians as 'supercilious and touchy'.[32] He may have been sensitive to criticism by academics since he did not possess a university degree, having studied mainly at seminary schools. He chides theologians for not recognizing the help he has given them. They are slavishly attached to Scholasticism with all its metaphysical obscurity. "They abound in newly coined expressions and strange-sounding words… and interpret hidden mysteries to suit themselves."

Theologians concern themselves with how the world was created and designed and the means by which Original Sin is passed on to Adam and Eve's posterity. They deal with questions concerning Christ's stay in Mary's womb and how the 'accidents', that is the appearance of bread and wine can

---

31   This theological tenet holds that the bread and wine are turned into the body and blood of Christ when the priest utters the words at Mass, "This is my body", and "This is my blood". There is an essential change in the nature of the bread and wine and these become the body and blood of Christ retaining only the 'appearances' of bread and wine.

32   Erasmus, D. 1993, *The Praise of Folly and Letters to Marten Van Doorp*, trans. B. Radise (London: Penguin) p. 86.

subsist in the Eucharist without retaining their substance and on and on.[33] All these are echoes of the ultimate question of the Scholastics, "How many angels can dance on the head of a needle?" Of course, angels can't dance anywhere, they are spirits and as such have no feet.

These criticisms are harsh condemnations of 'ivory tower' thinkers who have drifted away from the real world in which Christ lived. Rather than concern for the suffering of souls overwhelmed by pain, hunger and homelessness the 'Schoolmen', as the Scholastics are called, were firmly positioned with their heads in the clouds. Voltaire, as noted earlier, was to continue such sardonic salvos in *Candide*.

Erasmus compares members of the hierarchy to secular monarchs. He suggests that the pope, cardinals and bishops might reflect on the meaning of their ecclesiastical robes and recall that the white they wear at Mass symbolizes a 'pure and spotless life'.[34] Similarly, the bishop's crosier stands for the "watchful care of his flock entrusted to him". There are many such symbols of his office and if a bishop would reflect on these for a moment they might realize that their lives are less than the ideal life that Christ set as an example before them. Erasmus levels similar criticisms on the cardinals and popes. Their secular ways, their opulence and inattention to duty are all found to flow from Erasmus' pen. Simony, violence including poisoning their enemies, the sword in battle against Muslims and Christians alike and the condemnation to death of 'heretics' are all instruments unknown to Christ but frequently employed by the hierarchy in their attempt to maintain power, protect their lands and increase their wealth. They should listen to the words of Christ. Erasmus goes on to say that it would be sufficient:

> To rid them (the hierarchy) of all their wealth and honors, their sovereignty and triumph, their many offices, dispensations, taxes and indulgences, all their horses and mules, their retinue, and their countless pleasures.[35]

Erasmus leaves very few of the Church's people, clergy, myths and liturgy untouched by his satire. He is possibly more direct in his censure of the Church than Dante, Boccaccio or Chaucer. In due course, the *Folly* made

---

33   Aristotle maintained that 'accidents' i.e. the characteristics of a thing can only 'subsist' when supported by the 'substance' or essence of the thing. The substance or essence is that which makes a thing what it is. This kind of metaphysical talk is what Erasmus objected to. In the Eucharist, if the substances of bread and wine are replaced by the substances of body and blood, how can the 'accidents' or appearance of bread and wine remain?
34   Ibid, p. 107.
35   Ibid, p. 108-9.

it onto the Church's list of forbidden books. It is no surprise that Erasmus lived and wrote on the threshold of the Reformation.

The height of the Church's worldliness came with the papacies of Alexander VI and Julius II, around 1500. Julius reigned from 1503 to 1513. Alexander is noted for his opulence, unchaste life and several children including the militant and Machiavellian Cezare Borgia. Julius, the warrior-pope, personally led his troops into battle. Leo X, who followed Julius, failed to recognize the seriousness of Luther's ninety-five theses, attempted to impose restrictions on Luther without success. Later Clement VII, for political reasons, yielded to the demands of Phillip of Spain, and refused to annul Henry VIII's marriage to Catherine of Aragon and thus suffered the dire consequences of this fateful decision. Reforms were beginning to snowball with ever increasing speed and size. Neither the Inquisition nor the counter-Reformation was to quell this storm[36] of religious and cultural change–much of this spawned and sustained by the corruption of institutional religion.

PROTESTANTISM

As noted earlier, Protestantism has not been untouched by violence, corruption, scandal and irrational beliefs. The case of Michael Servetus and his death, fostered by John Calvin was chronicled earlier. Many of the 'power plays' associated with the Roman Church are not unknown to Protestants. Reformers frequently sponsor theocracies of a most 'heavy-handed' sort. This was true in Europe and America. Burning of 'witches' in New England by Puritan groups is a well-known example of religious fervor gone astray. Much of the American Revolution involved battles over religion and religious freedom. Thomas Jefferson[37] and Thomas Paine[38] among others fought vigorously for religious freedom. Many of the colonies were established for religious reasons and the founding fathers wanted to ensure that no individual state or the Union as a whole would restrict freedom of faith while at the same time making sure that there would be separation of church and state.

We are aware today of the religious polarity that has developed in this country over the last several decades. Fundamentalists are fighting to rescind Roe v. Wade, prevent gay marriages, stem cell research and introduce

---

36   Grant, R. 2006, *Storm* (Eugene, OR: Wipf & Stock Publishers). This recent novelized version of Luther's life emphasizes the impact Luther had on religion and the Reformation.

37   Gibbons, J. C. 2009, *The Faith of Our Fathers* (Charlotte, NC: Tan Publishing).

38   Paine, T. 2003, *Common Sense, Rights of Man and Other Essential Writing s of Thomas Paine* (New York: Signet Classics).

creationism and intelligent design into public schools. At the same time a number of evangelists have been tainted by sexual and/or financial scandals.

The negative aspects of religion seem endless but one must remember that institutionalization of any movement spawns many ills; the economists call this the 'diseconomy of scale'. For religious groups this means hyper-organization, theological tentacles that spread endlessly and corruption among the clergy that seems self-perpetuating. Nonetheless, religion remains a vital force in America and worldwide. It will not go away any time soon. We must learn to accept and work with it, utilizing its pluses and minimizing its minuses. Part of this process, however, involves change so that religion can be properly integrated into modern society. Change is difficult for some religious persons. But change is always hard no matter what field with which one is dealing.

In the next section we look at three religious tenets that test the rational bases of theology. We investigate the supernatural realm, creationism and the question of grace, free will and predestination. There are many such doctrines that have developed over the past two millennia and defy rational analysis. The three issues I have chosen to look at are personal interests of mine. They do however relate to the question of how one defines God.

CHAPTER 5

RELIGION: THE UNBELIEVABLE

THE SUPERNATURAL WORLD

One of the first tasks with which we must deal and the most difficult of all the dualisms one confronts in any religious debate is the supernatural/natural dichotomy. This is a dualism that many, including Stephen J. Gould, say can never be bridged. The supernatural world has a long history dating, most likely, to prehistory. Prehistoric *Homo sapiens* buried their dead with supplies to carry them into the next world. The ancient Sumerians, Babylonians, Egyptians and Greeks all professed belief in an afterlife by spirits of a supernatural nature.

The concept of the supernatural includes notions of the immaterial, spiritual, the human soul, angels, devils, ghosts and God. We are, however, creatures of a material world. The only things we know for sure are those objects of the physical world that surround us and are known through the five senses. We believe in the supernatural through faith, Scripture, personal feelings and/or ancient authority. Religious tradition, the Bible, Qur'an and other holy writings provide a source for what many would call 'truth' but all these are suspect, for they spring from a variety of sources that often are inconsistent or contradictory, are disputed by conflicted religious authorities, cannot be tested by other than anecdotal means and often result in ever increasing divergent views that create confusion rather than consensus. Empirical research has the advantage of leading to convergent opinions and general agreement rather than divergent and conflicting views. In addition, science provides practical confirmation of their data, that is, they work. They offer concrete, useful results that most would agree help people live a better, more convenient or safer life. This is not the case with religious tenets such as the concept of the supernatural. Wars have been fought over such theological concepts that spring from human imagination or emotional, egoistical and/or avaricious desires. Ideas that feel right or seem commonsensical may turn out to be in error. Many sincere people believe very fervently in a variety of religious doctrines that support them in their emotional or physical lives but what works for one believer may not work for another. As we are seeing today, religious views may lead to disruption and destruction over conflicting ideologies. The resulting discord, devastation and death are daily in the news. Currently it seems to be Islam against Christianity and/or Judaism. Too often, it is Christians against Christians, Muslims against Muslims or Hindus against Muslins and Sikhs. Many authors such as Richard Dawkins and Sam Harris make much of the cruelties spawned by religions, both past and present. The origins of all these disputes are not always clear but whether ethnic, economic, territorial or egotistical, religious tenets often are given as the excuse for such discord.

THE BODY-MIND PROBLEM

As mentioned, of all dualistic religious beliefs, the supernatural/ natural debate accounts for more intellectual, emotional and physical discomfort than perhaps any other dualistic concepts. The supernatural world is accepted by most, if not all religions and certainly this is true for the three monotheistic faiths. How the spiritual realm came to play such a prominent role in modern religions is not entirely clear. The notion of a domain above and beyond the physical, though ancient, came to the fore in the Middle Ages.[1] Although the definition of this 'other' world may have differed from this concept as used today, we continue to find differences of opinion as to how one should view the supernatural. Spiritual or immaterial status may be applied to God, the soul, ghosts, séances, extrasensory perception (ESP), magic, stars, comets, mythological figures, monarchs, emperors, angels, devils, haunted houses, incantations and many such objects and ideas. If one asks for a definition of the supernatural, the responses given may run the gamut from religious to romantic.

Because a spirit is not accessible to the five senses, the immaterial can mean many things to many people. It is not, however, the lack of a precise definition that concerns us here but, rather, the supernatural and natural as disparate domains. The supernatural/natural dualism forms the basis for almost all the dualistic debates found in theology and philosophy. Whether dealing with the mind and body, good and evil, free will and determinism, good works and grace, the transcendence or imminence of God, the metaphysical or anthropomorphic character of God or a number of other issues. The supernatural/natural divide underlies all these controversies.

Many attempts to bridge the gulf between these two realms or magisteria (as Stephen J. Gould calls them) have been attempted. None of

---

1   Bartlett, R. 2008, *The Natural and Supernatural in the Middle Ages* (New York: Cambridge University Press).

these, however, has successfully resolved this issue. Gould has settled on calling these two worlds 'non-overlapping magisteria' (NOMA). In other words, the supernatural and natural are separate spheres that cannot be viewed or studied using any common instrument. The supernatural is known only through authority, sacred writings, tradition, philosophical and/or theological reasoning, while the natural world is accessible only through the five senses and empirical research. According to Gould, there is no way that one can unite these two disciplines. This is dualism in its most extreme form. The two spheres are separate; never to be connected and in Gould's mind there is no reason to connect them. This would be a vain, senseless task in his view.

Descartes attempted to unite the soul with the body, placing the former in the pineal 'gland' of the brain. This approach has been labeled 'interactionism' since the mind (soul) interacts with the body (brain) in some manner. This, of course, solves nothing, for we are still faced with connecting the immaterial with the material. Claiming that the spirit can direct or control the material because it is 'superior' or has 'power' over matter explains nothing. We are left with no more information, no better an explanation than previously. To say that the spirit has power or control over matter including the body is an empty statement.

Other approaches to elucidating the nature of the mind and body interaction have been tried—some are dualistic, some monistic. Dualism of the sort Gould posits holds that the mind and body are fundamentally different and each exists independent of the other. Descartes attempted a kind of union of the two, though most would agree that this was unsuccessful. Baruch Spinoza (1532-1576) denied Descartes' idea that the soul was located in the pineal gland[2] and suggested the mind and body were but two aspects (attributes) of God, so that they are simply different views of the same thing united in God. God possesses an infinite number of attributes however only those of thought (spirit) and extension (matter) are known to humans. This explanation has a certain appeal but in the end is just another metaphysical explanation that really says nothing we can get our reason or imagination around. And, of course, his approach is not empirically verifiable.

Another way of dealing with the body-mind duality was provided by Gottfried Leibniz's (1646-1716). In contrast to Descartes, he realized that there was no way for spiritual and material systems to connect with one another. In his scheme, the mind and body do not interact but exist side-by-side in parallel worlds. Leibniz called this 'Pre-established Harmony'. Leibniz proposed that God, at the time of creation, set the spiritual and material

---

2   The pineal gland is a 'pea-sized' structure located in the center of the brain that produces melatonin and is involved in sleep control.

worlds ticking at exactly the same rate, like two synchronized clocks, so that all material events were accompanied by a simultaneous spiritual event. These two happenings perfectly matched each other as though there were a cause and effect relationship between them. Early on Leibniz had rejected 'Occasionalism' because this theory required that God continually adjusted the two spiritual and material 'clocks' in order to keep them synchronized, making God an imperfect 'watchmaker' or intelligent designer.

Strict materialism is a form of monism. Karl Marx labeled this Dialectical Materialism. The very word materialism carries negative connotations for most theists. Modernism and materialism have been condemned by many theologians in the past two centuries as being anti-spiritual and, thus, providing a sure path to Hell. In the late nineteenth and early twentieth centuries, the Catholic Church was particularly exercised by the idea of modernity.

Materialism has the one advantage of eliminating the body-mind problem entirely. However, it leaves the apparent reality of the mind and its corollary, the soul, unexplained. The concepts of consciousness and self-awareness also remain enigmatic within a materialistic system.

Epiphenomenalism is a monistic materialism that claims that what is viewed as mind or soul is only an accidental by-product of brain activity. Consciousness is no more than an intricate interaction of trillions of nerve cells. Francis Crick promotes this theory in, *The Astonishing Hypothesis*.[3] Broom believes it is superfluous to separate 'mind' and brain:

> It is my view that there is no useful distinction between mind and brain and only the word brain is needed.[4]

George Berkeley (1685-1753) proposed a monistic idealism or mentalism to solve the body-mind problem. He is called by some an 'objective idealist' because his approach is not strictly solipsistic.[5] The world, in other words, is not contained entirely within a person's mind. Ideas are the only real things but these ideas are in your mind and my mind but also in the mind of God. Like Plato's Ideas or Forms, these images or ideas are the only truly real things. In contrast to Plato, however, there are,

---

3   Crick, F. 1994, *The Astonishing Hypothesis: The Scientific Search for the Soul* (New York: Simon & Schuster).
4   Broom, D. M. 2004, *The Evolution of Morality and Religion* (Kindle Edition) p. 90.
5   Solipsism is 1. The theory that the self is the only thing that can be known and verified; and 2. The theory or view that the self is the only reality, everything else is a construct of the mind, in other words there is nothing outside my mind—no people, matter, souls etc.

according to Berkeley, no shadowy imitations of these Ideas in what we call the physical world. Berkeley was a clergyman and resisted the mechanistic physics of Newton as anti-spiritual and potentially evil. Berkeley's monism has the advantage of eliminating any dualistic puzzles. There is but one domain, the mental and, therefore, there can be no debate about soul-body or spiritual-material interplay. All reality is one. Berkeley's system flies in the face of scientific evidence that there is something that we call matter/energy. This something may be strange and incomprehensible, especially in quantum terms, but it is still a part of reality that cannot be ignored. Thus, the materialistic monism of Marx eliminates the spiritual whereas Berkeley's idealism eliminates the material realm, *ergo*, no dualism and no body-mind problem. Both systems leave unanswered questions raised by 'real-world', practical events and concepts. The physical cannot be denied any more than the mind or consciousness.

There have been other solutions to the mind-body issue. Bernhard Rensch in 1971 offered a theory suggesting that all matter has a kind of primitive consciousness. Accordingly, every bit of matter has some consciousness. In this approach, the mind is an aspect of matter–the two are not really separate. This still leaves the nagging question of how the two (matter and consciousness) exist and interact with one another. It's the same dualism only on a microcosmic scale. This is more metaphysics–long on concepts, short on explanations. At present, there seems no good solution to the body-mind conundrum so let us move on to the question of the soul and its nature.

THE SOUL

Is there such a thing as a soul? And if there is, what is its nature? Is it simple or complex? Is it immaterial or corporeal? What are its functions? Is it immortal and eternal? Can it be rewarded or punished for past good or evil deeds? Can it sin? And if it sins grievously, does it turn black (as the nuns used to tell us)? Can a spiritual soul burn in Hell? Or can an immaterial soul have a color such as white or black?

The concept of the soul has a long history. We have already discussed Animism. According to this theory, all things, animate and inanimate[6] possess a soul–trees, rivers, fountains, ponds, winds, storms, seas, mountains, forest groves, plants, animals and, of course, humans. Greek mythology is full of such souls, be they nymphs, spirits, shades in Hades or gods.

---

6   Of course, to say that an inanimate thing has a soul is an oxymoron, inanimate meaning 'without soul'.

The Sumerians believed in a nether world where souls resided after death. These souls were called shades and they went to Kurt (Hades). On occasion, they could return to the land of the living, as was the case with the Sumerian mythical figure, Enkidu, who was welcomed home by none other than the epic hero, Gilgamesh. There are similar resurrections in Greek literature such as the case of Persephone who spends six months each year in the underworld with Pluto and the same period with her mother, Demeter, the goddess of agriculture.[7] Similar tales are written in the Bible (I Samuel 28:11-15) where King Saul retrieves the prophet, Samuel, from Sheol, the Jewish version of Hades. And, of course, Lazarus (John 11) and other NT persons returned from the dead, including Christ himself.

The Greeks debated the nature of the soul at length. Plato claimed that the soul is immortal. Death was merely the separation of the soul from the body. A soul cannot be created out of nothing some claim. This would imply that the soul, in fact, all souls, have existed eternally. Whether Plato's Forms are eternal, spiritual essences is not clear. The soul is however, according to early writers tripartite, that is the soul has reason, appetites and a sense of honor. These might be analogous to the cognitive, appetitive and moral aspects of human nature that some authors claim. The soul, though composed of these "parts" or "aspects" or "functions" is, nonetheless, said to be simple; that is, not partitioned. Material things have parts because they are extended in space and time but the soul as immaterial cannot have dimensions or parts. It is undivided–a simple unity according to many theologians.

Aristotle sought 'wisdom' first and foremost. Of all things to be studied, he ranked the soul as the number one most "honorable and prized" subject to pursue. He also readily admitted that gaining knowledge about the soul is most difficult. Its essence is, indeed, elusive. For Aristotle, discerning the nature of the soul is a strictly metaphysical process that leaves us with no certitude about the soul's true nature. We have seen how fallible metaphysical reasoning can be. In spite of this view, Aristotle posits a number of characteristics of the soul that he feels define its essence. For Aristotle all earthly things consist of form and matter, both of these are metaphysical entities. Form provides the essence of a thing, its essence makes a thing what it is, a thing's defining principle. Naming such a vital principle an essence unfortunately, tells us nothing about how its Form or essence gives something functional characteristics. It is a fatuous or empty term.

---

7   The six months Persephone spends in Hades is winter and the other six months she spends with her mother, Demeter, on Earth accounts for the agricultural growing season.

Matter, in Aristotle scheme, is "prime matter," that is, the metaphysical stuff that the Form uses to make something a physical thing. How prime matter accomplishes this 'materialization' of the body is unexplained. How can a metaphysical thing (prime matter) act on another metaphysical factor (the Form or substance) to make a material being? The body is the material part of a human being and is fashioned out of prime matter, though the latter is not truly physical. It is the metaphysical basis of physical things that have been given reality by its Form and this Form is the soul, also referred to as its substance. Whereas the body is physical, the soul is immaterial and spiritual. It is the vital principle in all living things–vegetable, animal or human. Animism had first offered a spiritual, vital principle to explain all motion and change. The soul was Aristotle's version of this concept. These verbal constructs provide no real information about how any living being is fashioned. One can see why Erasmus and Voltaire lampooned metaphysics.

The body requires a soul so that it may be a body. The soul expresses itself through the body. The emotions, for example, are evident in bodily behavior. And the human soul contains the functions found in the vegetative and animal soul but in addition it is capable of thought and deliberation. Thought has for its object 'truth for truth's sake', while deliberation seeks practical and prudent truth. Aristotle calls this part of the soul, *nous*. It is the *nous* that is immortal and may exist separate from the body. The vegetative and animal parts of the soul, however, die with the body. Aristotle also refers to the *nous* as the 'active intellect'. One can see how Aristotle influenced Christian theology of the soul.

Aristotle does not view the soul as entombed in the body, as Plato did. Rather the soul and body form one close union. The soul must have the body in order to exercise its various faculties.

Plato and Augustine of Hippo saw the body as a drag on the soul. The soul was superior to the body. The latter led humans into sin, was prone to diseases and was responsible for most of one's miseries. The body was base and the soul sublime. The soul participates in the divinity of God. The sooner the soul can rid itself of this bodily millstone the better. Again, it is easy to see the effect that this Platonic view of human nature had on future religions dogma especially sin and Luther's concept of total human depravity.

In the Middle Ages, the body was seen as sinful. Even such necessary functions as sexual intercourse were considered to be a necessary evil with the emphasis on 'evil'. Sex even within marriage was sinful according to Augustine. Venial sins, lesser infractions against God's laws, included laughter, enjoying material pleasures and being too gregarious. These are sins I try to commit on a daily basis! These venial failings, according to church doctrine, could result in many years of purgatorial fire in order to cleanse one's soul of such indiscretions.

Aristotle claimed a closer union between body and soul than did Plato and Augustine. He was less of a dualists in this regard and in *De Anima* notes that there is nothing wrong with scientists and philosophers using different methods in defining or studying the soul. This appears to be an attempt by Aristotle to overcome the dualism of soul and body–a problem of which he was well aware. Aristotle has much to say about the soul that will not be reviewed here. Needless to say, he found difficulties wherever he looked. One example may suffice for now. The soul had several parts only one of which was immortal–the *nous*. However, the soul as supernatural must be simple, that is, without parts. Anything with parts is corruptible–its parts can be disassembled. If corruptible, the soul cannot be immortal. If it were not immortal, how can it be rewarded or punished in Heaven or Hell as later religions taught. On the other hand, if the soul is simple and not complex, how can it perform complex functions such as thought, reasoning, initiate motion, produce emotions and/or demonstrate free will? These and other questions face us when analyzing any supernatural entity.

Augustine of Hippo was a Platonist, nonetheless, there were elements of Aristotelianism in his thought. He spoke of a kind of prime matter that had the potential to receive Form and thus become a 'real thing'. This was important to Augustine because in following Genesis he required that God create the physical world *ex nihilo*, out of nothing. Unlike Aristotle, however, Augustine did not believe that the world was eternal and uncreated by God. He also believed that matter was co-created with Form. The latter was not infused into matter at a later time. As a result, his idea of the soul was based on Plato's view of the Forms or Ideas. Aristotle spoke of substance as that which 'subsists' in prime matter in order to make a thing what it is. As an example, a human is composed of prime mater and substance (soul). Its particular substance is 'human nature'. This makes it a human whereas matter provides a being's individuality. There is a problem with this scheme because if the human substance is a universal template then why would not all humans be essentially the same even if individuals? We should all be clone's of one another just as the Trinity is but one God though with three persons. On the other hand, if God is one but with three persons how can there be three persons without a material individualizing principle such as matter? Theologians 'solve' this problem by saying that God has but one substance or essence in which 'subsists' three 'hypostatic' persons. Does this explain anything?[8] Such metaphysical verbiage fills theological texts without actually clarifying the nature of God or humans.

A 'universal' is Aristotle's generic principle that exists in all humans and which makes humans, human. A substance is not just a mental construct or idea of humanity, that is, a notion abstracted by the mind in order to make sense of the world by mentally grouping or classifying things. Aristotle believed, as did many medieval theologians and philosophers that there was actually an entity called substance (or universal) that exists within each individual. This is called 'realism', that is there 'really' is such a substance that each class of individuals share. Later on, beginning with Abelard (1096-c.1153) some thinkers came to believe that human characteristics are only similar features that each individual possesses. This was called 'conceptualism' or in its more fully developed form, 'nominalism'. This concept held that there was no substance or universal existing in each individual, only similar features that we grouped together in our mind and to which we give a specific name, thus the label nominalism.

The medieval Church condemned nominalism because it undermined the concept of soul that was essential to many religious tenets, including life after death,[9] Heaven, Hell and the distinction between humans and brutes. Animals and plants had souls but according to Aquinas, they were vegetative or sensitive but not rational as was the human soul. The latter was ordained as special by God. We had to be unique. After all, the Universe was made for us and the proof of this was the "fact" of geocentrism–the Earth was the center of the Universe. The Bible supported this belief as did Church tradition. Earth had to be at the center of the Universe because we humans were the apotheosis of God's creations.

From very early on, Plato's Ideas, Aristotle's substances and Thomas Aquinas' essences were all considered spiritual or supernatural entities. This

---

8   To further confuse things here are the various dictionary definitions of hy·postasis:
1. Philosophy: The substance, essence, or underlying reality.
2. Christianity:
        a. Any of the persons of the Trinity.
        b. The essential person of Jesus in which his human and divine natures are united.
3. Something that has been hypostatized.
4.   a. A settling of solid particles in a fluid.
        b. Something that settles to the bottom of a fluid; sediment.
5. Medicine: The settling of blood in the lower part of an organ or the body as a result of decreased blood flow.
6. Genetics: A condition in which the action of one gene conceals or suppresses the action of another gene that is not its allele but that affects the same part or biochemical process in an organism. Hypostastasis comes from the Greek meaning 'to stand below'.
9   It is now known that DNA accounts for the many characteristics that define us as individual humans.

did not change with the Reformation. We still had souls that not only made us rational beings but also provided eternal life with the prospect of Heaven. Moreover, there were many aspects of humans that needed explaining. Obviously, matter can neither think, explain consciousness nor free will. Purely physical things are corruptible and changeable. If we were to have eternal life there had to be a non-physical element to make this possible. Besides, how can the psyche be accounted for? Imagination, reason, free will, logic, mystical and/or religious experiences, dreams, extrasensory perception, near-death or out of body happenings all demand something other than a purely physical, material part to *Homo sapiens*. There is just too much for us to explain with simple matter, humans must have a soul, or at least this is what theologians tell us.

GOD, ANGELS AND DEVILS

If humans are half supernatural then, indeed, God must be entirely supernatural. God is not only eternal into the future but has existed from all time past. Even before time God is: *sum qui sum*, I am who am. Furthermore, God is believed by many theologians to be infinite, all-perfect, immutable, omniscient and omnipotent. IT created the entire Universe, keeps it in existence and watches benevolently over all creatures. In order to be such a being as described above, God cannot be in any sense physical. Only a spiritual being by definition can possess all these attributes. We know of no material being that could perform all these functions.

The concept of God as supernatural begins with Genesis. In Genesis 1:2, it is said that God's *spirit* came over the world. In John's gospel, IT is said to be a 'spirit'. Origen of Alexandria (c.185-c.254) wrote that God could not be a body, that is, IT was not material. God's supernatural status has been posited by the early Church Fathers, by medieval theologians and Reformation writers. This view of God is sacrosanct today just as it was in the early Church. Only a spiritual being could provide for all that we ask of a divine being. For many there is no other explanation for all the mysteries of the Universe.

This aspect of God is so important that God, according to many theologians, is composed of three persons, one of which is called the Holy Spirit. Presumably, it was this person of the triune God that swept over the world when it came into being. The Holy Spirit has been labeled the "Sanctifier" and it was this Spirit in the form of tongues of fire that came down upon the faithful at the first Pentecost. (Acts 2: 1-41).

In addition to supernatural souls and a supernatural God, there have been posited supernatural beings of other sorts. The Jewish tradition has held that there are angels that mediate between God and humans. This idea was accepted by Christian theologians, based in part, on Neo-Platonic thought. In ancient philosophy the stars were divine beings and later these divinities became somewhat less than divine but remained supernatural, angelic functionaries of the one true God. The angels were entirely spiritual without material elements and as a consequence, though created, were eternal, immutable and capable of great feats. In some religious systems they took over the task of worldly creation.

Angels serve, as intermediaries, betweens God and humans and in the OT act as destructive agents, though God was certainly capable of such deeds on ITs own.[10] An angel provided Mohammed with the revelations found in the Qur'an, on which Islam is based. Similarly Joseph Smith was visited by an angel out of which came the *Book of Mormons*.

Satan or Lucifer and the other devils are said to be fallen angels. As such they are also entirely spiritual or supernatural. They are immortal as are all such beings. One function of spiritual creatures is free will and these fallen angels chose to revolt against God, some say through a sin of pride and as a result were cast down into Hell for all eternity and have been, according to theologians both ancient and modern, the source of many human sins.[11] The three great sources of sin are said to be the world, the flesh and the devil. We are tempted by the devil and often fall prey to his enticements.[12] Satan, early on, was more of a trickster than a tempter but Christian theology has made him much more evil.

All of the above mental and metaphysical machinations concerning the supernatural represent a complex system of theology that is very imaginative and meets many emotional, religious and philosophical needs. However, in the end this is a house of cards, which on close scrutiny collapses under the weight of its meaningless verbiage. None of the beliefs about the spiritual world can be verified. All the doctrines that constitute what we call pneumatology, that branch of theology dealing with the supernatural or spiritual, are purely speculative and in spite of what 'spiritualists', paranormal psychologists and seers tell us, there is absolutely no basis for any claims made about the spiritual world except as founded on some authority or authoritative source such as the Bible.

---

10   In Exodus, God sent an angel to kill the oldest child in each Egyptian home whereas in Joshua, God ITself rained down boulders upon the Gabaonites.

11   Devils have had a checkered history, playing different roles at different times in history. See Carus, P. 1900, *The History of the Devil and the Idea of Evil* (Kindle Edition)

12   Devils are generally considered male though angels may be either male or female. Spirits, by definition, of course, are genderless as is God. Gender can be applied only to physical beings that procreate sexually.

Today we know that DNA and the environment to which we are exposed account for what we are. If we have a soul, it works through our DNA. The soul is then superfluous in light of modern day genetics and the known influence of environmental factors. The concept of a soul would violate Ockham's razor[13]. The supernatural domain is simply not necessary in explaining our world. In addition, eliminating this domain also eliminates a host of logical problems that the body-mind dualism creates. The supernatural simplifies theology and philosophy but raises more issues than it resolves.

There are many people that experience 'spiritual' feelings. I mentioned peering through a telescope or hearing vespers at Notre Dame Cathedral as producing spiritual experiences. Many find a beautiful sunset, viewing an art piece or intimate communion with a loved one as very spiritual. Elkland has even identified 'spiritual atheists' among the 1700 'elite' university scientists she polled.[14] These are not supernatural phenomena but what I would call Neo-Natural experiences. They are feelings that many people are conscious of and which they call religious but are not always associated with religious events. William James (1902) discussed these in *The Varieties of Religious Experience*. However, more recently Argyle has studied the psychology of religion and found that a significant percentage of people, religious or otherwise, are aware of spiritual experiences (SE).[15] The incidence figures range widely from 31% to 72% of the population that was surveyed. Others believe the incidence is much lower.[16] Spiritual feelings can be associated with meditation, prayer, dance, music, sacred spaces and a variety of drugs, such as psilocybin and peyote in addition to the aesthetic experiences mentioned above. Depression, schizophrenia, schizotypal personality disorder and epilepsy have all been associated with SE. Some authors suggest that religion is actually an attempt to explain these SE.

There have been neurobiological (brain) associations reported by Newberg and others[17] regarding religious experiences. Hamer claims he has

---

13   Ockham's Razor was first formulated by William of Ockham (c. 1285-1349) and is often stated as, "the simplest explanation is more likely the correct one". This is not always the case, as we shall see later.

14   Elkland, E. H. 2010, *Science vs. Religion: What Scientists Really Think* (New York: Oxford University Press).

15   Argyle, M. 2000, *Psychology and Religion: An Introduction* (New York: Routledge).

16   Thomas, L. E. & Cooper, P. E. *Mystical Experiences: A Exploratory Study*, Journal for the Scientific Study of Religion, 1978, 17(4): 433-37.

17   Newberg, A. 2009, *How God Changes Your Brain: Breakthrough Findings from a Leading Neuroscientist* (New York: Ballantine).

discovered the "God gene" i.e. VMAT2.[18] This is a neurotransmitter (passes information from one neuron to another) that is associated with SE. His findings have been hotly debated and at best the gene may indicate that there has evolved a selective advantage in those who more often meditate or have SE. All of these findings do not prove there is a God or a supernatural world. However, such studies support the idea that there are spiritual, emotional or psychological experiences that are real and cannot be denied even if we don't know their exact nature. These data also support the importance of religion, SE and related events. Religion and the need for SE cannot be dismissed in spite of what Dawkins and others assert. We are not strictly rational beings. We possess faculties beyond pure cognition. We are not automatons like Star Trek's Spock that function only on a logical level. To deny SE, religion or other psychological phenomena, just because we don't currently fully understand them is to ignore a very important aspect of human nature.

A supernatural explanation for these data is not necessary or useful in our quest to understand humankind and the world as a whole. The supernatural realm offers only an empty explanation. It tells us nothing about how the world works. The supernatural is magical and fanciful but not revealing. The more we search for the underpinnings of the Universe, the more we find. These underpinnings are often puzzling and counterintuitive but they are nonetheless pregnant with fascinating, definable and empirically defensible mysteries. And it is in relativity theory, quantum mechanics, astrophysical, mathematical, psychological and biological disciplines that we can find God but not a God as classically defined.

Whenever atheism is mentioned, it is always facing off against the God of traditional religion. It is forever countering the providential, personal, omnipotent omniscient God of time-honored religions. But all these views of God are either anthropomorphic and/or metaphysical. We have to stop looking for a God using human eyes. IT will not be found in any world that we humans comprehend intuitively. We still look for the God of religion and the 'non-God' of atheism where these 'Gods' cannot be found. There is a God out there that avoids all the pitfalls into which the traditionally defined God falls. We have the tools to find a God worthy of our modern, scientific world. This God will not meet the needs of everyone. Traditionally religious persons will balk at this God. If they must have a loving father for their deity, so be it. I would not deny them this option. But for those who want more than a mythical figure that meets only emotional rather than fully human, rational needs, IT can be found in the Neo-Natural God and in the spirituality of the world around us.

---

18   Hamer, D. 2005, *The God Gene: How Faith is Hardwired into Our Genes* (New York: Anchor Books).

THE UNBELIEVABLE

CHAPTER 6

CREATIONISM VERSUS EVOLUTION

CREATIONISM

The Bible[1] is the most popular book in the Western World. Its sales still surpass that of all other written works, even Harry Potter! It is undoubtedly one of, if not the most influential books of all time. The Bible is uplifting, instructive, calming and spiritually fulfilling for millions of religious faithful. The Qur'an enriches the lives of millions upon millions of Muslims just as the Bible has for Christians and Jews. In spite of this, the Bible is full of contradictions and variations that make it difficult to interpret. Bible scholars are at odds with one another as to how to approach these many difficult and/or ambiguous passages. When there are apparent inconsistencies found in the Bible, what is one to make of them?

Some Churches allow interpretation only by scripture scholars or theologians. The Catholic Church is one example of this. But even here, there are persistent disagreements among these experts. Other Churches teach that the light of the Holy Spirit guides the individual's understanding of the Bible so that they may know and follow the will of God in all things. Some claim the Bible provides literal truth and any seeming contradictions can be explained away in one manner or another. Others believe the Bible speaks to us metaphorically, offering moral rules, truths about the nature of God or the world IT created. The Bible tells of the origins of the Universe, of all living things and the course of events that are to unfold over time. Many view the Bible as beautiful poetry that informs and transforms as it eases the burdens of life. Some suggest the Bible must be read as myth, metaphor or allegory. Others claim historical accuracy for the Bible. Many consider it mainly a code of conduct. Fundamentalists believe it should be

---

1   Here the Bible includes both the Christian Old and New Testament, recognizing that the Jewish Bible refers only to what Christians call the Old Testament and especially the Torah, that is, the first five books of the Bible said to have been written by Moses.

interpreted literally. Just how literal one should be in interpreting the Bible is a major contemporary issue. Is each word infallible or should only phrases or concepts be considered inerrant?

No religious issue facing society today exemplifies this problem more than the debate over Creationism and evolution. Science increasingly brings new data and with these data, theories that help to explain the origins of the world in an increasingly more precise way while at the same time providing a happier, more useful life. Unfortunately, these data and their consequent theories appear to be at odds with what the Bible seems to be saying about many controversial issues. The words of Genesis have perhaps caused more enmity between scientists and theologians than any other chapters of the Bible. Because of the vitriolic nature of this dispute and the potential and real harm that has and continues to flow from Genesis, I will spend some time analyzing the creation/evolution controversy. This is not necessarily done to prove that the weight of evidence supports evolution, which I believe it does, but rather to offer some thoughts about religious beliefs as opposed to scientific, empirical research.

CREATIONISM AS A BELIEF SYSTEM

The Creationism-evolution debate in many ways comes down to a matter of values. Karen Armstrong sees the conservative-liberal dichotomy as a product of two contrasting views of reality–*mythos* and *logos*.[2] *Mythos* is the symbolic, metaphorical representation of the human condition, whereas *logos* offers a 'rational' approach to our understanding of the world. Both are necessary aspects of humanity. They each meet certain human needs; neither one is 'right' nor 'wrong'–each has a role to play in the workings of the human mind and emotions. These two views of the world are not mutually exclusive, for they arise out of the two parts of our lives as rational animals. Neither is fully understood and neither holds a monopoly over our worldview. In general, creationism tends to be espoused by traditionalists and evolution by liberal scientists. We have already seen that nearly half the U.S. population believes in creationism. In this chapter I shall attempt to analyze the underlying warrants for both creationism and evolution; the points of contention between these two systems and look at the social and religious aspects of these two views of the origins of life especially as they relate to our concept of God.

There are essentially two warrants or bases for creationism: the Bible as expressed primarily in Genesis and an argument from 'intelligent design'

---

2   Ibid, p. 95.

(ID). There are many other creationist polemics, but these two, by and large, are the main arguments for creationism.

Let's review Genesis:
1. In the beginning God created the heavens and the earth.
2. Now the earth was formless and empty; darkness was over the surface of the deep and the Spirit of God was hovering over the waters.
3. And God said, "Let there be light," and there was light.
4. God saw that the light was good, and He separated the light from the darkness.
5. God called the light "day," and the darkness He called "night." And there was evening, and there was the first day.
6. And God said, "Let there be an expanse between the waters to separate water from water."
7. So God made the expanse and separated the water under the expanse from the water above it. And it was so.
8. God called the expanse "sky." And there was evening and there was morning–the second day.
9. And God said, "Let the water under the sky be gathered to one place, and let dry ground appear". And it was so.
10. God called the dry ground "land" and the gathered waters he called "seas". And God saw that it was good.
11. Then God said, "Let the land produce vegetation: seed-bearing plants and trees on the land that bear fruit with seed in it, according to their various kinds". And it was so.
12. The land produced vegetation: plants bearing seed according to their kinds and trees bearing fruit with seed in it according to their kinds. And God saw that it was good. 13. And there was evening, and there was morning—the third day.
14. And God said, "Let there be lights in the expanse of the sky to separate the day from the night, and let them serve as signs to mark seasons and days and years,
15. and let them be lights in the expanse of the sky to give light on the earth". And it was so.
16. God made two great lights—the greater light to govern the day and the lesser light to govern the night. He also made the stars.
17. God set them in the expanse of the sky to give light on the earth
18. to govern the day and the night, and to separate light from darkness. And God saw that it was good.
19. And there was evening and there was morning—the fourth day.

20. And God said, "Let the water teem with living creatures and let birds fly above the earth across the expanse of the sky".

21. So God created the great creatures of the sea and every living and moving thing with which the water teems, according to their kinds, and every winged bird according to its kind. And God saw that it was good.

22. God blessed them and said, "Be fruitful and increase in number and fill the water in the seas and let the birds increase on the earth".

23. And there was evening, and there was morning—the fifth day.

24. And God said, "Let the land produce living creatures according to their kinds: livestock, creatures that move along the ground, and wild animals, each according to its kind. And it was so.

25. God made the wild animals according to their kinds, the livestock according to their kinds, and all the creatures that move along the ground according to their kinds. And God saw that it was good.

26. Then God said, "Let us make man in our image, in our likeness, and let them rule over the fish of the sea and the birds of the air, over the livestock, over all the earth and over all the creatures that move along the ground."

27. So God created man in his own image, in the image of God he created him; male and female he created them.

28. God blessed them and said to them, "Be fruitful and increase in number; fill the earth and subdue it. Rule over the fish of the sea and the birds of the air and over every living creature that moves on the ground."

29. Then God said, "I give you every seed-bearing plant on the face of the whole earth and every tree that has fruit with seed in it. They will be yours for food.

30. And to all the beasts of the earth and all the birds of the air and all the creatures that move on the ground–everything that has the breath of life in it–I give every green plant for food." And it was so.

31. God saw all that he had made, and it was very good. And there was evening, and there was morning–the sixth day.

In these few passages of Genesis are contained the essentials of the biblical basis for creationism. In the creationist's view, the Bible is the infallible word of God transmitted to humans and can only be interpreted in its literal sense.[3] This includes the concept that creation was a supernatural event not to be explained on a material basis.[4] For many creationists, if one denies the literal biblical account of creation, it is not possible to be a 'Christian'–such

3   MacArthur, J. 2001, *The Battle for the Beginning: The Bible on Creation and the Fall of Adam* (www.ThomasNelson.com: W Publishing Group).
4   Ibid, p. 11.

views are, in fact, anti-Christian.[5] The inherent dichotomy in this debate, as seen by the creationists, is 'naturalistic' materialism facing off against the divine, supernatural creative act.[6] This creative process took place in six, 24-hour days, as we know days to be today and occurred in the sequence described in the Bible. All of this happened within the last 10,000 years and, finally, that all the known world is, today, as it was at the time of creation—no new species, genera, families, orders, classes, phyla, kingdoms or domains have evolved since the time of Genesis. The only change that has taken place in the biological hierarchy of plants and animals is one of decay, degradation or extinction. Some creationists don't believe in the extinction of species claiming that dinosaurs, for example, still live, hidden, in caves in Africa.[7] So, although, the various species were the result of 'special creation', they do not change or improve by evolutionary forces; they can only deteriorate and possibly disappear. By 'special creation' is meant that all species were willed into existence by God at the moment of creation and are, as species genera etc., unchanging and un-evolving. Each species was created individually. This same static concept of living beings applies to the entire Universe—our Solar System, the stars, galaxies and all other heavenly bodies that make up the Universe.

A Gallup poll dated March 5, 2001, found that 37% of Americans believe that humans developed as a result of the guiding hand of God (theistic evolutionists); 12% believe humans developed without God having anything to do with this process (atheistic evolutionists) and 45% accept the literal creationist's view as presented in Genesis. Six percent had no opinion.[8] These figures are little changed from 1982. According to a 1987 Gallup pole, 55% of American scientists are strict atheistic evolutionists. Thus, although a minority (12%) of the general population is atheistic, a true majority of scientists fall into this category.

INTELLIGENT DESIGN

ID theory is based on speculative reasoning not backed by empirical data. Scientists have presented empirical data and their interpretation of that data, as we shall see, while the creationists give their critique of this data

---

5   Ibid, p. 16.
6   Wikipedia, The Free Encyclopedia, 2002, http://en.wikipedia.org/wiki/Creationism.
7   Smolin, L. 2006, *The Trouble with Physics: The Rise of String Theory, the Fall of Science, and What Comes Next.* (Boston, MA.: Houghton Mifflin) pp. 25-6.
8   Gallup Poll, 2001, http://www.ul.edu/rhames/courses/current/creation/evol-poll.htm.

based on reason alone. They do not offer new empirical evidence but rather speculative reasoning to refute the interpretation of scientific data.

An example often used by creationists concerns the development of the human eye. There is geological, paleontological and biological evidence that the human eye has evolved over past eons. Creationists counter that such a complex organ could not evolve through a series of gradual genetic steps. The intervening structures would have no function, they claim, and thus no survival value. The eye would have to be created complete and whole at one time and this precludes the evolution of this organ or any human organ. This is called the argument from "irreducible complexity". The organs of the human body are so complex that they cannot evolve over time. Genesis provides a faith-based argument for creation. ID, on the other hand, puts forth a reasoned but speculative polemic for Creationism based on the principle of 'cause and effect' with God as the cause.

David Hume (1711-1776) first presented ID in his *Dialogues Concerning Natural Religion*.[9] His argument for the existence of God is based on natural theology utilizing the workings of the world. Basically, he argues that the natural world points to a divine creator. This theme was expanded upon by William Paley (1743-1805). He is famous for expressing the ID argument as, "If there is a watch there must be a watchmaker". Paley doesn't say this specifically in his book and mentions, "the intelligence of the watch-maker" only once.[10] Paley discusses at great length the issues of how a watch found on a heath in England may come into being, basically saying that unlike a stone found on the heath, a watch must have a designer and then extends this argument to creation as a whole even though he admits that it is possible the stone, "had lain there for ever". Paley covers several arguments including the law of order as evident in nature. He seems to deny self-ordering of natural things. Self-ordering in fact does occur in nature and this will be discussed latter.

Between the naturalist and creationist's views of the beginning, there is for some a middle ground. On the one end of this spectrum is the atheistic evolutionist who believes there is no God and the entire Universe is based on matter, energy and the physical laws that rule the Universe. There may have been a 'Big Bang' but no God was involved in its initiation. Theistic or deistic evolutionists believe that, while evolution is empirically justified, there must also be an intelligent force behind the design of the Universe.[11] ID is a concept much in the news today since it is at the heart of the creationist's argument for teaching their view in public schools. Strict creationists, as

---

9   Hume, D. 2010, *Dialogues Concerning Natural Religion* (Kindle Book).

10   Paley, W. 2006, *Natural Theology* (New York: Oxford University Press) p. 9.

11   Ibid.

described above, represent the third view, which only admits of a theistic, special creation unencumbered by evolutionary forces. Darwin's natural selection and random genetic mutations are unnecessary concepts in this scheme, since God is the force directing evolution.

The most recent development in Creationism is that of 'Scientific Creationism'. This movement claims well over one thousand academics with advanced degrees as supporters of this position. These are generally strict creationists who wish to provide a 'scientific' basis for their arguments against evolution and promote ID as the basis for their beliefs. The Creation Institute located a few miles north of San Diego, California is one of the centers for this movement and it maintains a museum of Scientific Creationism. There is also a Discovery Institute in Seattle, Washington, as well as, a Museum of Creationism at the Columbus Center in Baltimore, Maryland.

The creationists' response to evolution is in part based on a refutation of the scientific evidence for evolution. The theory behind Creationism is intelligent design, as noted above and this is essentially a speculative, metaphysical argument not supported by experimental data. As a result, the only 'scientific' avenue open to the creationists is a critique of evolutionary experimental methods. From reading the creationists' literature there does not appear to be any research that they have carried out on their own. Their refutations consist in an analysis of work done by evolutionary biologists, geologists and paleontologists. This approach deviates from, or more properly, supplements, the biblical basis for Creationism by employing a 'scientific' polemic based on analyses of evolution literature.

The argument from ID has developed out of the evident complexity of the Universe. It is counterintuitive, according to creationists, that such an intricate Universe could be explained on the basis of chance alone. MacArthur notes that all living organisms are self-sustaining and self-repairing; both of these capacities involve highly organized biological processes, too complex to be based on random evolutionary events. This complexity cries out for an Intelligent Designer, that is, God, according to MacArthur.[12] Concerning DNA, MacArthur says:

> There is no viable explanation of the Universe without God. Coded information as found in the genetic structure of every living being does not arise by chance. It is not produced by nothing. It has a source and that source must be an Intelligent Designer.[13]

---

12   Op. cit. MacArthur, J. 2001, p. 132.
13   Ibid, p. 40.

Thus, the complexity of the Universe, the law of cause and effect and reason all speak to a divine designer according to the creationists. A basic element in their system is a belief in teleology. Everything has to have a reason for its existence. God has made everything for a purpose. All creatures are aimed at an ultimate end. For humans this means eternal bliss with God. Evolution is too random; too pointless. Complex organisms can't just 'happen' based on chance i.e. natural selection.

Fig. 6.1. Charles Darwin (1809-1882). The Father of Evolution Theory. A naturalist who developed the basic tenet of evolution– natural selection.

EVOLUTION

What follows in the next several sections is an attempt to outline the scientific and thus empirical evidence for evolution. This may be 'too much information" for some readers. Nonetheless, evolution is one of the key elements in defining and understanding the Neo-Natural God and it must be dealt with in some detail in order to demonstrate the validity of evolution. Using Darwinian theory and the evidence for natural selection that is based solidly on geology, physics, archeology, molecular biology and other scientific disciplines, there can be no question about the truth of evolution. It is no longer a 'theory' but firmly established fact.

The theory of evolution begins with Charles Darwin's[14], *The Origin of Species*, first published in 1859 and last revised in 1872.[15] Darwin freely admits his indebtedness to early workers such as Jean Baptist de Lamarck, who first proposed the idea of evolution in the early part of the nineteenth century. Lamarck, however, believed that environmentally induced characteristics,

---

14   Darwin was one of many naturalists who actively and intensively studied natural phenomena in the 19th century. These researchers from all parts of the world are recognized by Darwin in the *Origin of Species*.

15   Darwin, C. 1979, *Origin of Species* (New York: Hillard Wang).

such as tanned skin, resulting from exposure to the Sun, could be passed on to one's offspring. Darwin's grandfather, Erasmus Darwin (1731-1802), had actually proposed the theory of evolution in the late eighteenth century but his ideas were not generally circulated. It was Darwin who developed the concepts of "modifications' or "change in character" (Darwin knew nothing of genetics) as something that developed within a species or variety which, if beneficial, were then passed on from generation to generation as a result of natural selection.[16] Darwin was, as many scientists or naturalists, before and after him, a theistic evolutionist. He did not deny God's 'hand' in the workings of Nature[17] but did not believe in 'special creation'. Rather, he held that all species including *Homo sapiens*, evolved from lower forms. Darwin did not have the benefit of Gregor Mendel's (1822-1884) laws or the concept of genetic mutations but he did understand that change or modification, useful to a species, must somehow occur over time before natural selection determines whether a species benefits from this change and thus persists rather than dies out. In other words, all species are in competition within their environment, including predators and those preyed upon. In order to continue as a species they must adapt to the world around them. The environment is always changing and in order to survive the individuals of a given species must change as well. Mutations, if beneficial, help individuals adapt to their environment.

All of Darwin's ideas were based on his or other naturalists' observations of the flora and fauna of England and other parts of the world, including the Galapagos Islands, where Darwin carried out research in the 1830's. The varieties of species he found there and in England, along with their local environments, convinced him that natural selection worked to improve species or, more precisely, helped them adapt to their environment in a beneficial way so that they would flourish. On this point, Darwin differs from the strict creationists who do not believe that there has been any 'improvement' in species since the original creation described in Genesis took place.

Although Darwin's theory of evolution is based on observations, much of his theory has to be considered speculative in type. Very frequently, he makes statements such as, "it seems reasonable" or "these observations would suggest" followed by some conclusion based on his observations. He was a meticulous student of nature. Thus, all of his ideas are founded on empirical data but his conclusions could be faulted as not necessarily following from these data. The causal relationships he develops are not always correct. Nonetheless, the great majority of his concepts have held up

16   Ibid, chapter 4.
17   Ibid, pp. 14, 57.

in light of modern genetics and molecular research. He did have access to Charles Lyell's *Principles of Geology*–the benchmark work on paleogeology, before he left for South America and the Galapagos Islands on the H.M.S. Beagle in 1831.[18] Thus, Lyell's concepts played a major role in his theory of evolution, even though geological time-scales were not well understood then. Lyell was convinced that the 6000 years proposed by Archbishop James Usher in 1650 for the age of the Earth, was not consistent with the geological record.[19]

In addition to the concept of natural selection, the theory of evolution rests on the fossil record, geological dating methods and modern genetics. These are the four 'warrants,' as philosophers would say, that support the notion of evolution and its many ramifications.[20]

NATURAL SELECTION

Natural selection was fully developed by Darwin in his *Origin of Species*. Darwin's numerous observations of nature made it clear that natural selection was the driving force behind "modification" of the species. He puts it this way:

> When we see leaf-eating insects [that are] green and bark-feeders, mottled-grey, the alpine ptarmigan[21], white in winter, the red grouse the color of heather, we must believe that these tints are of service to these birds and insects in preserving them from danger.[22]

Darwin gives many such examples in great detail and his most famous 'proof' of natural selections deals with the finches of the Galapagos Islands. These finches are geographically isolated on the several Galapagos Islands and their eating habits have led to modifications of their beaks, depending on the type of food they eat–large beaks for eating seeds, small sharp beaks for insects and so on.

In order to strengthen the case for natural selection as envisioned by Darwin, one needs access to modern methods for establishing the role of evolution in nature. That a hierarchy of species exists is not enough to support the theory of evolution, as proposed by Darwin and his nineteenth

---

18   Lyell, C. 1997, *Principles of Geology* (London: Penguin).
19   Ibid, p. 13.
20   Hutton, N. 1968, *The Evidence of Evolution* (New York: American Heritage Publishing).
21   Ptarmigan is a species of grouse.
22   Op. cit. Darwin, C. 1979, p.78.

century colleagues, such as Thomas Huxley.[23] It was not until the fossil record became more complete and geological dating appeared on the scene that the theory of evolution matured into a true science. Today this more complete theory of evolution is called 'Neo-Darwinism'.

FOSSIL EVIDENCE

Natural selection is evident in the macroscopic, microscopic and molecular world. The fossils that have been discovered over the last 150 years or more have helped to fill in the gaps of our human genealogy, although there are still a myriad of mysteries to be solved and many actors on the stage of evolution are yet to make their appearance. The evolutionary record of *Homo sapiens* and its progenitors is complex and marked by many twists and turns, some of which lead to dead ends. Life appears to have begun on Earth some 3.8 billion years before the present epoch as unicellular organisms. Metazoans (multicellular organisms) emerged 2.5 billion years ago.[24] The first organisms were anaerobic,[25] since there was essentially no oxygen (O_2) in the atmosphere at the time. The Ediacarans[26] developed later, as aerobic metazoans, after the Cyanobacteria[27] produced enough O_2 to allow aerobes to evolve.[28] Beginning with the Cambrian Period, 540 million yeas ago, there was a mushrooming of many new phyla.[29] In addition, over the course of many eons, there have been numerous mass extinctions, some occurring as the result of climate changes,[30] catastrophic events, such as asteroid or comet strikes[31] or the impact of humans on the environment.[32] After each mass extinction, new forms of life evolve to fill the ecological niches that

---

23   Huxley, T. 2001, *Man's Place in Nature* (New York: Modern Library).

24   Knoll, A. H., & Carroll, S. B. 1999, *Early Animal Evolution: Emerging Views from Comparative Biology and Geology*, Science, 284:2129-37.

25   Anaerobic: not requiring oxygen.

26   Ediacaran: Of or relating to a soft-bodied marine organism of the Precambrian Era, thought to be the earliest multicellular form of life.

27   Cyanobacterium: A photosynthetic bacterium of the class *Coccogoneae* or *Hormogoneae*, generally blue-green in color and in some species capable of nitrogen fixation. Cyanobacteria were once thought to be algae. Also called *blue-green alga*.

28   Brasier, M., & Antclife, J. 2004, *Decoding the Ediacaran Enigma*, Science, 305:1115-17.

29   Op. cit. Knoll, A. H., & Carroll, S. B. 1999.

30   Bains, S., et al. 2000, *Termination of Global Warmth at the Palaeocene/Eocene Boundary through Productivity Feedback*, Nature, 407:171-74.

31   Ward, P. D., & Brownlee, D. 2000, *Rare Earth: Why Complex Life is Uncommon in the Universe* (New York: Copernicus Books).

32   Barnsky, A. D., et al. 2004, *Assessing the Causes of Late Pleistocene Extinctions on the Continents*, Science, 306:70-75.

then became available. An example of evolution related to climatic change is that of the Woolly Mammoth, whose evolution has been recently worked out.[33] They came on the scene as an adaptation to Ice Age conditions and later disappeared as a result of over-hunting by Neanderthals and humans.

The genera of our human lineage have been partially elucidated over the past 150 years.[34] And, of course, new *Homo species* are being found in Africa and Asia on a regular basis.[35,36] There are hominids dating to four million years B.C. E. However, the earliest *Homo sapiens* fossils date to 160,000 years B.C.E.

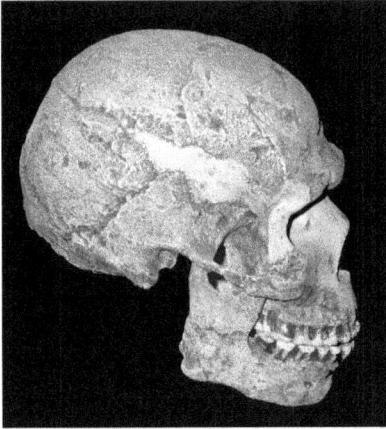

Fig. 6. 2. Oldest know *Homo sapiens* skull dating to 160,000 years ago. The skull shows typical modern human features with a high forehead, small supraorbital ridges and no prognathism (forward projecting jaw).

From the fossil record there is ample evidence of human evolution. The earliest humans are usually classified as Archaic *H. sapiens* because there are some minor anatomical variations present when compared to present day humans. Beginning around 50,000 years ago, truly modern humans emerge and this is confirmed, in part, by the evidence of cultural advances, such as the cave paintings found in Europe and, to a lesser extent, in Africa.[37] Evidence of a developing human culture is seen as early as 2.5 million years ago.[38] Thus, there is not only evidence of anatomical evolution,

---

33   Lister, A. M., & Sher, A. V. 2001, *The Origin and Evolution of the Woolly Mammoth*, Science, 294:1094-97.

34   Cela-Conde, C. J., & Ayala, F. J. 2003, *Genera of the Human Lineage* PNAS, 100:7684-7689.

35   Brown, P., et al. 2004, *A New Small-Bodied Hominim from the Late Pleistocene of Flores, Indone'sia*, Nature, 431:1055-1061.

36   Gibbons, A. 2002, *In Search of the First Hominids*, Science, 295:1214-19.

37   Balter, M. 1999, *Restorers Reveal 28,000-Year-Old Artworks*, Science, 283:1835.

38   Ambrose, S. 2001, *Paleolithic Technology and Human Evolution*, Science, 291:1748-53.

but also cultural evolution.[39] Such cultural changes are found in many activities, such as sewing,[40] burial rituals,[41] fire making,[42] flint mining,[43] jewelry making,[44] hunting equipment, such as spears,[45] the fashioning of knives and farming.[46] In addition, there are anatomical changes that suggest evolutionary developments in cognitive function, beginning around 50,000 years ago.[47],[48]

There are literally thousands of studies indicating evolutionary processes in animals, plants and humans, not to mention evolutionary developments in the Universe including the evolution of planets,[49] stars[50] and galaxies.[51] The data are convincing.

GEOLOGICAL DATING

Until the discovery of geological dating techniques in the early twentieth century, many of the claims made by evolutionists remained unproven. After100 years' experience with radiometric dating methods, along with stratigraphy (the study of geological sedimentary layers), dendrochronology (counting tree rings), glacial ice core studies (counting

39   Klein, R. G., & Edgar, B. 2002, *The Dawn of Human Culture* (New York: Hahn, Wiley & Sons). Culture in this and other papers, refers to all information transmitted to subsequent generations by other than genetic means. Technology, language, writing, art and all types of learning would be included in the definition of 'culture'.
40   Balter, M. 2004, *Dressed for Success: Neanderthal Culture Wins Respect*, Science, 306:40-41.
41   Op. cit. Klein, p.147.
42   Goren-Inbar, N., et al. 2004, *Evidence of Hominim Control of Fire at Gusher Benot Ya'aqov, Israel*, Science, 304:725-27.
43   Verdi, G., et al. 2004, *Flint Mining in Prehistory Recorded by* in situ-*Produced Cosmogony* [10]Be, PNAS, 101:7880-84.
44   Kuhn, S., et al. 2001, *Ornaments of the Earliest Upper Paleolithic: New Insights from the Levant*, PNAS, 98:7641-46.
45   Ibid, p. 159.
46   Denham, T. P., et al. 2003, *Origins of Agriculture at Kuku Swamp in the Highlands of New Guinea*, Science, 301:189-93.
47   Chou, H- H., et al. 2002, *Inactivation of CMP-N-acetylneuraminic acid Hydroxylase Occurred Prior to Brain Expansion During Human Evolution*, PNAS, 99:11736-41.
48   Conroy, G. C., et al. 1998, *Endocranial Capacity in an Early Hominid Cranium From Sterkfontein, South Africa*, Science, 280:1730-31.
49   Buckle, R. van, et al. 2004, *The Building Blocks of Planets within the "Terrestrial Region" of Protoplanetary Discs*, Nature, 432:479-82.
50   Abel, T., et al. 2002, *The Formation of the First Star in the Universe*, Science, 295:93-98.
51   Buser, R. 2000, *The Formation and the Early Evolution of the Milky Way Galaxy*, Science, 287:69-74.

ice layers) and other non-radiometric methods, the science of geological dating now rests on firm experimental foundations.[52] There are about 40 radiometric methods currently available. The first to be used was the Uranium/Lead system. Certain elements are physically unstable and will 'decay', that is, are converted into different elements or isotopes over precisely predictable time periods.[53] There is a defined 'half-life' of each of these unstable elements. One half-life is the time it takes for one-half of a given amount of an element to be converted into another isotope or element. Fig.6. 3. shows several radiometric systems and their half-lives.

Radioactive Isotope (Parent)	Product (Daughter)	Half-Life (Years)
Samarium-147	Neodymium-143	106 billion
Rubidium-87	Strontium-87	48.8 billion
Rhenium-187	Osmium-187	42 billion
Lutetium-176	Hafnium-176	38 billion
Thorium-232	Lead-208	14 billion
Uranium-238	Lead-206	4.5 billion
Potassium-40	Argon-40	1.26 billion
Uranium-235	Lead-207	0.7 billion
Beryllium-10	Boron-10	1.52 million
Chlorine-36	Argon-36	300,000
Carbon-14	Nitrogen-14	5715
Uranium-234	Thorium-230	248,000
Thorium-230	Radium-226	75,400

Fig. 6. 3. Radiometric isotopes commonly used in geological dating of sedimentary strata and fossils of various types. The isotope, is produced by radioactive decay and its half-life is shown. Note that each isotope has a different half-life–some very long, others much shorter. Many of these half-lives overlap in time and, thus, can be used to check the accuracy of other radiometric methods.

---

52   Wiens, R. C., 2002, *Radiometric Dating: A Christian Perspective*, http://www.Talkorigins.org/faqs/dating.html

53   In the nucleus of an element, there are protons and neutrons (with the exception of hydrogen which has only one proton). If a uranium atom loses one or more of its neutrons it will have the same 'atomic number' i.e. same number of protons in the nucleus and thus will still be an uranium atom, though with a lighter nucleus, that is, its atomic weight will be less. Uranium with a total of 238 protons and neutrons in its nucleus is U^{238}. If this molecule loses three of its neutrons, it is converted into the uranium isotope U^{235}. On the other hand, if, by radioactive decay, (because U^{238} is unstable) it loses a total of 32 protons and neutrons, it is converted into a new element, that is, lead (Pb^{206}). Loss of neutrons makes an element lighter becoming an isotope of the same element. With the loss of one or more protons it becomes another element entirely.

The half-life of a given isotope can be used to determine the age of a fossil or rock that contains the fossil, even if the isotope is present in very small amounts. If the amount of the 'parent' isotope is known and the 'daughter' isotope is determined, then the age of the fossil or rock (or both) can be determined.[54] The half-lives of over 40 isotopes have been determined directly, either by using a radiation detector to count the number of atoms decaying in a given period of time or by measuring the ratio of parent to daughter isotopes, where the original amount of parent material is known. These measurements are very precise and can give accurate dates up to 10 half-lives, so that carbon dating is valid to 45,000 years and several of the isotopes listed in Fig. 6. 3 can give accurate ages for the Earth, meteorites or Moon rocks dating back even billions of years. Potassium 40/Argon 40 is often used to date hominid fossils. Usually the value obtained by one dating method is compared to one or more additional methods in order to verify a given result. This makes geological dating a highly reliable research tool.

Radiometric methods can be checked by non-radiometric methods, such as counting tree rings. Using long-lived trees, carbon dating has been verified to 6800 years and by combining living tree ring counts with long-lived, but dead trees that were alive for a time when the living tree was first growing, carbon dating verification has been extended to 11,600 years. Because of the variation in yearly rainfall, tree ring patterns from tree to tree are the same for the same years and, thus, the pattern from dead and living trees will overlap and extend the period that dendrochronologic methods are useful.

Using these techniques, thousands of studies have been carried out in order to date a variety of fossils and rocks. This has included accurate dating of the onset of the Cambrian flowering of life,[55] the age of feathered

---

54   A 'parent' isotope is the original form of the element present in a fossil or rock when it is formed. In the case of rocky material the parent isotope is present at the time the sediment is laid down or, for an igneous rock, it is the amount of isotope present when the nascent, volcanic rock begins to cool. For plant or animal life, it is the amount of C^{14} present when the organism dies. There is a certain concentration of C^{14} in the air we breathe. This is incorporated into living cells and when the plant or animal dies, the C^{14} begins to decay to C^{13} and finally C^{12} (which is stable). The ratio of C^{14} to C^{12} can then give the age of the material, knowing the half-life of this reaction.
55   Knoll, A. H., et al. 2004, *A New Period for the Geological Time Scale*, Science, 305:621-22.

dinosaurs,[56] dates of the woolly mammoth,[57] timing of early hominids,[58] antiquity of early human settlements,[59] occurrence of early modern humans,[60] chronology of Neanderthal burial sites,[61] and dating of cave paintings,[62] and many other such studies.

Although creationists have criticized some of these dating methods based on earlier errors that have been reported,[63] the mountains of evidence, crosschecking of data and improved technology leaves no room for doubting their validity.[64]

MOLECULAR BIOLOGY

Molecular biology has been the most recent scientific advance in evolutionary research.[65] Genetic studies have not only defined the nature of humans and lower animals but they have also provided demographic data concerning geography, as well as, the timing of major migrations by *H. sapiens*. Genetic studies have provided one more way of correlating data obtained from fossil finds, geological dating methods and linguistic studies.[66] They have also helped us understand what separates humans from lower species especially our nearest relative, the chimpanzee.[67]

---

56   Swisher, C. C., et al. 1999, *Cretaceous Age for the Feathered Dinosaurs of Liaoning, China*, Nature, 400:58-64.

57   Op. cit. Lister, A. M., & Sher, A. V. 2001.

58   Leakey, M. G., et al. 1998, *New Specimens and Confirmation of an Early Age for Australopithecus anamnesis*, Nature 393:62-66.

59   Holden, C. 1997, *Archeology: Tooling Around—Dates Show Early Siberian Settlement*, Science, 275:1268-70.

60   Tinkaus, E., et al. 2003, *An Early Modern Human from the Pester cu Oases, Romania*, PNAS, 100:11231-36.

61   Valladas, H., et al. 1987, *Thermoluminescence Dates for the Neanderthal Burial Sites at Kebara in Israel*, Nature, 330:159-60.

62   Valladas, H., et al. 2001, *Paleolithic Paintings: Evolution of Prehistoric Cave Art*, Nature, 413:79.

63   Op. cit. Morris, H. M. 1985, pp. 161-2.

64   Godfrey, l. R. 1983, *Scientists Confront Creationism* (New York: W. W. Norton) pp. 37-40.

65   Foley, R. 1998, The *Context of Human Genetic Evolution*, Genome Research, 8:339-47.

66   Cavelli-Sfoza, L. L., et al. 1988, *Reconstruction of Human Evolution: Bringing Together Genetic, Archeological, and Linguistic Data*, PNAS, 85:6002-6.

67   Gibbons, A. 1998, *Which of Our Genes Makes Us Human?* Science, 281:1432-34.

The Y-chromosome has allowed the identification of time and place of our oldest male ancestor[68] and mitochondrial DNA has provided the same information regarding our oldest female ancestor.[69] DNA studies of *H. sapiens* and *H. neanderthalensis* have settled the question of the relationship between humans and Neanderthals–showing that the two are not directly related and that Europeans are not descended from Neanderthals.[70] It is not certain if humans and Neanderthals ever intermarried. There is DNA evidence, however, for an association, even descent of humans from lower forms. This has been established by molecular studies.[71] The genome of *H. sapiens* is very close, for example, to that of the chimpanzee where 98% or more of their DNA is the same as ours. More and more animal and plant genomes have been elucidated, further establishing the genetic evolutionary processes present in all species of all biological domains.[72]

The Genographic Project has and continues to clarify our origins and migration patterns since *H. sapiens* left northeast Africa some 50,000 years ago.[73] These data have been chronicled in Spencer Wells' *Deep Ancestry* and his earlier book, *The Journey of Man.* [74] Wells describes the methodology used in the project and the information that has come out of it so far. In brief, by studying DNA in geographically isolated populations worldwide, it has been possible to find DNA patterns as they evolve over time. Mutation rates, though low, are temporally predictable and from this the timing of migratory movements can be determined. Since each geographical group develops a specific DNA sequence over a short period of time, about 200 years, it can be determined by comparison with other geographic populations as to where they came from and when this occurred. They have determined, for example, that the vast majority of European males come from seven ancient 'fathers' and where these 'fathers' originally lived. Five 'racial' types have been identified. These five types developed, that is evolved, after leaving Africa. The five, as one might anticipate are the Blacks, Whites, Native Americans, Asiatics and Australian Aborigines.

---

68   Bertranpetit, J. 2000, *Genome, Diversity, and Origins: The Y-chromosome as a Storyteller*, PNAS, 97:6927-29.

69   Klicka, J., & Akin, R. M. 1998, *Pleistocene Speciation and the Mitochondrial DNA Clock*, Science, 282:1955-59.

70   Ovchinnikov, I. V., et al. *Molecular Analysis of Neanderthal DNA from the Northern Caucasus*, Nature, 404:400-3.

71   Op. cit. Gibbons, A. 1998.

72   Biology Analysis Group, 2004, *A Draft Sequence for the Genome of the Domesticated Silkworm ((Bombyx more)*, Science, 306:1937-40.

73   Wells, S. 2007, *Deep Ancestry: Inside the Genographic Project* (Washington, DC: National Geographic).

74   Wells, S. 2002, *The Journey of Man* (New York: Random House).

The genomic record is quite convincing and combined with other measures of evolution, leave no doubt that evolution is an established biological process which adequately explains all of the living organisms found on Earth, now and in the past. God may have devised this system as the Intelligent Designers claim but it is certain IT need not be a hands-on deity that keeps it going. The fact that an Intelligent Designer can never be proven makes the issue moot. This brief discussion will suffice for now in defining the role of genetics as one of the bases for the theory of evolution. More will be said regarding molecular biology below

THE CREATIONIST'S REBUTTAL
RELIGION AS SCIENCE

As noted before, creationists use the Bible, especially Genesis and ID as their warrants in support of Creationism. In addition they raise questions about the validity of evolutionists' research. John MacArthur portrays 'naturalism'[75] as a belief system similar to any religious belief system.[76] He sees 'naturalism' as essentially "anti-theistic" and naturalism as based on a belief system which rests on the 'assumption' that the Universe is rational and cohesive. Scientific experimentation is founded on these assumptions, Evolutionary theory can thus be viewed as a 'secular religion' no different from traditional religions. Scientist have nothing more than 'faith' in these scientific suppositions to support their claims. Philip Johnson considers naturalism a metaphysical construct just as is religion, though the latter has additional support from Scripture and ancient authority, making it more solidly based than naturalism.[77] Johnson also separates naturalism from science because of its non-empirical, metaphysical character. In addition, MacArthur states that 'naturalism' is based on the "presupposition" that there are no supernatural forces at work in the Universe and that this "presupposition" is taken as a matter of faith. Therefore, the theory of evolution uses as its warrant, a belief system unsupported by scientific data. MacArthur quotes Paul (Romans, 1:20-22) in describing 'naturalists', "Professing to be wise, they became fools".

Furthermore, MacArthur speaks of the "spiritual barrenness of naturalism". He goes on to point out the dire consequences of 'naturalism', which, because it denies God, can only lead to immorality and the consequences of immorality, i.e. Hell. A depraved society necessarily follows

---

75   Some use naturalism interchangeably with materialism or atheistic materialism.

76   Op. cit. MacArthur, J. 2001, p. 11.

77   Op. cit. Johnson, P. p. 205.

upon atheism.[78] This is one of the most emotional of all the traditionalists' arguments because, in their view, the very fabric of society is threatened by such an atheistic system. The moral underpinnings of society are therefore under attack.

Haught in *God and the New Atheism* also asserts that scientists require an unsupported belief system that differs little from religious faith.[79] Haught, however, does accept evolutionary theory. This is a theme basic to the creationist's objections to evolution because if science requires the unproved warrant that nature is essentially uniform and its laws universal, then the scientific method differs little from faith-based theology.

Naturalists do not necessarily deny the existence of God. Charles Darwin as a naturalist was a spiritual person though he moved toward agnosticism later in life.[80] The Catholic Church does not see evolution and religion as mutually exclusive. Deistic dogma holds to a scheme in which God created both the world and the forces that carry evolution forward.

MacArthur's concern regarding the association between naturalism and immorality, an issue often raised by religious writers, has not, to my knowledge, ever been shown to be statistically valid. Atheists appear to be as moral, if not more so, than the general population and since most are humanists they may be more attentive to and understanding of the needs of others than some adherents of fundamental religious groups. In fact, there is some evidence that fundamentalists tend to be more immoral than their contemporary atheist friends. According to one Christian source atheists are more immoral.[81] On the other hand, if one looks at "Ask Atheists" they are not.[82] This latter source states that although 10% of Americans are atheists only 2% of convicts are atheists. Convicts, on the other hand, are said to be more often fundamentalists and murders are more often committed fundamentalists.

MacArthur insists that there is no essential conflict between a literal interpretation of Genesis and current scientific literature.[83] He asserts that the scientific literature, if interpreted properly, confirms the biblical view of creation. As a corollary of this, he condemns "theological liberals" who deny the literal truth of the Bible, because they distort science so as to undermine

---

78   Ibid, p. 15.
79   Haught, J. F. 2008, *God and the New Atheism* (Louisville, KY: Westminster John Knox Press).
80   Clayton, P. & Schloss, J. 2004, *Evolution and Ethics* eds P. Clayton, & J. Schloss (Grand Rapids, MI: Wm. B. Eardmans Publishing) p 312.
81   Evidence for God: http://www.godandscience.org/apologetics/atheists_more_immoral.html.
82   Ask Atheists: http://www.asktheatheists.com/questions/7-are-atheists-immoral/.
83   Op. cit. Haught, J. F. 2008, p. 17.

the word of the Bible. MacArthur maintains that the "day" spoken of in Genesis is, indeed, one, 24-hour day and not some "long age" or epoch. There are other fundamentalists that interpret the biblical day as longer.

MacArthur also believes that "all sorts of theological mischief" ensues when one rejects or compromises the literal truth of the Bible.[84] There must have been an Adam and Eve who sinned and were ejected from Paradise for if there were no Adam, there was no Fall, and, thus, no need for redemption or Christ, the Redeemer. The whole basis of Christianity collapses. Several other basic religious tenets are also undermined, if one denies a literal interpretation of the Bible: divine revelation, divine providence, personal responsibility for our sins and the punishment in Hell all disappear and we are left once again with a corrupt society. The fundamentalists take this as a serious responsibility and are intent on saving the world from such moral and theological disasters.

MacArthur, also, defends the Bible against attacks based on apparent contradictions found in it. More will be said of this later. In sum, MacArthur offers these arguments as a defense against "anti-theistic hypotheses". All the evolutionary claims, since Darwin, amount to nothing more than unfounded, speculative hypotheses, not to be believed anymore than the speculations of the Ancient Greek philosophers.

SCIENTIFIC CREATIONISM

It is the defined task of Scientific Creationists to demonstrate the weaknesses of all the scientific arguments used to support evolution. Many aspects of the biological sciences are used to show the complexity of nature–a complex system that cannot be explained on the basis of chance alone. This is the argument from ID discussed above. Such a complex world as ours cannot have happened by chance alone. Another major argument against evolution is based on the first two laws of thermodynamics. The creationists' refutation of evolution based on these laws, as well as, those relating to natural selection, fossil evidence, geological dating and molecular biology will be covered in what follows.

THE FIRST AND SECOND LAWS OF THERMODYNAMICS

The first law of thermodynamics is the 'Law of Conservation of Energy', which states that energy can neither be created nor destroyed. The total amount of energy in the Universe is unchanging. Energy can be

---

84   Ibid, p. 19.

converted to matter by Einstein's famous equation, $E = mc^2$ but energy, as such, can neither be created out of nothing nor be destroyed; it can only be transferred from one part of the Universe to another.[85] This law applies to 'isolated or closed systems' anywhere in the Universe and to the total potential and kinetic energy within a closed system. A 'closed system' is one to which no energy can be added, although energy can be lost from such a system. The internal energy of the system applies to all the atoms and molecules in the system, that is, all the energy in the system that can be transformed into heat.

The creationists contend that Creationism theory implies "conservation rather than innovation".[86] This conforms to the creationist's concept that God made the Universe in six days and that the world as it was then, remains essentially unchanged today, except for the "degradation" that has occurred over time. All species of the three biological domains and five kingdoms that make up the animate world are stable and no new domains; kingdoms, phyla, classes, orders, families, genera or species have evolved since God's initial creative act. To evolve new and higher forms of life, would defy the law of conservation of matter and energy, according to the Scientific Creationists. Energy would have to be created in order to improve a species and, as we have seen, this is impossible as stated in the law of conservation of energy. God created all the energy and matter in the Universe at the time of the initial creative act as described in Genesis and no additional matter or energy has been made since. It follows that if there is no new energy or matter; there can be no evolution.

The second law of thermodynamics can be stated as follows: the entropy of a closed system increases with time.[87] Entropy is viewed in Creationism as a process of progressive disorganization within any closed system, including biological ones.[88] The Universe, if it is a closed system, is gradually becoming more disordered, because as it enlarges, its temperature

---

85   Isaacs, A. 1996, *A Dictionary of Physics* (New York: Oxford University Press), p. 427-28.

86   Op. cit. Morris, H. M. 1996, p. 38.

87   Op. cit. Isaacs, A. 1996, p. 428.

88   Ibid, p. 428. Isaac defines entropy as "a measure of the unavailability of a system's energy to do work in a closed system, that is, an increase in entropy is accompanied by a decrease in energy availability." Mathematically this is stated, $DS = DQ/T$ where S = entropy, Q= the energy in the system and T = thermodynamic temperature of the system. So if the temperature in the system rises the entropy decreases and vice versa. "Heat death" then is characterized by enough heat loss, so that disorganization (entropy) of a system reaches its maximum level.

falls[89] and, thus, there is more entropy (disorganization) in the Universe over time. Rudolph Clausius (1822-1888) predicted the 'heat' death of the Universe based on the Second Law of Thermodynamics.[90] When all large-scale samples of matter in the Universe are at a uniform temperature, entropy will be maximal. In other words, everything in the cosmos has been going downhill since its creation. Creationism does not allow for "innovation" in the biological world and this excludes the possibility of evolution. There can, however, be extinctions. Extinction is an accepted creationist concept held by most, though not all of its adherents. It is, however, a creationist tenet that all species, including saber-tooth tigers and woolly mammoths, were created at the same time as dinosaurs and humans. Fossil findings of extinct species can, therefore, be explained using Creationism theory. All species were created at the same time though this does not mean they will all become extinct at the same time. So, the second law of thermodynamics allows for "disintegration but not integration".[91] Because evolution posits improvement in species, it contradicts not only thermodynamic laws but also the Bible and cannot be countenanced by creationists.

THE ARGUMENTS AGAINST NATURAL SELECTION

The creationists believe that there is "nothing really novel" in nature though DNA is accepted as a valid biological concept and that Mendel's (1822-1884) Laws show that various characteristics can be transmitted genetically, in a limited number of ways. However, creationists deny there are any new traits ever seen in any species, no matter how long a given species is observed.[92]

89　As the size of a body increases, its heat (energy) is dispersed more widely causing its temperature to fall. If a body is compressed, it heats up; if expanded, it cools down. Refrigeration is based on this principle.

90　Ibid, p. 177.

91　Op. cit. Morris, H. M. 1996, p. 38.

92　Ibid, p. 51.

Genetic traits can be re-shuffled or even re-combined[93] but they cannot mutate for the benefit of i.e. improvement in a species. If one assumes that beneficial mutations do not occur in nature or in the laboratory, then the basic support for evolution is eliminated, since recombination or any other variation in DNA position, will not allow true evolution but only variations among subspecies. Morris uses the example of the peppered moth, a common species of English moth.[94] This example involves the adaptation of the light-colored peppered moth to urban pollution by developing a grey-coloration in order to be less obvious to predators as the moth rests on soot-darkened trees. Indeed, this would appear to be a natural selective advantage gained by this transformation, however, it does not necessarily indicate an evolutionary change, merely a new variety of the same species, according to Morris. The creationists do not deny natural selection as a force in nature but, rather, deny that this selective process supports the theory of evolution. They accept only limited changes that do not include improvement in a species leading to an entirely new species. Any higher biological organism is excluded in Creationism as noted above.

THE FOSSIL EVIDENCE

Creationists are quick to point out that there are gaps in the fossil record. If evolution is a gradual process, then there should be no gaps. According to Morris, the evolutionists teach 'gradualism', that is, evolution as a gradual and progressive process, spanning many eons, while creationist theory offers a 'cataclysmic' view of creation–all species appeared at one time though some have become abruptly extinct.[95] If the gradual genesis of new species is to be given credence, then the fossil record should show a progression of new species as one excavates the ascending sedimentary

---

93   Thain, M., & Hickman, M. 2001, *The Penguin Dictionary of Biology* (New York: Penguin), p. 551-52. Recombination occurs when a segment of DNA, containing several genes on a given chromosome, is either moved to a different part of the same chromosome or to an entirely separate chromosome. This can account for different varieties of species but not new species. A phenomenon called genetic or allelic drift may occur at the time chromosomes of the mother and father are randomly distributed to an ovum or sperm. Every gene has two alleles (genes for one genetic trait) and only one of these can be passed on to an offspring. For example, the mother may have an allele for blue eyes and the father an allele for brown eyes. This is a random process, which through natural selection may lead to the elimination of a trait or its being distributed to 100% of the population. If a mutation occurs then the allele involved will be weeded out or perpetuated depending on its effect on survival of the species.

94   Op. cit. Coyne, J. A. 1998.

95   Op. cit. Morris, H. M. 1996, p.78.

strata. However, the stratigraphic evidence doesn't support a gradual process for there is the sudden emergence of many phyla during the Cambrian period with many gaps in the fossil record. Also, there is no evidence of the so-called 'missing link' that would tie humans to their ape-like progenitors.[96] Morris suggests that the fossil record, in fact, shows that all kingdoms, phyla and classes known today have been present since the Cambrian, with the exception of the moss-corals (Ordovician), insects (Devonian), and the graptolites[97], which appear over the Cambrian to the Carboniferous periods. The trilobites emerged in both the Cambrian and Permian, according to Morris. All plant phyla began in the Triassic, with the exception of the bacteria, algae and fungi, which originated in the Precambrian and several other phyla that appeared somewhat earlier than the Cambrian period.

Similarly, according to creationists, the fossil record seems to show that essentially all classes, orders, families, genera and species have appeared abruptly, so that there is a "horizontal" but not a "vertical continuum" as Morris phrases it. He asserts that evolutionists rely on "secondary assumptions" to explain these fossil gaps (and other weaknesses in evolutionary theory). An example of a secondary assumption is the idea of "punctuated equilibrium" which evolutionists use to explain evolutionary gaps.[98] This concept states that there are bursts of evolutionary activity with long periods of evolutionary stability in between. Morris calls this an "imaginary process" which has no genetic basis. He does not elaborate on the specific lack of genetic evidence to which he refers.

Those phyla that emerged over several geological periods do not present a polemic problem, according to creationists, because these geological periods were very short and occurred during the six days of creation. The Precambrian, Cambrian, etc. periods all occurred within the one week of creation, rather than separated by millions of years, according to creationist's estimates–all this is supported by the words of Genesis.

In terms of fossil evidence, Morris speaks of evolutionary "uniformitarionism", which describes the evolutionists' belief that rocks and fossils "formed slowly over vast eons of time by the same processes now at work within the Earth."[99] The creationists espouse the concept of 'catastrophism', which holds that rocks and fossils formed over a short period

---

96   Ibid, p. 79.
97   Any of numerous extinct colonial marine animals chiefly of the order *Dendroidea* and *Graptoloidea* from the late Cambrian to the early Mississippian periods, provide fossil remains often used by paleontologists to date the rocks of the Silurian and Ordovician periods.
98   Ibid, p. 90.
99   Ibid, p. 91.

of time. Uniformitarionism implies two major concepts: first, that the Earth has been around a very long, time during which evolution continues to unfold and, second, that the same physical forces that are in play today were present when the Earth was in its infancy. Morris denies both aspects of the principle of uniformitarionism. The Earth is not as old as geologists claim and the physical laws we know today do not work at the same pace as they did in the past. These laws, Morris asserts, functioned much more rapidly than they do today and, thus, six days was ample time to create the world. We will present the geologist's view of these processes in the next section.

As for the fossil record related to *H. sapiens*, Morris finds these data wholly unconvincing. He states that the various strata in which human fossils are found are often mixed with older fossils.[100] One such site is in Belgium and he cites a reference by Edwin Colbert, *Men and Dinosaurs*, which seeks to prove that humans and dinosaurs lived together at the same time. It is Morris' contention that the very existence of numerous fossils mixed together speaks to the cataclysmic nature of their origins. He goes on to argue that sandstone and other sedimentary layers must have formed rapidly. He includes shale, limestone and coal strata in his analysis, all of which must have formed over a short period of time. He cites two references here, one from the Quarterly of the Creation Research Society.[101] Morris also details how the 'Great Flood' impacted the geological data and how it explains many of the geological findings that evolutionists use to support their 'gradualism' theory.[102]

Morris analyzes hominoid and hominid fossils and finds the evidence for the evolution of humans inconclusive.[103] Either the specimens are too scanty, that is, they very often consist of only a tooth, part of a mandible or maxilla or the fossils are consistent with an ape or *H. sapiens* but not an intermediate species. Either way, he finds no solid evidence of evolution in any of the specimens reported in the "scientific literature".[104] He specifically deals with ape progenitors of humans, as well as, several hominids, including *Australopithecus*, *H. erectus*, *H. neanderthalensis* and *H. sapiens*, finding inconsistencies in the evidence, often quoting various researchers, such as Louis Leakey. Morris notes that at one point, Leakey "changed his mind"

---

100   Ibid, p. 99.
101   Rumpke, N. A. 1966, *Prolegomena to a Study of Cataclysmal Sedimentation*, Quarterly of the Creation Research Society, 3:16-37.
102   Op. cit. Morris, H. M. p. 129.
103   Ibid, Chapter VII.
104   Ibid, pp. 172-76.

regarding the bipedalism[105] of *Australopithecus*, thus, casting doubt on the taxonomy of this intermediate hominid.[106]

Space doesn't permit further review of Morris' objections to the fossil record as interpreted by evolutionists but the foregoing gives a brief outline of Morris' major objections to evolutionary theory as based on the fossil record.

GEOLOGICAL DATING

Morris finds deficiencies in both stratigraphic (geological layers) and radiometric data (radioactive decay of elements). He provides theoretical evidence that the various strata must have been deposited in a very brief period of time, noting that:

> The adjacent strata may be of the same material, contain the same types of fossils and look very much like it.[107]

Thus, one stratum (layer of earth) cannot be distinguished from another making distinctions between strata impossible. He also points out that trees spanning several strata have been found and the same fossils may be found in more than one stratum indicating they span more than one epoch. The biblical Flood can explain much of what is found in the various strata, according to Morris. See Fig. 6.4.

In terms of the radiometric record, Morris believes they can be explained away by denying their scientific validity. "Not even uranium dating is capable of experimental verification, since no one can actually watch uranium decay for millions of years."[108] Similarly, he finds "fallacies" in other radiometric techniques, such as potassium-40/argon-40 and carbon 14 dating, noting that there have been errors and inconsistencies in several studies using these techniques.[109,110]

---

105   Bipedalism or walking on two feet is the feature used to separate apes from hominids.
106   Staff, 1971, *Australopithecus: A Long-Armed, Short-Legged Knuckle-Walker*, Science News, 100:347.
107   Op. cit. Morris, H. M. 1996, p. 112.
108   Ibid, p. 137.
109   Ibid, pp. 160-1.
110   Kieth, M. S., & Anderson, G. M. 1963, *Radiocarbon Dating: Fictitious Results with Mollusk Shells*, Science, (August 16, 1963, no volume given), p. 634.

Standard System	Corresponding Stage of the Flood
Recent	Period of post-Flood development of modern world.
Pleistocene	Post-Flood effects of glaciation and pluviation, along with lessening volcanism and tectonism.
Tertiary	Final phase of the Flood, along with initial phases of the post-Flood readjustments.
Mesozoic	Intermediate phases of the Flood, with mixtures of continental and marine deposits. Post-Flood possibly in some cases.
Paleozoic	Deep-sea and shelf deposits formed in the early phases of the Flood, mostly in the ocean.
Proterozoic	Initial sedimentary deposits of the early phases of the Flood.
Archaeozoic	Origin of crust dating from the Creation Period, though disturbed and metamorphosed by the thermal and tectonic changes during the Cataclysm.

Fig. 6.4. This table shows how The Flood can explain the several geological periods having occurred as a result of sedimentary forces at the time of the Noachian flood described in the Bible.

MOLECULAR BIOLOGY

As noted earlier, Morris believes that there are no beneficial mutations that occur in DNA. He puts it this way:

Modern molecular biology, with its penetrating insights into the remarkable genetic code implanted in the DNA system, has further confirmed that normal variations operate only within the range specified by the DNA for the particular type of organism, so that no truly novel characteristics, producing higher degrees of order or complexity can occur. [111]

Morris does not necessarily deny the occurrence of mutations however he sees them as trivial, minor and rare events that cannot be responsible for evolutionary changes as claimed by scientists.[112] In addition, the second law of thermodynamics precludes any mutation as beneficial and, thus, such changes, even if they take place, cannot result in higher or more complex organisms. Each such change must be positively helpful in

---

111   Op. cit. Morris, H. M. 1996, p.51.
112   Ibid, p. 5.

the environment if it is to be preserved by natural selection and contribute to evolutionary progress.[113]

Since mutations are random events, it would be very unlikely, in Morris' view that chance mutations could result in beneficial biological changes. "The net effect of all mutations is harmful."[114] Also, since mutations are rare events, even the time-scales claimed by geologists would not be long enough to produce the complex world we see before us. Furthermore, "good mutations are very, very rare" making the possibility of developing a higher organism even less likely. In sum, mutations could only lead to extinctions, in Morris' opinion.

Morris offers many arguments against evolution–too many to review here. His approach is echoed in several other creationist books on the subject.[115,116,117] In addition, there are many websites that present similar arguments.[118] The following section deals with the evolutionists' rebuttal to these creationist arguments.

THE EVOLUTIONISTS' REBUTTAL
SCIENCE AS RELIGION

The evolutionist would say that science is not religion. Science is surely based on hypotheses, as the creationists suggest but there is more to science than just hypothetical speculation.[119] Hypotheses are only educated guesses as to how the world works based on preliminary data. These hypotheses must be verified by further observation and experimentation. This can be done in a chemistry laboratory, through a telescope or even by pure mathematics (though this last must ultimately conform to the 'real' world of empiricism). In fact, the foundations of the scientific method

---

113   Ibid, p. 54.

114   Ibid, p. 56.

115   Hanegraaff, H. 1998, *The Face That Demonstrates the Farce of Evolution* (Nashville, TN: World Publishing).

116   Bethe, M. 1996, *Darwin's Black Box: The Biochemical Challenge to Evolution* (New York: Simon & Schuster).

117   Op. cit. MacArthur, H. M. 2001.

118   Proof of Creationism, 2004, http://proofofcreationism.com.

119   Berra, T. 1990, *Evolution and the Myth of Creationism* (Stanford, CA: Stanford University Press).

involve observation, data collection, null hypothesis testing [120] and most importantly, a hypothesis must predict outcomes or future events.

An example of such a hypothesis can be found in Percival Lowell's prediction that an unknown planet existed at the far-reaches of our Solar System. This claim was based on perturbations (anomalies or irregularities) in the orbits of Neptune and Uranus and mathematical calculations using Kepler and Newton's laws of planetary motion. Lowell died in 1916 before finding Pluto[121] but Clyde Tombaugh, in 1930, using Lowell's calculations was able, finally, to identify Pluto by telescopic observations. Thus, there was preliminary data–orbital irregularities–a hypothesis that another previously unknown planet was causing these perturbations and finally observational evidence of Pluto.

The warrant evolutionists use to support their claims rests on the scientific method, along with the physical, chemical, mechanical and electrical laws that have been shown over the years to be capable of predicting a variety of natural events. There is, certainly, a belief that these laws are enduring, consistent and reliable. This belief, however, is not based solely on ancient authority or faith in science–in contrast to religious beliefs. 'Faith' in scientific laws rests upon a long history of testing these laws using a variety of disciplines and finding them, more often than not, capable of accurately describing and precisely predicting events in the world around us. As seen by the example above, such empirical evidence is not limited to things that are earth-bound. Helium was found on the Sun studying its spectrum of electromagnetic radiation (solar light) before it was isolated on Earth. Now every child loves a helium-filled balloon and all Goodyear blimps floating over football stadia are filled with helium–both practical demonstrations of the validity of Pierre Janssen's 1868 discovery of helium in the spectrum of light coming from the Sun.

A 'belief' in science, cannot be considered analogous to a belief in Genesis. Scientific facts are practical and tangible. They provide workable and beneficial improvements in our daily lives. They are reproducible and allow us to land men on the Moon. We cannot deny the validity of these scientific outcomes.

In addition, scientific research tends to converge into one accepted, consensus opinion regarding a specific question such as, "Is there a planet beyond Neptune and Uranus?" or "Does penicillin cure syphilis?" Religion

---

120   A null hypothesis is a statistical method that indicates the probability that a given statement about a 'population' being studied might be in error. If the result falls within the 5% range of error, that is, one chance in 20 that it is false, then it is considered statistically significant and, therefore, it is very likely the hypothesis is true.

121   Of course, Pluto is no longer considered a full-fledged planet.

on the other hand, has no accepted endpoint. Is there a God? Are some people predestined to go to Heaven? Was Mary a virgin and the mother of God? None of these questions can be answered with a high degree of certitude. In fact, religious questions are divergent in nature. Rather than leading to one defined answer nearly everyone agrees upon, they almost always produce more and more differences of opinion. The fact that there are 20,000 different Christian sects worldwide points to religious divergence. Religion has no ability to predict outcomes. It has no way of developing consensus opinions. The Bible's veracity relies solely on faith and authority. Theology cannot be empirically verified but then, if we require such demonstration, we may be missing the whole point of religion as discussed earlier. Religion doesn't deal with facts; it deals with feelings and feelings are as diverse as there are feeling beings.

THE LAWS OF THERMODYNAMICS

In terms of the law of conservation of energy/matter (the first law of thermodynamics), there is no conflict between this law and evolution. Matter and energy are not lost or gained in evolutionary processes. In fact, radiometric dating methods are based on this law. When uranium decays to lead, the atomic weight and energy released during this process can all be accounted for–there is no 'missing' energy or matter.[122] In order to have evolution, energy is not created but rather added to a biological system from some other system, such as the Sun, which provides most of the energy required by virtually all systems on Earth, whether they are chemical, geological, atmospheric or biological.[123] While one system loses energy (the Sun) another system (the Earth) gains energy.

The same refutation applies to the creationists' argument concerning the second law dealing with entropy. It is true that all 'closed systems' tend to become disordered over time but this only applies to 'closed systems.' Any 'open system,' and this includes biological systems on Earth–can take energy from other 'open systems' (such as the Sun) which then is used in maintaining or even increasing order within the system. This happens every time a new child is conceived. The embryo receives energy from its mother and, thus, is able to develop and grow. The Universe, as a whole, is

---

122   For example, in uranium decay: ^{238}U à ^{206}Pb + 8^4He, that is, uranium with an atomic number of 238 (238 protons and neutrons total) is converted to lead with an atomic number of 206 with the release of 8 helium nuclei (32 protons and neutrons). Each helium nucleus has 2 protons and 2 neutrons. Mass and energy are both conserved in this reaction.
123   Patterson, J. W. 1984, *Thermodynamics and Evolution in Scientists Confront Creationism*, ed. L. Godfrey (New York: W.W. Norton & Co.), pp. 101-2.

considered to be a closed system by physicists but within the Universe there may be transfer of energy from one system to another. Many tons of matter are added to the Earth from outer space every year, brought by meteors and comets.[124] We receive energy in the form of gamma rays from other galaxies every second in addition to solar energy. It is quite clear that the Universe is evolving just as biological systems do.[125] The error creationists make in enlisting entropy in their arguments against evolution lies with their failure to distinguish open from closed systems. As we have noted above, there is evolution everywhere in the Universe. Planets, stars and galaxies are all in various stages of evolution. We can see the Universe evolving just by looking into outer space. The more distant the view of the Universe using the Hubble or other telescopes, the farther back in time we are looking because the light we see today represents light from the past. If an astronomer sees a billion light years into space, he or she is seeing history that is a billion years old. It is like time travel; we can literally see into the past. This gives a living history of the Universe and we see its evolution, just as the fossil record on Earth provides us with a similar view of Earth's past.

THE FOSSIL EVIDENCE

As noted above, the arguments advanced by creationists with regard to the fossil record include the limited fossil finds, often consisting of only a tooth or jaw. There are many gaps in the fossil record and there is difficulty in classifying fossils. Morris, however, ignores the bulk of fossil research over the past 150 years. Some fossil finds, indeed, are fragmentary. This is true of the Java Man but continued excavations at the original and nearby sites have helped complete the fossil record of the Java Man, *Homo erectus*.[126] In addition, paleo-anatomists have found that, even a single tooth, especially a canine or molar, can tell a great deal about any given species. The size of the skull or hypoglossal canal, for example, yields clues to intelligence or language development.[127]

---

124   Jupiter's gravitational pull on its first moon, Io, is responsible for Io's volcanic activity, that is, Jupiter's gravitational energy is converted into Io's thermal energy.

125   Eggers, D., et al. 2005, *Hubble Space Telescope Observations of Star-Forming Regions in NGC 3994/3995*, Astronomical J. 129:136-148.

126   Baba, H., et al. 2003, *Homo erectus Calvarium from the Pleistocene of Java*, Science, 299:1384-88.

127   Kay, R. F., et al. 1998, *The Hypoglossal Canal and the Origin of Human Vocal Behavior*, PNAS, 95:5417-19.

As far as gaps in the fossil record, this does not preclude evolution.[128] We are dealing with thousands of species that are, in some cases, billions of years old. Earth has changed a lot since many of these fossils first came to rest. If punctuated equilibrium, as a concept, holds true and geological as well as fossil evidence strongly support this claim, then the transition periods during which species were rapidly evolving into empty ecological niches would be short and transitional species less numerous. Also, the fossil record continues to be filled in over time. Some of these findings are dead-end species others may well be transitional precursors to new species, that is, 'missing links'; only time will tell. Only a small number of fossils remain after individuals die. Fossil finds are a numbers game. Since only very few individuals yield fossils, there are bound to be gaps, nonetheless, ongoing digs continue to fills in these gaps.

MOLECULAR BIOLOGY

We have already seen the evidence for celestial evolution. There are data to show that there is biological evolution on both the micro- and macro-scales. Proteins evolve,[129] as do enzymes.[130] This is the case, as well, for DNA,[131] dinosaurs,[132] parasites,[133],[134] woolly mammoths,[135] finches[136]and hominids[137],[138] among many other species.[139] The study of Darwin's finches, as already noted, is of particular interest because one of the creationists' concerns is that evolution has never been observed in progress. The finch

128   Godfrey, L. R. 1983, *Creationism and Gaps in the Fossil Record*, in. *Scientists Confront Creation*, ed. L. Godfrey (New York: W. W. Norton & Co.) p. 193.
129   Williams, E. J. B., & Hurst, L. D. *Proteins of Linked Genes Evolve at Similar Rates*, Nature, 407:900-7.
130   Chou, H., et al. 2002, *Inactivation of CMP-N-acetylneuraminic Acid Hydroxylase Occurred Prior to Brain Expansion during Human Evolution*, PNAS, 99:11736-41.
131   Holden, C. 2001, *Oldest Human DNA Reveals Aussie Oddity*, Science, 291:230-31.
132   Serene, P. C. 1999, *The Evolution of Dinosaurs*, Science, 284:2137-47.
133   Marti, M., et al. 2004, *Targeting Malaria Virulence and Remodeling Proteins to the Host Erythrocytes,* Science, 306:1930-33.
134   Ebert, D. 1998, *Experimental Evolution of Parasites*, Science, 282:1432-35.
135   Op. cit. Lister, A. M., & Sher, A.V. 2001.
136   Grant, P. R., & Grant, B. R. 2002, *Unpredictable Evolution in a 30-Year Study of Darwin's Finches*, Science, 296:707-11.
137   Cela-Conde, C. J., & Ayala, F .J. 2003, *Genera of the Human Lineage*, PNAS, 100:7684-89.
138   Trinkets, E. 1997, *Appendicular Robusticity and the Paleobiology of Modern Human Emergence*, PNAS, 4:13367-73.
139   Knoll, A. H., & Carroll, S. B. 1999, *Early Animal Evolution: Emerging Views from Comparative Biology and Geology*, Science, 284:2129-37.

study provides direct observational evidence of evolution in a higher species than a virus or bacterium. In the influenza virus one sees evolutionary changes virtually every year.[140] The *Drosophila* fruit fly has been known to evolve rapidly and such changes in the wild have been observed, as well.[141] Human evolution has involved the insertion of bacterial genes into human cells so that bacteria and humans have evolved together.[142] There is evidence that archaic *H. sapiens* evolved into modern *H. sapiens*. We have already reviewed DNA studies of body lice indicating that humans first began sewing clothes around 72,000 years ago and not before.[143] Language did not develop until 50,000 B.C E. and cave art not until 10,000 years later. It could be argued that these observed evolutionary events are no more than variations in species as the creationists suggest but enzymatic evolution that accounts, in part, for developing intelligence is more than a subspecies variation. It indicates the evolution of not only intelligence but also self-consciousness, both associated with the genus *Homo*. There is evidence of evolution wherever one looks whether in the fossil record or DNA.

Geological dating and molecular studies are the primary bases for the evolutionary nature of the data cited above. Without these supports, the creationists would have as good a case for their view as do scientists, however, combining the above evidence with the data to follow in the next two sections, it is certain that evolution is more than just a hypothesis.

THE CASE FOR GEOLOGICAL DATING

This topic was covered earlier but I would like to emphasize certain points because geological dating is a pivotal technique used in evolution studies. Creationists criticize geological dating methods in several ways. The main of these asserts that there are a number of inconsistencies in the various techniques used and that these variations invalidate radiometric-dating methods.[144] That there are difficulties encountered in geological dating is unquestioned.[145] All of the problems found in a given method of

---

140   Smith, D. J., et al. 2004, *Mapping the Antigenic and Genetic Evolution of Influenza Virus*, Science, 305:371-76.

141   Huey, R. B., et al, 2000, *Rapid Evolution of a Geographic Cline in Size in an Introduced Fly*, Science, 287:308-9.

142   Salzburg, S. L., et al. 2001, *Microbial Genes in the Human Genome: Lateral Transfer or Gene Loss?* Science, 292:1903-6.

143   Wade, N. 2007, *Before the Dawn: Recovering the Lost History of Our Ancestors* (New York: Penguin).

144   Raup, C. M. 1983, *The Geological and Paleontological Arguments of Creationism*, in. *Scientists Confront Creation*, ed. L. Godfrey (New York: W. W. Norton & Co.) p.149.

145   Op. cit. Wien, R. C. 2002, p. 7.

dating, however, can be compensated for and, when there are errors in the determinations, the resulting data often indicate there is something amiss and re-testing is needed. In addition, virtually all studies are verified by using two or even three methods to confirm the age of a given specimen. Since there are over 40 radiometric techniques, all having overlapping ages for which they are valid, each of the methods can be validated by comparison with results obtained from other methods. In addition, dendrochronology or other non-radiometric methods can be used to verify results.

One of the criticisms of radiometric dating is that it cannot be verified in the laboratory, since a scientist is unable to check a specific half-life over millions or billions of years. The fact is that U^{238} decay has been measured for 100 years and several of the other techniques have been tested for over 60 years. This may seem like a short time when dealing with half-lives spanning millions or billions of years however the precision of measuring radioactive decay is so accurate that the release of one alpha particle (helium nucleus) can be detected. The Geiger counters used are very sensitive and counting decay rates for even 10 years can give accurate data for elements that decay at very slow rates. The physics and mathematics of radioactivity is fairly simple.[146] Sources of potential error are ever present but all of these can be accounted for. Radiometric dating has been used for many purposes including determining ages for feathered dinosaurs,[147] diets of early hominids,[148] age of extraterrestrial particles,[149] timing of asteroid impacts on Earth,[150] the periods of mass extinctions,[151] dates of flint

---

146   For potassium-40 to argon-40 decay, the formula is:
t = $t_{1/2}$ X ln [1 + (argon-40)/{0.112 X (potassium-40)}[/ln(2).where t = the age of the sample, $t_{1/2}$ = half-life, ln is the natural log (found in any scientific calculator), argon-40 and potassium-40 are the amounts, by weight, of each element found in the sample, 0.112 is a constant and ln(2) is the natural log of 2 (also found using a calculator). It's all simple algebra without any of the differentiations or integrations used in calculus.

147   Swisher, C. C., et al. 1999, *Cretaceous Age for the Feathered Dinosaur of Liaoning, China*, Nature, 400:58-61.

148   Sponheimer, M., & Lee-Thorp, J. A. 1999, *Isotopic Evidence for the Diet of an Early Hominid, Australopithecus africanus*, Science, 283:369-70.

149   Flynn, G. J., et al. 2003, *Chemical and Mineralogical Analysis of an Extraterrestrial Particle in Aerogel, Lunar and Planetary*, Science, 35:18-22.

150   Kerr, R. A. 2004, *Evidence of Huge Deadly Impact Found Off Australian Coast?* Science, 304:941-42.

151   Mundil, R., et al. 2004, *Age and Timing of the Permian Mass Extinctions: U/Pb Dating of Closed-System Zircons*, Science, 305:1760-62.

mining,[152] the antiquity of stone tools[153] and the age of hominid remains,[154] and many others. The creationists, in fact, simply choose to ignore the bulk of geological dating research.

Carbon dating, in particular, has been criticized by the creationists but, even here, the technology has improved in recent years.[155],[156] A source for error in carbon-14 dating can arise, if the C^{14} level in the atmosphere at the time an organism dies, differs from current levels. Ancient C^{14} levels can be determined by various non-radiometric methods. In one study, glacial sedimentary layers were sampled to develop a graph of the fluctuations in atmospheric C^{14} levels over the past 45,000 years. This is a very accurate method–it is like counting tree rings. With such comparative methods, radiometric dating has become very precise–truly beyond question as a dating technique. If radiometric dating is valid and there is little doubt about this, then the claims made by creationists regarding the age of the Earth, the timing of sedimentary deposits, the contemporaneous existence of humans with dinosaurs, the Flood, age of new and extinct species and the creation of Earth in six days cannot be true. Critical assessment of dating methods leaves no doubt about the validity of this technology.

As with all scientific statements, one can only claim a high probability for its accuracy. There are no scientific absolutes. Science is a convergent discipline. Usually several scientific methods are used to confirm data obtained by a given dating method. This is certainly the case with evolution where molecular biology, paleontology, geology, archeology, chemistry and physics all point to the same conclusion, namely that evolution is a valid paradigm.

Molecular biology has helped undermine one other tenet of creationist theory–the argument from ID. This is not to deny the possibility of an Intelligent Designer but, rather, to support a non-biblical, empirical basis for creation, which allows for a 'prime mover' (to use Aristotle's terminology) that incorporates physical, chemical and biological forces into the process of creation.

---

152   Verdi, G., et al. 2004, *Flint Mining in Prehistory Recorded by* in-situ *Produced Cosmogony* ^{10}Be, PNAS, 101:7880-84.

153   Rink, W. J., et al. 2004, *Confirmation of Near 400 ka Age for the Yabrudian Industry at Tabun Cave, Israel,* J. of Archeological Science, 31:15-20.

154   Smith, F. H., et al. 1999, *Direct Radiocarbon Dating for India G_1 and Velika Pecina Late Pleistocene Hominid Remains,* PNAS, 96:12281-86.

155   Bard, E. 2001, *Extending the Calibrated Radiocarbon Record,* Science, 292:2443-44.

156   Kitagawa, H., & van der Plight, J. 1998, *Atmospheric Radiocarbon Calibration to 45 yr B.P.: Later Glacial Fluctuations and Cosmogony Isotope Production,* Science, 279:1187-90.

The creationist's view is that the chance creation of all living organisms is a statistical impossibility.[157] They liken evolution to a hurricane blowing through a junkyard and leaving a fully assembled 747 in its wake. Evolutionists, however, see no problem with random, genetic mutations and natural selection in producing all past and present species.[158] The evolutionists' rebuttal centers on the molecular evidence found in the biological world. Let us see just how random nature really works.

MOLECULAR SELF-ASSEMBLY

Nature is filled with recurring non-random patterns.[159] These include bacteria, snowflakes, seashells, trees, sand dunes, urban sprawl and the atmosphere of Jupiter. Molecular self-assembly has been known for the past two decades or more,[160] Atoms and molecules react with each other in predictable ways–they tend toward self-assembly. We seldom marvel at snowflakes, bubbles forming on seashores or a crystal of salt. These are everyday phenomena: they are not, however, random occurrences but rather consequences of the physio-chemical principles that govern all matter. We are not carbon-based organisms (as Spock would say it) by chance. If the chance proximity of molecules were the basis of our organic world, then we would be iron-silicon creatures because the vast majority of elements on Earth are iron and silicon. The fact is that carbon, hydrogen, oxygen and a host of other elements are 'on the lookout for each other' all the time. They have an affinity defined by chemical laws. Terms such as 'hydrogen bonding', 'metal coordination', 'Octet rule', or 'van der Waals stacking' are used to describe various physical forces that determine how molecules react with one another. These forces account for molecular 'self-selection', 'self-recognition' and result in the formation of complex molecules such as nucleic acids, DNA and proteins–all building blocks of living organisms. A brief search of Science magazine turned up 272 articles on molecular self-assembly. DNA acts as a template to facilitate (using RNA intermediates) the self-assembly of proteins which are the essential building blocks of all biological systems.[161]

157   Op. cit. Morris, H. M. 1996, pp. 59-69.

158   Doolittle, R. F. 1983, *Probability and the Origins of Life*, in *Scientists Confront Creationism*, ed. L.R. Godfrey (New York: W.W. Norton & Co..) pp. 85-97.

159   Ball, P. 1999, *The Self-Made Tapestry Pattern Formation in Nature* (New York: Oxford University Press).

160   Lehn, J- M. 2002, *Toward Self-Organization and Complex Matter*, Science; 295:2400-03.

161   Yan, H., et al. 2003, *DNA-Templated Self-Assembly of Protein Arrays and Highly Conductive Nanowires,* Science, 301:1882-84.

Nucleic acids have been developed using nanotechnology.[162] Protein-based elements of inheritance can be created in the laboratory.[163] Artificial RNA is used to produce self-assembling molecules for a variety of purposes.[164] Even 'artificial cells' have been constructed.[165] These are not true cells, since they cannot replicate on their own but they are capable of protein synthesis–the job 'living' cells do all the time. This will, in due course, allow the mass-production of such products as insulin, human growth factor, antibiotics and many more biological products useful in medicine and other related sciences. These products are produced now but utilize living organisms.

This kind of research clearly demonstrates that the world, including the biological world, is not produced by random events. There is rhyme and reason to the world. Evolution is one of these processes that is not random in spite of what the creationists say. Mutations occur at a predictable rate. The ever-changing environment then determines which mutations hang around–at least until the environment changes once again. There are laws governing the organization of nature. Evolution is not, however, a teleological process. It is not aimed at defined ends or outcomes. Instead of being pushed in a given direction it is pulled along by the need to adjust to the environment. This is what natural selection is all about. In spite of what Dawkins claims, genes are not 'selfish'. Selfishness requires consciousness or some kind of awareness of the environment. The concept of selfish genes is an anthropomorphism just like the theistic notion of God. It is a catchy phrase but doesn't truly describe the genetic, biological realm.

What is behind all this complexity is the quintessential philosophical and theological question. Is it God or an uncreated, unending material Universe or as I will contend a Neo-Natural power that one might call God but a God of a different ilk? The theists or deists may well be right in believing that there is a God behind all of what we see around us. If it is a God, then what can we know of IT. Is God transcendent and totally unknowable? Or are our weak intellects simply too primitive to comprehend this deity? One thing is certain; all of this vast, unbelievably sophisticated world was and is not based on the abrupt, one-time creative act of an anthropomorphic divine being. There is continuous creation every instant with every new being that is born and each being does not 'pop' into existence by a stroke of divine will–there are biological processes that take place with the conception,

162   Yan, H. 2004, *Nucleic Acid Nanotechnology,* Science, 306:2048-49.

163   Li, L., & Lindquist, S. 2000, *Creating a Protein-Based Element of Inheritance,* Science, 287:661-64.

164   Yan, H., et al. 2004,*Building Programmable Jigsaw Puzzles with RNA,* Science, 306:2068-70.

165   Ball, P. 2004, *Artificial Cells Take Shape,* Nature, 6 December 2004 (Online News).

development and growth of each of these 'creations'. There is obviously much more to our Universe than what is depicted in Genesis and this includes its beginning and evolution over the eons.

SOCIO-RELIGIOUS ASPECTS

There are significant socio-religious aspects to the creationism/ evolution debate. As we have seen, 45% of the population believes in the literal biblical rendition of creation, another 25% adhere to some creationist concept of how the world began, while 55% of scientists do not accept God's 'hand' in the creation of the Universe and 12% espouse a strict secular atheism. It is not surprising that this debate stirs emotions and consequent activism.

Religion and science have long had a precarious co-existence beginning in Antiquity.[166] As Draper says:

But faith is in its nature unchangeable, stationary; Science is in its nature progressive; and eventually a divergence between them [science and religion], impossible to conceal, must take place.

Socrates was forced to take hemlock because he was 'poisoning' the minds of young men with his ideas about the world that did not necessarily include the ancient Greek gods.[167] In the Middle Ages, the Church initially denounced Aristotle because he taught that the world was eternal. This idea was in opposition to the biblical version found in the Apocalypse.[168] The Galileo affair is well known[169] Isaac Newton wrote on theological issues, most of which remained hidden in his study, for fear that his views on the Trinity might result in a heretic's hanging.[170] When the idea of evolution first surfaced in the late eighteenth and early nineteenth centuries, resistance to it was quick and vigorous.[171] Charles Lyell (1797-1875) in the *Principles of Geology*, first published in 1830, anticipated an outcry from the public

166   Draper, J. W. 2007, *History of the Conflict Between Religion and Science* (Charleston, NC: Nab Press).
167   Plato, 1981, *Apology*, in *Plato: Five Dialogues*, trans. G. M. A. Grube (Indianapolis, IN: Hackett).
168   Grant, H. 1996, *Planets, Stars, and Orbs: The Medieval Cosmos*, 1200-1687 (New York: Cambridge University Press), pp. 52-3.
169   Ibid, p. 202.
170   Manuel, F. E. 1974, *The Religion of Isaac Newton: The Fremantle Lecture 1973* (New York: Oxford-Clarendon).
171   Schmid, R. 1882, *The Theories of Darwin and Their Relation to Philosophy, Religion and Morality* (Kindle Edition, BiblioBazaar).

regarding his attack on catastrophism.[172] Lyell's name continues to come up in creationist writings even today.[173] And Charles Darwin's name remains anathema in creationist circles.[174]

The demographics of creationists and evolutionists have been studied in the past two or three decades, beginning in 1983.[175] These studies were carried out using only college students from five universities in three sections of the country: California, Texas and Connecticut.

As one might expect, there is a greater tendency in Texas to believe in strict creationism, although among these college students, a plurality accepted evolution as the explanation for the origins of life.[176] Forty-seven percent agreed with an evolutionary cause of life versus 45% who did not. In California and Connecticut, over 60% favored evolution. When asked if there was ample scientific evidence to support evolution, 43% of Texas students said 'yes', whereas over 50% of the other two groups of students said 'yes'. Twenty-eight percent of Texans believed that humans were created 10,000 years ago but 45% disagreed with this statement. In California and Connecticut, nearly 60% disagreed with this time frame for creation. In terms of media use such as TV, books and journals, there was no correlation except in those students that read Nature magazine, in which case, creationists were under-represented. If they did read such scientific journals, especially in Texas, their 'creationist score' was lower.[177] Those identified among the Moral Majority had higher creationist scores, as did those holding conservative religious and/or political views. Grade point average was inversely correlated with creationist tendencies, as was parent's educational level. In California, where both creationism and evolution are taught in the classroom, more students believed that the two ideologies should be taught together.

It is important to remember that the several studies that went into collecting these data were carried out on college students and, if one were to study the general population, it is likely that the 'creationist score' would approach 47% as suggested by the Gallup poll findings quoted earlier.

Creationism, in spite of the evidence against it, is here to stay at least for a while, maybe a long while. It has been with us for over 2000 years and shows no signs of disappearing from the minds and emotions of a significant

---

172	Op. cit. Lyell, C. 1997, p. xxiv.

173	Op. cit. Morris, H. M. 1996, p. 254.

174	Ibid, pp. 6, 48, 51, 52, 53, 70, 81, 179, 199.

175	Harold, F. B., & Eve, R. A. (Eds.) 1995, *Cult, Archaeology and Creationism: Understanding Pseudoscientific Beliefs about the Past* (Iowa City, IA: University of Iowa Press).

176	Ibid, p.73.

177	The 'creationist score' was derived from those questions more often positively correlated with a belief in creationism.

proportion of society. It provides a rallying point for many religious and conservative groups. Why this is and why such belief systems remain strong in the hearts of many will be discussed at greater length in the next chapter.

CONCLUSIONS

In the end, we come back to the concepts of *mythos* and *logos*. Just as society is complex, so, too, are the members of that society. We, as individuals, have varied physical, psychological, spiritual and intellectual needs. All of us have some needs in all these areas of our lives. There are those whose needs center more on the physical, others on the psychological, spiritual or intellectual aspects of humanity. Holding to the Bible or other religious authority, is most important to a significant sector of American society. Others feel strongly about science and the need-fulfillment it provides. One's need-fulfillment may come from various areas of life. A rabbi may be very tied to his religion because it provides not only a livelihood but also status. In addition, his religion offers comfort, as well as, intellectual satisfaction. The same could be said of scientists, historians, psychologists, physicians, lawyers or laborers. All these factors influence our belief systems. As a result, a belief system is not easily abandoned and strict logic will not easily dissuade the follower of a given religion, profession or political party. All the arguments provided above for or against creationism or evolution lay fallow in the minds of the dedicated believer in the 'other side' of the controversy.

All of us, I would submit, have need of both *mythos* and *logos*. There are many things we accept on the basis of empirical evidence: that our car will start in the morning, a certain antibiotic will cure an infection or the 'perm' we just got, will last the usual six weeks. There are many aspects of our world, however, that do not lend themselves to empirical verification and we must then rely on the myths of our culture to help us understand this mysterious world in which we live. In these myths we can at least find comfort, if not certainty. In religions, social clubs, service groups, political parties, academic societies, activist movements and the like, we find answers to and support for the many questions we face each day. It is easy to believe what our group of friends believes and this is partly why we like to belong to groups. They provide security and a sense of belonging. We are less alone and less 'scared'. All these human needs may be met, in part, by the belief system that binds us together with those with whom we live, work and socialize.

In a real sense, belief systems provide the 'glue' that holds us together, psychologically, spiritually and socially. As a result, we must be very careful when tampering with such sacred social and psychological cement. It is too easy for us to find fault with those of a different ideological 'persuasion', whether religious, professional, social, political or sexual. As 'stupid' as we might see these other views, it is important to realize that those that hold such views may see our views as equally 'stupid'. We need to see the belief systems of others as meeting human needs and to find ways to incorporate this diversity into the fabric of our society. In the long run, I firmly believe, differing views make for a stronger, more productive and robust society. The only caution I would add is that we allow everyone to believe as they wish, so long as these beliefs do not harm others. And please don't try to 'make' me accept your belief system as long as my system is not harming you!

CHAPTER 7

RELIGION: THE UNBELIEVABLE

FREE WILL, GRACE AND PREDESTINATION

Second only to the divinity of Jesus Christ is the controversy surrounding free will, grace and predestination. It is of special interest because both Martin Luther (1483-1546) and John Calvin (1509-1564) made salvation the cornerstone of their theologies. The question of human free will has a long history dating to the ancient Greeks and the concept of divine grace came to the fore with Christianity. There is a tension between free will and grace that developed when the two concepts met head-on in one theological system. This debate has rumbled on ever since. The tension created does not arise out of any intrinsic conflict between free will and grace but rather relates to the nature of God and this is one reason I include this issue in *Problem Gods*. An anthropomorphic God (AG) could provide grace, that is, 'help' that aids humans in acting morally and eventually in attaining Heaven. There are merciful judges, kindly teachers and benevolent parents who are ready to 'help' their inferiors–to give them another chance and to aid them in being good people. These benevolent acts are 'grace filled' gestures. God's grace is similar though more abstract. The Baltimore Catechism says that:

> Grace is a supernatural gift of God bestowed on us, through the merits of Jesus Christ for our salvation. [1]

God's grace appears to work something like parental direction and kindness. It helps us to behave in a better, more functional or moral way. As we will see later, studies have shown that kindly, supportive parents are blessed with better, more moral children. It is probable that God's grace is patterned after this paradigm. When I was a child, it seemed that God's grace was like some kind of light or liquid that washed over me when I went

---

[1]   Baltimore Catechism, No. 2, 1947.

to church, prayed or was absolved of my sins in the confessional. It was a refreshing or relieving experience.

The question comes up, "Why do people act immorally if Christ died for all humans and God provides this grace to everyone?" Wouldn't God make sure we all had enough grace so that we could enter into to Heaven after we die? And what is this grace God provides? Does it have something to do with our environment? We know, for example, that criminal behavior is fostered by parents who demean or abuse their children.[2] If there is a stepparent in the picture, children tend to be more sociopathic i.e. commit more crimes, use more drugs and have more babies out of wedlock. Therefore, is grace related to the situation in which God puts us or is grace some other kind of help that God provides? Is there some supernatural 'influence' that flows from God/Christ that inclines us to behave morally? Maybe it is a refreshing spiritual shower that washes over us that makes us more blessed. Or is this just metaphysical talk that explains very little?

Luther claimed that some people are 'elected' or 'predestined' by God to go to Heaven; everyone else goes to Hell. If so, what is the basis for God's decision to save some and condemn others? Doesn't God give everybody the same allowance of grace?

Part of the problem with free will and grace relates to how the theistic God is defined. As we have seen, an AG cannot fulfill the job description required of a modern day God. IT has to have metaphysical properties such as omniscience and omnipotence and be all-perfect. This means that a Metaphysical God (MG) has to be in control of everything. No one or no thing can out vote the MG. God is all-good and for one of ITs creatures to do evil would mean that God could be trumped by an inferior being with free will. This is OK for an AG but not allowed in a MG. Thus, the AG can provide grace and still permit human free will; a MG, on the other hand, cannot give grace and at the same time permit humans free will. An AG is flexible but not all-powerful; a MG is deterministic and not flexible by ITs very nature and could give grace but cannot allow free will and still be all-powerful. Everything has to go according to the divine plan–God's will is sovereign. Under a MG there can be no free will and, in fact, there would be no need for grace. All behaviors would be predetermined or predestined. An all-perfect God must make an all-perfect world. As covered earlier, most religions define God as having both human and metaphysical qualities–the AG/MG. God, as such, is a hybrid and IT cannot meet religion's need for an all-powerful yet kindly, personal God. Theologians cannot have it both ways.

---

2   Barber, N. 2004, *Kindness in a Cruel World* (Amherst, NY: Prometheus Books) p. 366.

Ignoring this problem for the moment, it is sufficient to say that Luther for various reasons wanted to have a sovereign God who could not be forced into granting grace as a consequence of meritorious human acts. God, he believed, cannot be forced to do anything and thus faith alone was all that was necessary for salvation and good acts were nothing more than evidence that a person was among the elect. Since God is totally free and cannot be forced, finagled or badgered into doing anything, both faith and grace have to be freely given by God. No human acts including prayer and meritorious deeds can 'earn' faith or grace for us, according to Luther and Calvin. It is likely that Luther structured this system of grace to meet his own psychological needs. In doing so, however, he created a logically insoluble theological conundrum. My friend and former high school classmate, Rev. Doctor John G. Lynch tells me that Luther viewed all humans as totally depraved. This is why Luther insisted on irresistible grace and election. This makes perfect sense if all humans are utterly depraved and incapable of a moral life on their own but leaves us with the question of why God saves some and damns others.

FREE WILL

Humans have free will–this seems self-evident. Intuitively we all know that we can make a decision to do this or that, depending on whether the act will benefit us or not. Should I go to work today? It would be nice to stay home but then I may lose my job. It would be great to buy a new outfit. But can I afford it? There are many decisions to be made, some of which are moral in character–lie or tell the truth; cheat on my spouse or remain faithful; withhold earnings from my tax form or not and many more. On a legal level, one might ask can I get away with speeding on the way to work this morning–I'm running late. In the criminal realm–should I use illicit drugs, drink alcohol to excess when I know I tend to argue and fight when I do so. These are not terribly complex decisions yet they all involve many components. There are social, legal, religious, family, economic, psychological, health and other consequences to be considered. Some of these elements may not enter consciously into the decision-making process. Many times it is a simple matter of, "I'd like to do it but can I get away with it?" And many decisions are determined by a host of influences beyond our control or are intuitive and not conscious. Are they all predetermined? In other words, are we not responsible for any of the 'decisions' we make and thus not culpable or blameworthy? Should we not suffer any of the negative consequences for our actions? Conversely, should we not wallow in the rewards earned by our actions, whether immediate and secular or ultimate and religious in nature?

Most people would say 'yes' to punishments and rewards, that is, we are responsible for our actions and deserve the just consequences of our deeds. Our parents would generally agree with this approach. So, too would our boss, the police, a judge, minister, priest or rabbi, unless one is deemed insane, coerced or blamelessly ignorant. Some thinkers have argued that all decisions are totally determined and see humans as devoid of free will, nonetheless, in practice this is not the way society treats our decisions and the behaviors that arise out of them. Most of the time we are considered culpable for any misdeeds and deserving of punishment.

The history of 'free will' dates at least to the ancient Greeks. It is evident from reading the Bible that the Jews and early Christians viewed humans as morally responsible. Free will was not in question for the authors of the Torah. There is sin and punishment throughout the Scriptures–God often exacted severe retribution for seemingly minor offenses such as eating an apple (Genesis 2:16-17).

THE EARLY GREEKS

Pythagoras (6th century B.C.E.) spoke of responsibility for sin and the need for purification in the course of transmigration (reincarnation) of one's soul after death–a concept also seen in Hinduism. The Eleatics[3] proposed an immutable, eternal principle that left no room for freewill. Democritus (c. 460-c. 370) was an atomist who claimed the world was composed of an infinite number of atoms that were uncreated, eternal and in constant motion within a void (or vacuum) bumping into each other at random. As a consequence, all actions are determined and this view precludes free will. All events, human or otherwise, occurred by random physical necessity.

SOCRATES AND PLATO

Socrates (c. 470-399) believed there was a moral aspect to all philosophical problems. However, he was convinced that no one would

---

3   A system of philosophy founded by Zeno of Elea (c. 495-c. 430 B.C.E) and Parmenides (c. 515-?) held that there is one indivisible and unchanging reality. Zeno formulated numerous paradoxes that challenged the ideas of pluralism and the existence of motion and change. His most famous involves a tortoise and hare in which the hare tries to catch up to the tortoise after a late start but never can because there are claimed to be an infinite number of intervals the hare must cross before reaching the tortoise and this would take an infinite amount of time, thus the hare never catches the tortoise.

knowingly do wrong. He equated the good with the true and from this it follows that if one understands the good s/he could not possibly do wrong. So with sufficient knowledge a person necessarily behaves morally. There is free will but knowing the 'truth' one was determined to do the proper thing. The 'truth' necessarily imposed itself on the will and intellect leaving no option but to follow the moral high road. So all properly instructed humans not only do what is morally correct but what is best for society at large. Ignorance is the source of all evil according to Socrates.

Plato (c.427-c.347 B.C.E.), Socrates' pupil, held the same view. Virtue is the determination of the will through knowledge of the good. Plato explicitly posited free will. However, if one knows the good, s/he then freely chooses the moral way.

ARISTOTLE

Aristotle (384-322 B.C.E.), a student of Plato, disagreed with both Socrates and Plato. Aristotle, in contrast to these men was an empiricist, he eschewed Idealism. The real world was not in Plato's perfect Ideas or Forms but rather found here on Earth. He observed his fellow wo/men and saw that they performed both good and bad deeds voluntarily. Decision-making is contingent on the many factors that go into our evaluation of the consequences of one's actions. We try to predict what will happen if we choose one behavior rather than another. A decision is based on the possible outcomes resulting from any given act; such choices are free, sometimes the choice is beneficial, sometimes harmful. An outcome cannot always be correctly predicted. We make mistakes and harm may result but the decision-making is voluntary unless there are overriding factors, that is, our parents, spouse, boss, police or friends say no. All factors involved in an outcome cannot be known and the result may be attributed to 'pure luck'–good or bad. God's prevision was not a problem for Aristotle and the fact that he posited God as the Prime Mover did not seem to interfere with his concept of free will, though this easily could have been a logical pitfall for him because the Prime Mover might be viewed as setting in motion a series of mechanistic, deterministic reactions leaving no room for free will. Aristotle did not address this logical problem so far as I know.

EPICURUS

Epicurus (331-270 B.C.E.) founded a new philosophical school that incorporated atomism with a peaceful, simple and moral life style. His followers lived in a commune outside of Athens since he advocated avoiding political activism. Simple pleasures were promoted and this lifestyle was aimed at reducing anxiety.

When Epicurus speaks of pursuing pleasure he means a peaceful existence, doing all things in moderation, not seeking after wealth or fame and striving for goodness. In contrast to the fierce God of the Jews, Epicurus believed that there was nothing to fear from the gods. He held that the gods were uninterested in human activities. They were not the angry, vengeful and emotional gods of Mt. Olympus. In fact, the Epicureans denied even the existence of gods but if they did exist, humans were of no concern to them. Punishment for humans here on Earth or in the life to come was a non-issue. Epicurus viewed Greek religion as oppressive and anxiety inducing. It provided little comfort and only induced more anxiety.

The Epicureans promoted four principle of living:

> 1. There is nothing to fear in God.
> 2. There is nothing to feel in death.
> 3. Good can be attained.
> 4. Evil can be endured.

These four maxims or 'four part remedies' as they were called, are aimed at lessening anxiety and promoting psychological peace. It is no surprise that the Epicureans ran afoul of Greek authorities and in later centuries Christian theologians. They denied the existence of God, an afterlife and the need for an organized religious hierarchy. As a consequence of their reclusiveness, they gained a reputation as being hedonistic and immoral (a reputation much like the early Christians had). In spite of their atomism, free will and responsibility for one's behaviors remained part of their philosophy, although some writers have claimed they were deterministic and denied free will. This seems not to have been the case.

STOICISM

Zeno of Cyprus (335-263 B.C.E) founded Stoicism, the name coming from the place where Zeno gave his lectures in Athens, the Stoa Poikile (Painted Colonnade). The Stoics have also been accused of determinism, however, they, in fact, advocated a well-developed ethical system. First and foremost, the stoic is to seek 'virtue'. The world is material, orderly and rational. Knowledge comes through sense perception and reason; proper judgments following from the former and a virtuous life is the end product of this process. Moral worth, duty to society and justice for all within the community are the three bases for a virtuous life.

Cleanthes of Assos (c. 331-c. 232 B.C.E.) succeeded Zeno, laying out stoic principles in his *Hymn to Zeus*. He was one of the first to speak of God as being providential–a concept we will hear more of later in this chapter. Chrysippus of Soli (3rd century B.C.E.) tried to prove there was no inconsistency in positing both fate and free will. The tension between these two concepts would play a major role in later Christian theology.

Though Stoicism contained deterministic, material elements, in the end all persons, according to stoic philosophy, are free to rationally choose the virtuous life. It appears that all the atomistic philosophical offshoots maintained some features of free will in spite of the logical conflict evident in a mechanistic world populated by seemingly free humans.

Lucretius[4] (c. 96-c. 52 B.C.E.) was a Roman philosopher, also an atomist, who was an Epicurean in most of his views. He posited a soul made up of very fine atoms. The soul had two parts, the *anima* that was distributed throughout the body and accounted for sensation and *animus*, located in the chest that was the center of consciousness. He believed that organized religion was oppressive and anxiety inducing, the gods had no commerce with humans and one was not to fear them. He was opposed to institutional religion.

Lucius Seneca (c. 4-65 C.E.) and Marcus Aurelius (121-180 C.E.) are the two best-known stoics. Seneca[5] was an advisor to Nero who eventually fell out of favor with the emperor and was forced to commit suicide. Marcus Aurelius was a Roman emperor who wrote the *Meditations*, which are a series of aphorisms such as:

> Dig within. Within is the wellspring of Good; and it is always ready to bubble up, if you just dig.

And also:

> Adapt yourself to the things among which your lot has been cast and love sincerely the fellow creatures with whom destiny has ordained that you shall live.

The first quote indicates a belief in free will. The second is in keeping with the commonly held view of Stoicism as promoting the placid acceptance

---

4   Lucretius is best known for his poem concerning the physical world, *On the Nature of Things.* 1951 (Baltimore, MD: Penguin).

5   Seneca's best-known wok is his *Letters From a Stoic,* 1969 (New York: Penguin).

of what fate deals you in life. This latter 'stoic virtue' influenced Christian aestheticism of later centuries. No matter what cards you are dealt, one can always look forward to a blessed afterlife in Heaven, if you follows the moral rules laid down by God and the Church.

There is some evidence that there were stoic influences in Paul of Tarsus' writings (ICor.11:14).[6] Several of the Church Fathers such as Ambrose of Milan and Origen of Alexandria may have used stoic concepts. In general, Stoicism was widely condemned by the Church, although it eventually incorporated stoic principles into Christian theology along with many other pagan elements. At any rate, free will was certainly a Christian tenet and Stoicism, in spite of its atomistic roots, provided support for the theology of salvation that was important in the Roman as well as the Reformation Churches.

AUGUSTINE OF HIPPO

Augustine of Hippo (354-430), has been a pivotal figure in the theology of salvation (soteriology) impacting both Catholic and Protestant thinkers. In the fifth century the logical conflict between God's grace and human free will was to meet head to head–a battle that has never ended. The two combatants were God's supreme sovereignty versus lowly human free will and intellect. This was a battle of the MG against *Homo sapiens*. God as metaphysical is sovereign over all creatures. God is boss and in control of the entire Universe. If this were not the case than IT would not be omnipotent and omniscient. Unless God is infinite in all respects, Christian theology must fall like a house of cards. On the other hand, if God is not also anthropomorphic IT cannot be providential. Divine love is intrinsically bound to free will, grace and salvation.[7] The promise of Heaven and sadly the prospect of eternal punishment in Hell require an AG. A MG by definition cannot be providential. The need to have such interactions with ITs creations limits the creator, as discussed in chapter 2. Recall that an infinite being has no boundaries and without boundaries there is no interface with which IT can contact, communicate with or impact another being. A supernatural, spiritual being has other problems in dealing with material beings because it has no way of connecting with the material world. Thus, a supremely sovereign MG must have total control over all things,

---

6   "Doth not even nature itself teach you that a man indeed, if he nourish his hair, it is a shame unto him?" The stoics taught that we learn from nature. It was a tenet of the early Church that men should not wear their hair long.

7   St. Augustine, 2010, *On Grace and Free Will* (Cambridge, UK: Cambridge University Press).

however, such an entity has no way of directly controlling ITs creations. An MG that is 'all-everything' automatically determines everything from all eternity. There is no room for chance or choice, the Universe is eternally etched in stone. In essence the MG as all-knowing and all-powerful is aware that all humans will sin and some will go to Hell. As omnipotent IT has the power to prevent this. If IT doesn't make it possible for all humans to go to Heaven, God is either not omnipotent or not all-good. Either way IT cannot be a MG; if not a MG, IT cannot have created and maintained the Universe. As omnipotent and omniscient God has to be able to devise a way that all humans can achieve Heaven but in so doing God limits free will. And on and on the debate goes. This in essence is the "problem of evil" in a nut-shell.

An AG could interact with the Universe, allow free will and choice but would not be the ultimate sovereign–the 'all-everything' being. A MG can only create automatons that are perfectly designed and function unerringly. If not automatons, humans would be equal to God, as equal to God in all respects they are then God ITself.

As noted above, Augustine affirms human free will but also says that we cannot act morally without God's grace. This raises the question, "If we cannot be good without grace then how are we free?" Without grace we can only sin, with it we can be good but not free to sin. On the other hand, if we are so depraved that we can only sin, how are we free to choose either good or evil? Thus, what good we do is entirely dependent on God's will, not our human free will. Either way we are not free, once again, round and round the theological carousel goes.

ORIGINAL SIN

Augustine is arguably the most influential theologian of all Christendom. He fully explained the theology of Original Sin, although the term dates to the second century C.E., introduced then by Irenaeus, Bishop of Lyon, as a tool in combating Gnosticism.[8] The concept is not explicitly mentioned in either the OT or NT though several passages are thought by some to support the idea of Original Sin.[9] Original Sin came, we are told, as a result of Adam and Eve's misconduct in the Garden of Eden. Augustine taught that the blessed state of Adam and Eve was lost not only for them but all their progeny thereafter. This sin was passed on to subsequent generations through the 'sin' of sexual intercourse and specifically transmitted via the

8   Irenaeus, 1992, *St. Irenaeus of Lyons: Against the Heresies* (Malwah, NJ: Paulist Press).
9   Paul of Tarsus in Romans 5:12-21 and 1 Corinthians 15:22, identifies Adam as the one man through whom death came into the world.

father's seed. The Roman Church does not accept this aspect of Augustine's theology maintaining simply that Original Sin is 'inherited' from Adam (although according to Genesis, Eve was the first sinner).[10] We all enter this world tainted by sin that is removed only through baptism. According to Augustine and early Christian theologians, we are born sinful beings. Original Sin predisposes humans to personal (actual) sins committed later in life. How vulnerable humans are to sinning depends on the theology one embraces. Augustine held that humans all have a depraved nature, lack the ability to do good deeds and can only respond to the will of God through divine grace. Grace in turn is irresistible, provides conversion to a holy way of life and allows the sinner to persevere in holiness. There are elements in Augustine's writings that suggest he believed in predestination, election of the saints and the impossibility of free will. However, he appears to have held that humans do have free will and are not predestined in the sense taught by Luther and Calvin. The Catholic Church denies that Augustine accepted election.

PELAGIANISM AND SEMI-PELAGIANISM

The conflict over free will and grace came to a head as a result of Augustine's dispute with Pelagius, a fourth century English monk. He was well educated, fluent in Latin and Greek along with a solid background in theology. Pelagius denied the doctrine of Original Sin and affirmed the ability of humans to be righteous by exercising their free will. A statement of Pelagius' views on free will and grace summarized by Celsius (c. 400) is as follows:

1. Adam would have died even if he had not sinned.
2. Adam's sin affected only himself, not all humanity.
3. All children are born in the same state as Adam before the Fall.
4. Humans neither die through Adam's sin nor are they saved through Christ's death.
5. The Mosaic Law can guide humans to Heaven just as well as the Gospels.
6. Even before Christ, there were sinless humans.

These statements imply that humans have free will and that they can will to do good deeds and these deeds gain for us the eternal rewards of Heaven. Thus, men and woman can 'earn' grace and Heaven. God is therefore

---

10   This belief probably relates to the fact that the female ovum was unknown until the last century. The woman was thought to be a passive partner in conception until recently.

required to dispense grace as a result of good works. In other words, this puts an irresistible demand on God and IT is no longer in complete control of all created things–no longer supremely sovereign–a heretical concept according to Augustine and later theologians. In spite of the contradictions inherent in a hybrid God (AG/MG) this mix was necessary in order to meet all the demands placed on God by virtually all religions, ancient and modern.

Semi-Pelagianism also required a hybrid God. It attempted to bridge the gap between a totally sovereign deity that undermined free will and one that was entirely anthropomorphic and consequently in some way limited. According to Semi-Pelagianists, such as John Cassia, Vincent of Lèrins and Faustus, Bishop of Ryes, there was Original Sin that made humans corrupt, grace that was necessary to overcome sinfulness and baptism that removed Original Sin. They did not, however, hold that the initiation of good deeds was beyond human free will. Wo/men by their unaided will could behave morally but would not be sanctified and go to Heaven without divine grace. So humans could take 'baby steps' toward goodness but to go all the way required the free gift of God's grace. Humans then could do some things toward goodness and in so doing would stimulate God to provide further salvific grace. The strong point in favor of Semi-Pelagianism is not only God's love that pours out grace to those who show some degree of holiness but also ITs justice that functions fairly in the face of moral acts by humans while retaining human free will. Of course, this leaves the problem of sovereignty. Even a little free will impinges on divine omnipotence. God is not totally in control. The Catholic Church opposes Semi-Pelagianism, although if one looks closely at the Church's views on free will, prayer, indulgences and grace, it is hard to tell how the two theological views differ.

Augustine wrote several works denouncing Pelagianism. In *Predestination of the Saints* he states, "No one can on his own either begin or complete any good work."[11] Because of human depravity consequent to Adam's sin, humans are unable to be good without God's grace that flows from Christ as a result of his suffering and death on the cross. In Chapter 5 of *Predestination*, Augustine makes some statements that suggest he believes humans can merit God's grace. But in the following chapter admits that this opinion was in error and that God's grace is 'gratuitous', that is, a totally free gift that cannot be merited through good deeds. He states in Chapter 7 that, "I was in a similar error, thinking that faith whereby we believe in God is not God's gift but that it is in us from ourselves." Now this would seem to make Augustine a predestinationist–a claim denied by the Roman Church. He does say that the 'elect' are assumed into Christ and are predestined to this

---

11   Augustine, *Predestination of the Saints*, Chapter 2. New Advent, http://www. newadvent.org/fathers/15121.htm.

salutary act of God i.e. Christ's death on the cross. He compares the election of humans to the predestined state to that of Christ as the Son of God (though this connection seems to me untenable). In later Church decrees, Augustine's views are revised. I already noted that the Church did not hold that Original Sin was passed on via the father's seed. Original Sin was part of human nature as altered at the time of the Fall.[12] It is thus not the father's sin that is passed on to the offspring only the father's 'new nature'. This seems to save the child from bearing the blame for the sin of another–or does it? If the child dies before it is baptized can s/he gain Heaven? They used to go to Limbo but the doctrine of Limbo is no longer held by the Catholic Church. Mary, the mother of Christ was, according to the Church, freed of Original Sin at the moment of her conception (doctrine of the Immaculate Conception)[13] and thus sinless from conception to her assumption into Heaven. Was her nature different from other humans i.e. did she have different DNA? And are the natures of baptized babies different from their unbaptized counterparts? Are there phenotypical[14] differences evident in baptized persons? Changes in nature would imply some alteration of the person's DNA, which in turn should be apparent in one way or another– either behaviorally or genomically. The genome of unbaptized persons has not been compared to baptized genomes. However, we have already seen that there is a difference in the behavior of felons, who are very often baptized (many are evangelicals) as compared to atheists who are more often not baptized. If baptism improves one's nature the reverse ought to be true.

The Eastern Orthodox and Eastern Catholic Churches have not apparently accepted ancestral guilt. They emphasize the metaphysical dimension of the Fall. Humans are born into a fallen world but, nonetheless, remain free. This belief is more in line with that of the Semi-Pelagianists. Humans are not so depraved as Augustine thought and certainly not so corrupt as Luther and Calvin maintained.

---

12   If depravity is inherited through Original Sin this would, in today's terms, require a change in DNA that is passed on from father to son via the Y chromosome, so that only sons would be depraved. For daughters it would require inheritance through the mitochondrial DNA and then only daughters would be depraved. If the inheritance is through a somatic chromosome the 'depravity gene' would be lost along the way and not all of Adam's progeny would be depraved. The inheritance of Original Sin creates a host of biological problems, none of which has, up to this point, been addressed by theologians.

13   This was proclaimed an infallible doctrine in 1854.

14   Phenotype is the characteristic manifestation of a genotype, that is, a person can possess a gene for blonde hair (genotypically blonde) but have black hair (phenotypically black haired) because the black hair gene is dominant over the blonde hair gene. Genotype indicates the genes one has in their DNA, whereas the phenotype is the way the person actually looks.

THOMISTIC AND MOLINISTIC THOUGHT

If you hate being befuddled, skip this section. If you love metaphysical verbiage, read on! God's foreknowledge of things to come is a major element in the free will/grace debate. Because a MG is omniscient and knows all, IT knows everything past, present and future. If God is aware of what a person is going to do, given any set of circumstances, why is s/he not considered predestined or determined to act in the way God knows s/he will act? As theologians put it, God possesses an infallible knowledge of man's[15] future actions. This raises two issues. First, how can God have this prevision if human actions are free and not determined? Put another way, a person can choose among a number of actions when faced with several choices and the ultimate decision is not determined by a series of previous events in the person's life but based on free will and chance, not related to any specific circumstance, past or present. It would seem impossible for God to predict human behaviors. Actions are not mechanical responses. They involve many factors, conscious and unconscious. Most decisions are made with incomplete facts. Probability theory can tell us what a group of people may do in a given situation but not what the individual will do. Decision-making is a very 'iffy' business. Even if God could know how someone will act in a certain situation and IT allows him or her to act immorally, does this impugn God when IT could have given the person additional free grace to 'make' him or her do the right thing?

Thomas Aquinas explains this by noting that God does not exist in time; the past, present and future are as one happening for God. It is as if IT were viewing all human actions from high on a mountain seeing all events as if they are occurring simultaneously and not sequentially. As with all analogies, this one 'limps' especially for us who are time-bound and have experienced nothing but time our entire life. We cannot conceive of such non-temporal happenings. Since God is timeless, IT doesn't make a decision at a certain point in time. All that God wills is willed eternally. God cannot change ITs mind!

The second question raised by God's infallible prevision is, "If God knows all events beforehand even those that arise out of human free will, is the will truly free? If nothing happens outside of God's sovereign control how is it that all human acts are not predetermined by God?

---

15   Theologians have tended to be somewhat chauvinistic using man to mean humankind.

Thomas Aquinas in the thirteenth century attempted to solve this problem and later Luis de Molina (1535-1690) developed an alternate solution. Thomas, according to the Catholic Encyclopedia maintains that:

> God premoves each man in all his acts to the line of conduct, which he subsequently adopts. It holds that this premotive decree inclines man's will with absolute certitude to the side decreed but that God adapts this premotion to the nature of the being thus premoved. It (Aquinas' scheme) argues that as God possesses infinite power He can infallibly premove man…to choose a particular course freely.

It is further stated that:

> The premotive decree is thus prior in order of thought to the Divine cognition of man's future actions.

What exactly a 'premotive' is and how it impacts free will is unstated. Presumably a premotive is some divine motivation instilled in the human intellect and/or will that 'nudges' the person to select a particular course of action. Is this premotive irresistible as is divine grace or is it a 'take it or leave it' suggestion made by God? If the former, free will would be suspended, if the latter, then God is neither omnipotent nor omniscient. And since God is outside of time, what exactly does it mean when it is claimed by Thomas that the premotive decree is 'prior in order of thought to divine cognition'? This is all very abstruse, obtuse and bewildering!

The Molinist or Jesuit School of thought, takes a somewhat different stance in solving the free will/grace conundrum. Thomas' approach, the Jesuits agree allows for God's infallibility and providence[16] but fails to preserve free will. Francisco Suárez, who modified the Molinist view, proposed that God's motivation is *concurrent* (my italics) with the individual's act of free will. So there is no premotive; everything happens at the same time. Of course, for God everything happens outside of time–whatever that means for us time-bound humans. Also, whether God's moral 'nudge' is prior to or concurrent with divine thought seems moot for, either way, God is manipulating free will. The Catholic Church further states:

---

16   Infallibility and providence: these two terms together, as we have seen, are contradictory and incompatible. Infallibility is found in a MG; providence is a characteristic of an AG. The two are logically impossible.

God's knowledge of what a free being would choose, if the necessary conditions were supplied, must be deemed logically prior to any decree of concurrence or premotion in respect to that act of choice.

It is easy enough to claim 'logical priority' but does this materially impact the effect of God's will on human free will? Whether a decree is logically or temporally prior, in God's timeless nature is moot since ITs logic as well as actions occur outside of time. In fact, the very word 'action' implies a temporal aspect. Action is defined as: "The state or process of acting or doing". An action is a process. How can the noun 'action' be applied to God? Can any human attribute or action be truly used to describe a feature of a timeless MG?

If you've made it this far without your eyes glazing over or falling asleep, congratulations! If not, don't worry, you are in good company. Much of this theological befuddlement is intended only to emphasize the unbelievability of the free will/grace controversy. The arguments about free will and grace go on forever but take heart, we have only Luther and Calvin left.

LUTHER, CALVIN AND FREE WILL/GRACE

It has been suggested that Luther's extreme scrupulosity, arose out of his father's harsh attitude toward Martin as a child and young adult and this influenced his theology of salvation and sin. Luther was an Augustinian monk, (a vocation his father did not approve) and as such was well aware of Augustine's ideas on Original Sin and human depravity. As Luther interpreted Augustine's writings, he found ample support for the concepts of predestination (election), the irresistibility of God's grace and salvation by faith alone. Luther and Calvin both believed that humans were so corrupted by Adam's sin that none of Adam's progeny was free to resist the lure of sin. It was only through God's free gift of grace that anyone could be saved from Hell. Further, no one could earn divine grace, good works were of no avail. This idea stemmed from the concept of God's supreme sovereignty over all things. God as omnipotent, omniscient etc. was in total control. ITs 'will' alone controlled the world. In this regard Luther's God was a MG and his soteriology flowed logically from this definition of God. There were still theological problems, however. Luther and Calvin believed in prayer and providence, neither of which is consistent with a MG. These elements fit only with an AG. Their God was thus a hybrid–an AG/MG. This 'mixed' God meets a number of human needs as noted above–psychological, social even physiological. We have a natural need for solace, security and comfort. A providential AG meets these needs. There is a social need not only to interact with other people of like-mind but also to have a 'personal relationship' with God especially with Christ the human God. Many Christians voice this longing for a close union with the divine. Freud would lay this on a desire for a father figure–possibly the kindly, caring father he never had–as was the case with Luther. There is no doubt that most of us have such psychological requirements. Haught cites this desire as proof for the existence of God.[17] The mystics hold this view as well. This does not prove that there is such a divine fatherly figure somewhere in the Universe only that there is such an urge–possibly based on a Darwinian drive for survival. Real or not, this feeling of or need for a loving, fatherly God is 'real' to many people.

Possibly the most debated of Luther and Calvin's theology is that of 'election' or predestination. God assigns wo/men to eternal bliss in Heaven or to Hell fire forever from before birth. S/he has no say in this election. There is no human free will involved in this divine decision according to Luther and Calvin. Either you are elected or condemned. One cannot merit Heaven. Good works are for naught except that they may indicate that an individual is among the elect. The elect may sin and still achieve heavenly blessedness. Calvin put this even more strongly, claiming that good deeds occur by necessity flowing from God's grace alone and this grace cannot be resisted or rejected. The idea of cooperating with grace is impossible. There can be no 'nudges' toward God's grace as the Thomists claim, there is no free will to be nudged.

The question here, of course, is how can God justify assigning one person to Heaven and another to Hell? The answer usually given is that we, as mere mortals, cannot fathom[18] the 'mind' of God. ITs will is a mystery. This is a solution to God's seeming capriciousness that fails to account for ITs boundless reason and resourcefulness. We are rational beings, God is similarly rational though infinitely so. In ITs infinite reason and unbounded power God surely could find a way to give us humans an acceptable answer to this truly perplexing question. It only makes sense that a loving God would not play mind-games with us, ITs beloved children. Why would God make life more difficult to understand than it already is? This seems so unGod-like and so like us imperfect humans.

The Council of Trent (1545-1563) was a counter-Reformation council and it specifically condemned Luther's soteriology. The Council stated that the free will of man, moved and excited by grace, can cooperate with God's will but human will can also resist God's grace if it so chooses.

---

17   Op. cit. 2008f, Haught, J. F.
18   A fathom is only six feet. Maybe to probe God's 'infinite reason' would be a better phrase.

Though the human intellect and will are weakened by Original Sin, the Council maintains this does not preclude free will. We can still be partners with God. As noted earlier, this seems to limit God's omnipotence, though Catholic theologians would deny this. This view also sounds more like Semi-Pelagianism than Catholic theologians would like to admit.

COMMENTS ON THE UNBELIEVABLE

There is much more that can be said about salvation theology. It is not my intent or within my ability to fully cover this topic that has defied solution for 2000 years or more. Rather, this brief overview is presented only to give the reader some idea of the complexity of the topic and the insoluble nature of the debate surrounding soteriology.

There are many 'unbelievables' in theology. The three topics I have chosen, the supernatural, creationism and free will/grace just happen to be three of my favorite 'unbelievables'. They also relate to the theme of this book and help in defining the Neo-Natural God. The Trinity, divinity of Christ, virginity of Mary, resurrection of Christ, assumption of Mary, infallibility of the pope and the Immaculate Conception are just a few of the many theological tenets that defy reason. They may have a role to play especially for children but as a person becomes more sophisticated in his or her thinking, these more emotionally driven doctrines may not be necessary for many, as Ranke-Heinemann suggests in *Putting Away Childish Things*.[19]

Immanuel Kant (1724-1804) makes the point that there is no proper discipline called metaphysics[20]–that all of metaphysics is pure speculation not to be verified by any means available to humans. It is like building castles in the sky. Metaphysical concepts are fun to play with but they possess no reality of their own. They provide mental calisthenics, keeping the mind nimble but produce no tangible results. That there is truth in Kant's view is supported by the many venerated metaphysical notions that are obviously false. Aristotle's concept of substance is one such metaphysical entity. Substance, according to Aristotle is an object's nature or essence. It is what makes a thing what it is. A human being has a human essence or substance (a soul) as a result of which that person has all the characteristics, physical and mental, that define him or her as human. Exactly what this substance is, is never fully explained. It is a metaphysical notion and nothing more. In sum, it tells us nothing

---

19   Ranke-Heinemann, Utah, 2011, *Putting Away Childish Things; The Virgin Birth, the Empty Tomb, and other Fairy Tails You Don't Need to Believe to Have a Living Faith* trans. P. Heinegg (San Francisco: Harper).

20   Nonetheless Kant uses this term in analyzing morality: *Fundamental Principles of the Metaphysic of Morals* [Kindle Edition], 2004, Public Domain Books.

or, at least nothing we can get our reason around. Over time and based on the authority of Aristotle, who at one time was unquestioned, we came to accept the idea of substance as something truly meaningful when, in fact, it explains nothing. It feels good; we think it has meaning but it is all a façade. We now know that what makes us what we are is DNA and a multitude of environmental forces. We adapt to our circumstances and DNA provides the infrastructure for this adaptive process.

Like metaphysics, theology is all speculation and it is in large part metaphysical in nature. Besides reason the other source for theology is the Bible. We know that the Bible is flawed. It cannot have been inspired by a perfect, omniscient God, for the Bible is imperfect. If God inspired the Bible as the one and only source of truth (*sola scriptura*), as some believe, why would this omnipotent, omniscient being provide spurious information to live by? Why would IT create a guide that can be interpreted in manifold ways so that any person can find support for a host of, often contradictory, doctrines?

All sides of the free will/grace debate have a host of biblical passages that writers believe make their view absolutely correct–so much so that they are willing to wage war over one or another tenet. How can so many religions be infallibly right? How can so many religious groups be the 'chosen people'? To understand this mindset is to understand the puzzling psychology of the human mind.

In the end, what does all this theological speculation amount to? Does it give us any useful answers or does it simply represent the end product of someone's emotional need fulfillment, as may have been the case with Augustine and Luther? Most theologians admit we can know nothing about God yet we persist in analyzing God. As I think of it now, maybe I'm doing the same thing, only you the reader can decide.

In the end are we better persons for having sought the nature of God rather than the good of our fellow human beings? Is what we do to help family, friends, patients, clients, customers, parishioners and even strangers really where ethical and practical good can be found? Yes, indeed, use your brain and exercise it continuously but don't take all that comes from intellectual activities as 'gospel.' Again, the only theology Christ offered was to love God and one's neighbor. Might we not put neighbor first and God second? God does not need our love or glory or adoration or anything at all. God is God. God is sufficient unto ITself.

PART III

THE MYSTICAL PHYSICAL WORLD

CHAPTER 8

ASTRONOMY AS THEOLOGY

Science, especially in the twentieth century, has turned our conception of reality upside down. What was once certain and determined is now uncertain and merely probable. René Descartes (1596-1650), Isaac Newton (1642-1727) and Pierre Laplace (1749-1827) painted a picture of the physical world as absolutely deterministic, like bouncing billiard balls. A butterfly flapping its wings in China would have an effect on rushes rustling in Minnesota. This had not always been the case. For eons, the world was thought to be utterly unpredictable, it had been filled with vicissitudes. Aristotle spoke of chance and luck as part of life and ethics. The goddess Fate or Lady Fortune had plied her tricks of chance with impunity. Life was but a series of happenstances, not to be comprehended by humans.

Boethius (c. 480-c. 524), in *The Consolation of Philosophy*,[1] bemoans the hardships Fate has foisted upon him. He had been rich, blessed with a loving wife and two successful sons. He was a Roman senator and man of influence with the Emperor, Theodoric. But Fate took all this from him and in order to make sense of such evil, he developed a dialogue, while in prison, with Lady Philosophy. From time immemorial, disorder and persistent evil has plagued all humans and religion offered a means to make sense out of this turmoil. Astrologers, oracles, magicians, soothsayers, shamans and priests have all been enlisted in this task. Religion has certainly helped make some sense out of this pervasive confusion. Only God knew what was to happen–life was basically chaotic.

Beginning with the Renaissance and men like Copernicus, Galileo, Newton and Laplace, science began telling us that the philosophers had it

---

1   Boethius, 1962, *The Consolation of Philosophy*, trans. R. H. Green (Indianapolis, IN, Bobbs-Merrill).

wrong. Scientists were saying that everything had been etched in stone from the beginning. If we could only figure out all the forces at play in the present, we could look into the past with certainty and likewise accurately predict the future. This posed major problems for both philosophers and theologians. Were all humans simply automatons, responding to the inescapable laws and forces that define the Universe? And what about ethics, moral rules, rewards, punishment, Heaven, Hell, grace and, most of all, free will? Were Luther and Calvin right? Are we all predestined, allocated by the 'whims' of God to Heaven or Hell?

In spite of these inconvenient 'truths', such as Newton's universal law of gravity,[2] science began to fill some cosmological and theological gaps. It appeared that science might have strengthened the cosmological arguments for the existence of God. The Universe was beginning to seem more marvelous than anyone had previously imagined. With the telescope, microscope, the calculus, new elements, chemical reactions and the newly discovered physical laws of Newton, Hooke and Boyle, the world seemed more complex, more awe inspiring and more magnificent. As the world became more wondrous, so did God. God's greatness, if it can be discovered at all must be found in the cosmos, it is to this quest that we turn next.

ASTRONOMY AS THEOLOGY IN ANTIQUITY

Cosmology/cosmogony and theology have been linked since prehistory. There is evidence that stone circles, such as Stonehenge, were both celestial and sacred.[3] As prehistoric humans raised their eyes to the heavens, they seemed to find their origins and their originators in the skies. The ancient Egyptians saw Ra their principal deity, in the Sun.[4] Osiris was identified with our brightest star, Sirius, and the constellation, Orion, was the home of the gods.[5] Hesiod, in the *Theogeny* tells of the Hellenic gods, many of whom were associated with the heavens.[6] Uranus, the sky god joined with Gaea, the goddess of the Earth, to bring order out of chaos. The Greek word, *Kosmos* means harmony[7], order or beauty, from which comes, among

---

2   This is arguably Newton's most significant discovery, $F = GMm/r^2$, that is, the force, F, between two bodies, M and m, is equal to the gravitational constant, G, times the mass of M and m and inversely proportional to the distance between the two bodies, r, squared. A relatively simple formula but one that revolutionized science and was the major celestial law until 1905 when Einstein published his Special Theory of Relativity.

3   Castleden, R. 1987, *The Stonehenge People* (New York: Routledge & Kegan Paul).

4   Spence, L. 1990, *Ancient Egyptian Myths and Legends* (New York: Dover).

5   Bauval, R., & Gilbert, A. 1994, *The Orion Mystery* (New York: Three Rivers Press).

6   Hesiod, 1953, *Theogeny* (New York: MacMillan).

7   Plato 1977, *Timaeus and Critias* (London: Penguin Books).

other words, cosmetics. The Greeks saw harmony as the essential feature of the Universe. Medicine was based on this concept of harmony.[8] As noted above, Plato believed that the stars and planets were divine. The Christian Neo-Platonists in later centuries extended the power of Plato's creative god, or Demiurge, to intermediate spirits or angels that resided in the heavens as well. For Aristotle, God was in the heavens and though much of his theology was based on observation of the natural world, he was very much influenced by what he saw in the skies. The celestial bodies were, in fact, unchanging, composed of ether and differed from earthy things that were derived from the four elements of fire, air, water and earth. These elements were mutable and destructible, in contrast to the heavenly bodies composed of ether (the quintessence). The stars were 'fixed' that is, did not appear to move with respect to the other stars. Their motions were circular, which Aristotle viewed as the 'perfect' type of motion, since it had neither beginning nor end. The stars circled the heavens annually but their positions with respect to the other stars never appeared to vary. This 'perfect' circular motion differed from the 'rectilinear' motion of earthly objects. Such motion was imperfect because it had a beginning and an end, just as all things on earth have. Such motion was mutable and terminal, that is, corruptible as were all base things. So, the heavens were divine and earthly things corruptible and inferior. Aristotle's natural theology was to have a major influence on future theologians, such as Thomas Aquinas.

The Romans adopted this Greek cosmology. The god's names were adapted to suit their native mythology, which was carried over from pre-Roman cultures, so that Zeus was now Jupiter, Hermes became Mercury and so on, but the gods of Hesiod and Homer were simply Greek gods now dressed in Roman togas. The planets were all assigned divine names and assumed the same characteristics as the divine stars and were also composed of ether and were considered immutable and eternal.

One question about the stars went unanswered until Ptolemy developed his celestial system in the second century C.E. Divine beings such as the stars and planets moved in perfectly circular orbits according to Aristotle but why then did some planets have such irregular paths? Their name, in fact, means 'wanderer'.

Ptolemy solved this theological dilemma with his system of deferens (circular orbits of the planets) and epicycles (circular orbits superimposed on the deferens). It was evident from astronomical observations that the planets not only moved faster at times and slower at other times (such change was not allowed by Aristotelian cosmology) but also some planets,

---

8   Garber, J. J. 2008, *Harmony in Healing: The Theoretical Basis of Ancient and Medieval Medicine* (New Brunswick, NJ: Transaction Publishers).

such as Mars, exhibited retrograde motion, that is, it periodically moved backwards (east to west instead of the usual west to east) during their travels through the sky. The epicycles were perfectly circular, while at the same time, they explained retrograde motion and, therefore, maintained the required geometric perfection of Aristotle's divine planets. Only one problem remained unsolved in Ptolemy's system. The Earth traditionally was held to be at the center of the Universe. This was of critical theological importance in the Middle Ages. However, some planets appeared larger i.e. closer to Earth at times. To explain this, Ptolemy created an 'equant' at the center of his planetary orbits.

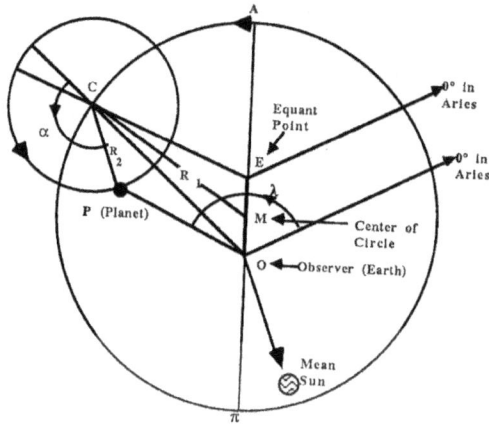

Figure 8.1. Ptolemy's system. The deferens (large circle) represents the orbit of a planet, including that of the Sun and Moon. The smaller circle is the epicycle in which the planet moves and the equant is the center of the deferens. The Earth is slightly off-center in order to explain the varying size of the other planets over the course of the year. Strictly speaking then the Earth isn't at the center of the Universe. A problem Ptolemy ignored.[9]

The equant was the geometric center of the deferens (large orbit) but several degrees away from the Earth itself. This off-set 'center' of the planet's orbit helped explain the variable size and speed of the planets during their annual circuit around the Earth. Unfortunately, this meant that strictly speaking the Earth was not at the exact center of the Universe. This was apparently a small point for the theologians of the time–small enough to be ignored. Only one other detail remained–Ptolemy's system did not quite account for real world observations. The heavens did not exactly follow his geometric scheme.

---

9   Crowe, M. J. 1990, *Theories of the World from Antiquity to the Copernican Revolution* (New York: Dover).

ASTRONOMY AS THEOLOGY IN THE MIDDLE AGES

With the evolution of medieval Christianity, came conflicts between ancient philosophy and theology as formulated by Church Fathers. The cosmogony of Genesis gives a very specific account of creation. This conformed to the celestial geometry of Aristotle[10] but was at variance with the biblical view that the world was to end in the course of time. As we have seen, however, Aristotle believed in an uncreated, eternal world. Moreover, in the case of the Neo-Platonists, such as Augustine of Hippo, it was acceptable to portray stars as playing a role in the divine plan as angels but they were not themselves divine, as Plato would have them. They acted only as intermediaries, doing the handiwork of God. A MG requires intermediaries to make contact with the material world and carry out divinely assigned tasks.

Angels as stars made it difficult, at times to separate theology and astrology and a tension between Church and society over this issue persisted for centuries. If the angels were stars and they influenced happenings on Earth, then pagan and, thus, heretical astrology was an embarrassment to Christian theologian. The 'sub-divine' angelic stars could provide some help for the medieval theologians by allowing their transcendent God to remain aloof by delegating all of the hands-on work to the angels, just as Plato's demiurge and the Gnostic's Sophia had done. But then what was God's relationship to the angels? And just how was God to be a providential God as the Church Fathers portrayed IT? How could IT look down on us with love akin to that of a benevolent father? All these were very perplexing questions for the medieval mind. So astronomy both helped and hindered theology in the Middle Ages.

These are only a few of the theological questions that troubled medieval theologians. Making the cosmogony of Genesis fit with that of the Ancients was no easy task. We will look at two medieval theologians of note who dealt at some length with the doctrinal debates generated by the astronomy-theology connection.

The first of these is Robert Grosseteste (1168-1253) who was a scholar and lecturer at the newly founded Oxford University.[11] He may have been the first chancellor of Oxford, though this is uncertain. He was later

---

10   Eudoxus was a pupil of Plato and was the first to construct a world composed of twenty-seven concentric spheres to explain the motion of the stars and planets including the Sun and Moon. Aristotle increased the number of spheres to fifty-five in order to better explain celestial motions.

11   McEvoy, J. 2000, *Robert Grosseteste* (New York: Oxford University Press).

appointed Bishop of Lincoln. Grosseteste was a polymath, writing on many topics including astronomy and theology. Arguably, his best know work is *De Luce*, a short treatise on the nature of light. His thoughts on this subject are of interest because they deal with a kind of rudimentary physics, as well as, the cosmogony of Genesis. He also wrote an exegesis on Genesis. In Genesis, light is mentioned twice (Genesis 1:3-5 and 1:14-16) and these passages have been the source of much controversy ever since.

> 1:3 Then God said, "Let there be light"; and there was light.
> 1:4 And God saw that the light was good; and God separated the light from the darkness.
> 1:5 God called the light Day, and the darkness he called Night. And there was evening and there was morning,[this happened on] the first day.

It appears that the OT writer was speaking of the Sun's light since this light was bright enough to make day distinctly separate from night. However in Genesis 1:14-16 it reads:

> 1:14 And God said, "Let there be lights in the dome of the sky to separate the day from the night; and let them be for signs and for seasons and for days and years,
> 1:15 and let them be lights in the dome of the sky to give light upon the earth. And it was so.
> 1:16 God made the two great lights—the greater light to rule the day and the lesser light to rule the night–and also the stars.

This second light seems to apply to the Sun, Moon and stars but the medieval readers of the Bible saw in these passages two distinct forms of light. Possibly, they were influenced by the Ancients' view that the Sun, Moon and stars were situated in separate crystalline spheres. At any rate, it stirred a lively debate. Grosseteste's solution to this problem involved positing two kinds of light–*Lux* and *Lumen*. *Lux* was a species of 'invisible' light akin to God ITself. God was the source of all light both physical and intellectual. IT is the 'light of light'. God's light was the source of the light in the stars and all illuminated heavenly bodies. God was also the light that provides all intelligent beings with self-awareness and knowledge of all kinds. Grosseteste took this type of light, *Lux*, one step further. He made it the source of all matter. The 'prime matter' of Aristotle was infused with *Lux* and from this came the Aristotelian 'substance' which accounted for all earthly things. Prime matter was combined with Aristotelian 'form' (not to be confused with

Plato's Forms) to produce substance. This 'form' was for Grosseteste *Lux*. *Lux* was the 'principle of corporeity' in Grosseteste' system—*Lux* produces all material things. On the other hand, *Lumen* (again light but using a Latin synonym for light) is visible light. This is the light with which we see objects along with their associated colors and heat. There is for Grosseteste a kind of kinship between *Lux* and *Lumen*. The one, *Lux*, generates *Lumen*. *Lux* was a basic principle of creation. It made more sense to Grosseteste than the five elements: ether, fire, air, water and earth. The latter four were in fact, derived from *Lux* rather than 'prime matter' and 'form' as Aristotle had suggested. This system seemed more tangible to Grosseteste. Light was everywhere; it was self-propagating and radiated everywhere instantaneously.[12] In a sense, this view gave the light of the stars (angels) a greater role in the makeup of the Universe. Light was in Grosseteste's system both a metaphysical and a physical concept. This approach combined these two domains in a way not previously imagined and all based on Genesis. This was one way of avoiding the dualism of traditional theology; it bridged the natural and supernatural. The concept of Neo-Naturalism that is to be covered later, is based on a similar approach but seeks its basis in quantum and relativity theory.

THOMAS AQUINAS

We return now to the most influential theologian of the Middle Ages, Thomas Aquinas (1225-1274).[13] He wrote the best-known medieval treatise on natural theology as presented in his five proofs for the existence of God. These proofs are in large part based on Aristotle's *Metaphysics* and *Physics*, though in expanded form. He is known for 'Christianizing' Aristotle's philosophy. Thomas believed that God was revealed in the Scriptures and was to be accepted as a matter of faith but he also maintained that ITs existence could be arrived at through reason based on nature and natural law.

Anselm of Canterbury (1033-1109) had earlier presented his 'ontological' proof for the existence of God. Anselm's proof was based entirely on reason. Anselm was a Platonist and, as such, believed in innate or *a priori* knowledge as defined in Plato's dialogue, *Meno*.[14] His proof of God's existence thus requires no foundation in nature. According to Anselm, the knowledge of God is present in the mind of all humans. This awareness of God is deemed *a priori*, since no prior experience of God or ITs works as expressed in nature are necessary to prove God's existence. Knowledge

---

12   It was not yet known that light moved at a finite velocity, i.e. 3×10^8 meters per second.

13   Copleston, F. 1962, *A History of Philosophy* (Garden City, NY: Image-Doubleday).

14   Plato, 1981, *Plato: Five Dialogues* (Indianapolis, IN: Hackett).

of God is in the human mind and imagination at birth. For Anselm, God "was that being of which no greater [being] could be thought". God is the supremely perfect being. No greater being is conceivable and God's essence is his existence. If one is able to conceive of the essence of God then God must exist since ITs essence and existence are one. Anselm asserts that an all-perfect being had to exist because otherwise IT would not be all-perfect. The greatest imaginable being would not be the greatest unless it existed. A non-existent 'all-perfect' being would be less perfect than an existent 'all-perfect' being. Thus, to be 'all perfect' implies existence. Since God's essence is to exist and since an *a priori* awareness of this essence is present in all intelligent beings then Anselm's proof is valid. His argument has always eluded me but the key, I think, is to remember that Anselm based his proof on the assumption that the awareness of God is innate and *a priori*. If one accepts this assumption, then his proof is valid. Kant attacked Anselm's proof by denying that existence is a predicate that can be applied to God. We discussed this question earlier as to whether one can speak of God 'being' in the same way we do for God's creations.

Thomas Aquinas denied Anselm's basic premise. For the 'Dumb Ox' as Aquinas was once called by his superior, the knowledge of God was *a posteriori*, that is, based on acquired, empirical knowledge found in the world around us. This is the so-called cosmological argument for God's existence–an approach also assailed by Kant. God was evident both in the heavens and on Earth, according to Thomas. In contrast to Anselm, Aquinas was an Aristotelian. He looked for God in the things of nature not in the 'Ideas' of Plato. As a consequence, Aquinas based his famous five proofs for the existence of God on nature. This approach is now labeled Natural Theology.

The proofs are principally derived from Aristotle's four causes: formal, material, efficient and final and are based on Aristotelian concepts, especially that of the 'unmoved mover' and denial of an infinite regress, as mentioned above. Though Aquinas was not an astronomer, he did look to the heavens for at least some of the evidence for God's existence.

The first proof given by Aquinas is derived from the concept of motion. This proof had been used not only by Aristotle but also Moses Maimonides, (1135-1204) the influential Jewish physician, theologian and astronomer who lived a century before Albertus Magnus (c.1206-1280), Aquinas' teacher, who also had employed this argument. Every object that is in motion has to be set in motion by another moving object, this is evident from nature. Since an infinite regression is not possible, there must, at some point, be an 'unmoved mover' and this is God.

The second proof also comes from Aristotle's *Metaphysics*.[15] This proof was used by Avicenna (980-1037) the great Arabic polymath. The proof is based on the assumption that nothing can be the cause of itself. Everything has an efficient cause, to use Aristotle's terminology but, again, since there cannot be an infinite regression, there must be finally an 'uncaused cause' and this we call God. It is of interest that some astrophysicists have recently claimed that there is no mathematical reason why something cannot cause itself.[16] This will be considered more fully later.

The third proof is based on the concept of contingency versus necessity. Natural things come into being and then go out of existence. Everything appears to be 'contingent', that is, nothing has had to exist always and forever. There is nothing in nature that is 'necessary', that is, nothing that exists in and of itself–it is possible that it may not have existed at some time and it is possible that it will not exist at some time in the future. But if everything were contingent then it is possible that nothing would exist. But since something exists, there must be a necessary being that by its very nature exists and has always existed and is responsible for all existent beings; this something we also call God.

The fourth proof comes from Aristotle's *Metaphysics*, as well, and was used by Augustine of Hippo as well as Anselm. This proof is based on the concept of the 'degree of goodness' or excellence. We know from experience that one thing is more perfect or beautiful than another. This is a judgment based on the observation of nature. Aquinas argues that such judgments have an objective foundation. 'Degrees of perfection' imply the existence of a 'best' being--the most beautiful, most good or perfect being. Again, this necessary ultimate perfection is God. This proof reflects Plato's notion of Forms, that are perfect and of which, earthly things are only imperfect copies. Plato's Form, the Good is often equated with the Christian God.

The fifth proof is based on an argument from final cause–the teleological proof. Everything in nature appears to have a purpose. Everything has some end or reason for its existence. This 'intentionality' of Nature implies directed order and thus a director of worldly order and we call this God. If there is a watch there must be a watchmaker as William Paley asserted six centuries later. The fifth proof is the basis for the idea of Intelligent Design as used by creation scientists.

---

15   Aristotle 1984, *The Complete Works of Aristotle* (Princeton, NJ: Princeton University Press).

16   Gott III, J. R., & Li, L. 1998, *Can the Universe Create Itself?* Physical Review, 58:1-43.

How valid these arguments are is not at issue here, the point, rather, is that Aquinas uses nature, including the heavens, to argue for the existence of God. This is pertinent to later arguments for Neo-Naturalism as a system that may offer advantages over classical theological or natural theological arguments for a higher power.

PLURALITY OF WORLDS

Another theme that persisted throughout the Middle Ages concerns the possibility of other worlds and civilizations elsewhere in the Universe.[17] The Atomists were the first to suggest the possibility of 'infinite' worlds and intelligences. Democritus (c.460-370 B.C.E.) and Epicurus (c.341-270) posited an infinite universe that was uncreated, eternal and composed of atoms that were also infinite in number, self-moved and in constant, chaotic motion. In between the atoms was an infinite void, since the atoms were in constant motion, random interactions resulted in the infinite universe with infinite worlds. Later, Lucretius (c.96-55 B.C.E.) adopted this cosmology in his, *On the Nature of Things*.[18] This system was a problem in the Middle Ages for several reasons.[19] For one thing, the medieval Universe, as created by God, recognized humans as central, unique and supreme among all species. Earth was at the center of the world. In addition, the world was not considered to be infinite–only God was infinite. All planets, along with the Sun, Moon and stars, revolved around Earth. Also, the concept of a void had been denied by Aristotle. Besides, the world was not chaotic, as the atomists had suggested. God was orderly and rational. The created world had to conform to this rational plan. So, a plurality of worlds and the Atomism that fostered this notion was at loggerheads with the theology of the Middle Ages. This may be why the old cosmology with earth, water, air and fire made more sense to the Medievals.[20] Whether this explained, in part, why the ancient atomic system of Democritus failed to gain support sooner is debatable. If we had thought in terms of atoms, might modern chemistry and physics emerged sooner is anyone's guess.

In the thirteenth century, the idea of other worlds was hotly debated. Christ, the 'Son of God' who died on the cross to save all humankind, would have had to die an infinite number of times to save all the beings living on

---

17   Op. Cit. Dick, S.J., 1982.

18   Op. Cit. Lucretius 1951.

19   Op. Cit. Dick, S. J. 1982.

20   Medievals like Ancients indicates the thinkers of these historical periods.'Medievals', however, is not a word found in the dictionary. Nonetheless, I have coined this term because it correlates with Ancients and is less cumbersome than 'thinkers of the Middle Ages'.

an infinite number of worlds. Humans are truly the ultimate egoists. The Universe had to be made for us and us alone. Consequently, Atomism and Democritus' ancient Greek atomic theory had to go.

In 1277 C.E., Ètienne Tempier, Bishop of Paris, promulgated a list of 219 condemned theological concepts.[21] Up to 27 of these dealt with cosmological issues. The Church had come out of the Dark Ages having consolidated its theology. The major 'heresies' had been suppressed and between the seventh and tenth centuries C.E., there were few doctrinal disputes to deal with, however, when translations of Aristotle's works reached the eyes of medieval theologians, they were forced to cope with concepts that often were at variance with orthodoxy. For the Parisian theologians, however, it was certain that God could not be limited and, thus, IT could accommodate any number of worlds or populations that needed salvation. Of course, as we have noted earlier, Aristotle posed other problems, including his belief in the eternity of Earth that contradicted Genesis.

Giordano Bruno (1548-1600), whom we looked at earlier, was a man ahead of his time. An Italian monk, he was defrocked because of his heterodoxy. He denied the Trinity, the divinity of Christ, promoted Arianism[22] and castigated the Church hierarchy for its corruption and cruelty. Ultimately, he was tried before the Inquisition and burned at the stake.[23] The issue that was probably most irritating and threatening to the Church at the time was his belief in infinite worlds and cultures. The proposition put forth by Copernicus (1473-1543) in *De Revolutionibus* that the Earth was not the center of the Universe and that humans were not the central reason for all of God's creative efforts, was too aberrant for the Church to accept. If Copernicus were right, then Aristotle was wrong and much of the Church's cosmology and theology would crumble as a result. Genesis was under attack and with it the basic underpinnings of Church dogma. This was a situation not to be tolerated and thus, Bruno and his books were both incinerated, though in the end, his books faired better than his body.

Galileo (1573-1642) is the most notable figure to have come under attack by the Inquisition. His sin was similar to Bruno's in that he not only accepted Copernicus' cosmology but also went a long way towards proving

---

21   Grant, E. 1996, *Planets, Stars and Orbs: The Medieval Cosmos, 1200-1687* (New York: Cambridge University Press).
22   Arius (c. 256-336) was a priest of the early Eastern Church who believed that Christ was only 'semi-divine', having been created by God the Father and as such was not co-equal to the Father. The Nicaean Council of 325 C.E. condemned Arius' view though it persisted for several centuries thereafter.
23   White, M. 2002, *The Pope and the Heretic* (New York: Harper-Collins).

that Nicholas was right.[24] There were other issues involved in his fall from ecclesiastical favor but this was the primary issue—a view Galileo recanted in order to avoid Bruno's fate. (Bruno had been executed only a few years earlier). Rene Descartes also believed in a plurality of worlds, as did Isaac Newton, but both suffered no major consequence as a result of their beliefs[25]

With the Reformation things changed, though the issue of many worlds was not well received by many Protestants including Luther and Calvin. The Enlightenment only accelerated theological debates that spawned Deism among other heterodoxies. But as the twentieth century unfolded, a new aspect to the debate developed.

ASTRONOMY AS THEOLOGY TODAY

Paul Davis' *God and the New Physics*, typifies the recent trend toward popular theology as a mix of astronomy, relativity and quantum mechanics.[26] Some of these authors use science to deny God, including Dawkins,[27] Harris,[28] Hitchins[29] and Dennett.[30] while others, such as Polkinghorne[31] and Kauffman[32] prefer to affirm God's existence with science. As noted above, my intention here is not to present arguments that prove or disprove either of these theses. Rather, I want to present a new view of the Universe, God's creation and God ITself. This involves astronomy, relativity and quantum theory and though I believe in something that one may call God, this term is misleading in a Neo-Naturalistic sense. The label 'God' carries so much baggage along with it that I hesitate to use it. As soon as one uses the term

---

24   Though strictly speaking this was not established until James Bradley (1692-1762) in 1728 discovered 'stellar aberration.' He showed that light rays fell on the Earth like rain on someone walking in the rain with an umbrella. The umbrella has to be angled in the direction of forward motion in order to prevent getting wet. So too the Earth in its annual revolution around the Sun moves toward and then away from the light rays of a given star, causing the star to make a small circle in the sky each year. As one views the skies through a telescope s/he has to angle the telescope slightly towards or away from the rays because of this effect. Bradley realized this meant the Earth was moving and not stationary at the center of the Universe. Copernicus and Galileo believed this but had not actually proved it.

25   Some of Descartes' works were put on the Index of Forbidden Books.

26   Davis, P. 1983, *God and the New Physics* (New York: Simon & Schuster).

27   Op. cit. Dawkins, R. 2008

28   Op. cit. Harris. S. 2006

29   Op. cit. Hitchins, C. 2007

30   Dennett, D.C. 2007, *Breaking the Spell: Religion as a Natural Phenomenon* (New York: Penguin)

31   Op. cit. Polkinghorne, 2007.

32   Op. cit. Kauffman, S. 2008,

God or naturalism, emotional barriers are immediately constructed that make valid discussion of any theology virtually impossible.

Advances in astronomy and astrophysics have changed our view of the world in major ways over the past few centuries. If Thomas Aquinas is right in claiming that God can be known through nature then our expanding view of the Universe should magnify our view of God. There are many astronomers who are atheists and see the world as purely material and mechanical–not requiring a divine principle to explain it.[33] On the other hand, there are still many in the field who find the often baffling quantum model of the Universe as even more evidence that there must be some primary principle to explain the Big Bang and the Universe that has evolved from it.

Davies deals with a variety of theological issues in his books, including creation, what life is, the mind and body debate, the self, quantum theory and its implications, time, free will, the fundamental structure of matter, chance or design in creation and other questions too involved to be dealt with in any satisfactory way here. These are issues for which one can find no ready answers. I will discuss the quantum question, however, in more detail in chapter 10. The point is that astronomy and astrophysics in the past century have opened up new avenues of theological inquiry. Not being limited by the theocracy of the Middle Ages has allowed new facts about the Universe to open up novel approaches to these questions.

Recent estimates suggest the Universe is 13.7 billion years old. As a corollary of this, the 'edge' of the visible Universe is 13.7 billion light years away–some 129,609,239,218,644 kilometers.(129 trillion plus kilometers[34]). The volume of the Universe, using these estimates, would be 2.9 X 10^{39} cubic kilometer–that's right, 2.9 with 39 zeros following it. There are as many as 400 billion stars in our Milky Way Galaxy and an equal number of galaxies in the Universe, each with similar numbers of stars and this number has been recently expanded. Our Sun has a mass of 1.99 X 10^{30} kilograms (one kilogram = 2.2 pounds). Thus, the Sun 'weighs'[35] almost 2,000,000,000,000,0 00,000,000,000,000,000 kilograms. The Sun has a mean surface temperature of just under 6000° K (Kelvin) (about 10,000° F). At its core the temperature is around 16 million degrees K. There are some stars with core temperatures of 100 million degrees K. The Sun and all the stars are powered by atomic energy, that is, hydrogen is converted by atomic fusion to helium at a rate

33   Stenger, V. J. 2009, *Quantum Gods: Creation, Chaos, and the Search for Cosmic Consciousness* (Amherst, NY: Prometheus Books).
34   A kilometer is 0.6 miles.
35   Strictly speaking this is its mass not its weight: m=f/a, i.e. force divided by acceleration.

not comprehensible by the human mind. We have all seen Einstein's famous equation, $E = mc^2$. This tells us that if one gram of matter is totally converted to pure energy, this energy would be equal to one kilogram times the speed of light squared, that is roughly 300,000,000 times 300,000,000 or 9×10^{16} Joules. Right again, 9 with 16 zeros after it.[36] This is more energy than we could ever imagine. Now it's true that only about 7% of the mass involved in a nuclear reaction on the Sun is converted into energy but the Sun fuses millions of tons of hydrogen every second. It is a huge 'furnace'[37] and yet is only a medium-sized stars. There are many stars much more massive that 'burn' their hydrogen at much higher rates. The Sun's life is about 10 billion years because it burns relatively slowly by astronomical standards. More massive, hotter stars use up their atomic fuel in as little as 10,000 years.

The Universe is stranger and more diverse than one can imagine. Wherever astronomers look, they find surprises. The Jovian moon Io, as one example, spews out volcanic gases made up mostly of sulfur dioxide. Its neighbor moon, Europa, is covered with water-ice sludge, crisscrossed with huge cracks and supported by extensive sheets of ice. Venus has an atmosphere composed of sulfuric acid and other toxic chemicals with a surface temperature of 900° F. Venus would not be a very hospitable hostess for us humans.

One could go on and on about the size, power and diversity of the Universe but you get the idea–if there is a God, IT is, indeed, very, very expansive and unimaginably powerful with an endless bag of tricks–a being, judging from what nature tells us, far beyond the comprehension of us mortals. What IT is, we do not or cannot know but certainly, God is much, much greater than anything depicted in the Bible or presented to us in Sunday school. Our Universe, both microscopic and macroscopic, is filled with astonishing mysteries, many of which, as we shall see, defy reason and human imagination. Thus, God must be equal to or surpasses these mystifying vistas.

CONCLUSION

All this information, some would argue, tells us many things about God–about ITs immensity and magnificence. The deists claim God works through physical laws. If matter can be self creating as suggested by reputable physicists,[38] then this argues for a transcendent God. Whatever God is, we

---

36   The formula for energy in ioules is: $J = 1kg(m/s)^2$ that is, one Kg times meters per second squared. For c, the speed of light, this is 300,000 m/s squared.

37   But not any furnace in the traditional sense that burns gas, coal or wood.

38   Op. cit. Giott, et al., 1998.

certainly can tell IT is phenomenally, incomprehensibly vast and powerful. ITs abilities reach far beyond anything we can imagine. God's ways are certainly mysterious, not because IT is some kind of magician waving a magic wand but, rather, because we can only begin to understand what God is and how IT works. It would be presumptuous and naïve to think otherwise. We know from what the Universe tells us that IT is not an anthropomorphic being sitting on a celestial throne. IT is not providential in the fatherly sense but this does not preclude involvement in our lives in ways beyond human understanding. We can only glimpse vaguely God's nature. We know some of the physical laws utilized in running the Universe. We get some sense of God's immensity from the size, age and workings of the Universe, however, in the final analysis, we cannot know God intimately or intuitively.

We as humans can strive for an ever-increasing knowledge of God through ever-increasing knowledge of the Universe. We will, however, never arrive at anything like a complete understanding of God, if, indeed, there is a God by any definition of IT one can devise. Does Thomas Aquinas prove there is a God or that there is a God responsible for the Universe? Will we ever elucidate the precise nature of God by studying the Universe? I think not. But if one believes in a God either through faith or the glorious cosmos around us, it is possible to know something about the divine through ITs handiwork. We must be humbled by all this. We humans are not as important as once thought and we ought to approach the nature of God with a humble heart. Whatever the case, we will be better off as a consequence of our quest for God. We may find more and more pleasure in our world as a result of these efforts. We may even make the world a better place through this ongoing search. I believe this is not a vain pursuit. For me this has been a passionate odyssey. An odyssey that is both enlightening and invigorating. It stirs the heart and mind. Astronomy as theology does have its place in our lives today. As we will see, there are even more mysteries to be encountered in this mystical, physical world of ours.

THE MYSTICAL PHYSICAL WORLD

CHAPTER 9

RELATIVITY, BLACK HOLES AND CAUSALITY

INTRODUCTION

What you don't grasp, you lack entirely;
What you don't touch seems miles away to you;
What you don't reckon, you think cannot be true;
What you don't measure, that is no amount'
What you don't coin, that, you think does not count. —Goethe[1]

Relativity could well be classified under Goethe's rubric quoted above. Goethe's admonitions apply to both Quantum and Relativity Theory. Many of the novel concepts in these two physical systems cannot be intuitively grasped by the human mind or imagination. The notion of black holes, an offshoot of relativity, can only be described mathematically. Such commonsensical ideas as space, time and distance take on new meaning in light of Einstein's relativity theory while at the same time adding to our concept of God just as astronomy does.

Einstein developed the theories of special relativity in 1905 and general relativity in 1916. Relativity deals with space, time and gravity– specifically, how massive objects like our Sun cause space to curve and in turn how curved space tells objects in what direction they are to move. More interestingly, relativity poses the question, "Can time go around in circles so that the past meets the present? Also, does time move slower for fast moving objects? And is a fast moving yardstick shorter than a slower moving one? The question also arises, "If mass can slow time, can it, in fact, bring it to a full stop?" If the arrow of time can be reversed then is time-travel into

---

1   Goethe, 1963, *Goethe's Faust*, trans. W. Kaufmann (New York: Anchor Books) p. 32

the past or future possible and, if so, could we create ourselves? Could one change the course of his/her life?

There is a famous puzzle in physics, the Grandfather Paradox which suggests that if we could travel to the past, would it then be possible to change the spouse his/her grandfather marries, thus, altering one's identity? More pertinent to our purposes here is the question, "Is it possible for our Universe to create itself or some other universe(s)?" All this sounds like something Isaac Asimov might concoct for one of his science fiction novels but there are theoretical mathematical bases to support such conjectures. In fact, many of these questions have been answered in the affirmative by experiments and shown to be true.

The development of non-Euclidean geometry by Jànos Bolyai (1802-1860) and others in the first part of the nineteenth century gave us a new way of looking at space and this set the stage, in part at least, for Einstein's Theory of Relativity. In the present chapter, we will go beyond non-Euclidean geometry to the geometry of space-time as defined by Einstein and others before and after him. This path takes us, inevitably, to the concept of black holes and the question of causality. In order to understand the journey upon which we are embarking in this chapter, we must first present some basic mathematical concepts that underlie relativity. Only by this background can we approach the modern idea of causality. I will attempt to explain in broad terms General Relativity then discuss black holes, present some of the theory behind self-caused universes and finally provide an analysis of the various theories of creation. All this is done in an attempt to delve into the mystical, physical Universe where we can truly find God in all ITs mystery and majesty. I shall not propose a pantheistic view of the world as Spinoza did but, rather, hope to provide a higher power more deserving of our awe and reverence than the traditional anthropomorphic deity as portrayed in traditional religions.

This is done with the hope that we can preserve the value of religion without reducing its tenets to the myth and contradictions we have discussed above. In the end we can make religion and God more rational and more worthy of respect and wonder. It is time to find a God that is more than a magician that simply waves ITs wand or 'breathes' life into inanimate beings or gives a divine command and creates all things in six days. My quest is to define a God that can be viewed in all ITs true wondrous grandeur. I think modern science can help us do this.

GENERAL RELATIVITY

Gravity, although the weakest of the four forces[2] that are found in the Universe, is nonetheless, considered the dominant universal form of energy. Relativity describes a new kind of spatial geometry–a non-Euclidean geometry. It also posits a four dimensional Universe. In an Euclidean world, there are but three dimensions defined by coordinates x, y and z.

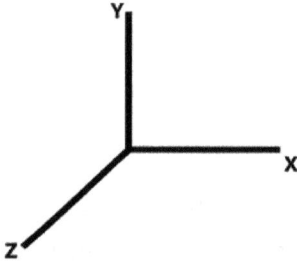

Fig. 9.1. A three-dimensional 'Cartesian' coordinate system. Euclid's geometry operates in a world defined by these dimensions, all of which are perpendicular to one another.

We live, and more importantly, develop our brains in this three-dimensional world. This is all we know. We are 'wired' to function within these three dimensions. When born, we have billions of neurons (nerve cells) in our brain. This represents a great redundancy of neurons. But this plethora of neuronal pathways offers the potential for knowing and relating to a myriad of microscopic and macroscopic worlds beyond that in which we live. It is a big world out there and we have little chance of contacting it without the aid of technology. As very young children, we have a nearly infinite capacity to learn languages. Most of us learn only one or two languages because they are the one's to which we are exposed. If we were required to survive in a world much different than the one in which we find ourselves, we would adapt and persist as individuals and as a species in this alternate environment. Billions of our redundant neurons would, over time, be enlisted to allow us to function, for example, in the world of relativity and quantum physics. One of the reasons we find this world of ours relatively congenial is that we have adapted to it. If we had not evolved to fit into this eco-system we call Earth, it would not be so livable. The problem with our nervous system is that its nearly infinite capacity is soon lost. Only those nervous pathways that help us deal with the environment in which we live, actually persist. All the other neuronal connections disappear in time for want of use–it is the 'use it or

---

2   The four forces are gravity, electromagnetic waves, such as light rays, the strong nuclear force that holds together all the positively charged protons of every atom in the Universe and the weak force that has to do with radioactive decay.

lose it' principle. If we lived in a non-Euclidian world we would not only adapt to it but would develop an intuitive understanding of the mysteries found in the worlds of relativity and quantum mechanics. The fact remains that we have not been directly exposed to many physical situations that are described in relativity and quantum theory. Because we lack exposure to this Einsteinian world, we have no intuitive or imaginative understanding of the events described by relativity.

It is my contention that our best hope of knowing God is to be found in the counterintuitive world of modern physics. Just as we find traces of God in this vast Universe of ours, so too, may we find IT in the world of physics–a world that is not immediately available to us. It is in the mystical, physical realm that we can find a God that is more mysterious than we have heretofore imagined–one that is more meaningful and truly rational.

The term relativity refers to time and space as being relative and not absolute.[3] Galileo was the first to conceive of time as relative. For Newton, however, space and time were absolutes. This idea persisted for over two hundred years. Space was like a container–there could be 'empty' space with nothing in it. There was space even if there was nothing occupying it. Space was fixed and unchanging. One could not alter space. Wherever an object occupies space, this space was just like space anywhere else in the Universe, according to Newton. Space could not be curved or altered in any way.

Similarly, time was thought to be the same throughout the Universe. Of course, time in Europe is different than the time in Australia but this is dependent on the Sun's position–time itself, however, is uniform. Time moves at the same rate everywhere. One minute in Europe is the same as one minute in Australia. Space and time were considered by Newton to be constants.

Objects could be located in space according to three-dimensional Cartesian (named after Rene Descartes) coordinates, x, y and z. Likewise, someone flying in an airplane and another person stationery on the ground were located in exactly the same time frame. Their clocks ticked away at exactly the same rate. The clock of a pilot flying west around the world recorded the same time as one flying east even though the one pilot was flying with and the other against the Earth's rotation. The one pilot may land later in the day than the other but the time elapsed will have been the same, if each pilot flew his or her plane at identical speeds and wind was no factor.

Einstein postulated and it has since been proven, that space and time are not absolutes. He did, however, claim that light moved at the same

3   Lorentz, H. A. 2009, *Einstein's Theory of Relativity: A Concise Statement* (Whitefish, MT: Kissinger Publishing) p. 3.

velocity (300,000,000 meters/second)[4] no matter how one views the light–head-on or moving away from the light ray. If two cars are approaching each other at fifty miles per hour they pass each other at a velocity of 100 mph. Not so with light. If someone riding a light beam in one direction passes another person riding a light beam in the opposite direction,[5] the two would measure each other's velocity as 300,000,000 m/s and not double this velocity, i.e. 600,000,000 m/s. The velocity of light does not depend on the velocity of the light's source. How can this be? This is not an intuitively evident fact.

Because the speed of light never varies, no matter how one measures it, there are strange consequences that follow. One is so-called 'time dilation'. It turns out that if someone is moving very fast, say 90% of the speed of light, her clock will register time at a slower rate than another stationery clock on Earth. The clock used by the high-speed astronaut will show less time has elapsed compared to the earth-bound timekeeper. The time difference depends on the velocity of the astronaut's spacecraft. The faster she moves, the slower the clock ticks (as viewed from Earth). Not only does the clock move more slowly but so does everything else in the spacecraft. The astronauts heart rate, thought processes, etc. all move just as slowly. The space jockey doesn't feel any different but from Earth she appears to be functioning more slowly and when the astronaut views the earthling, he appears to be moving faster in every way–heart rate, respirations, even age. The formula that describes the passage of time is shown below in a footnote.[6] The easiest way to visualize this is to imagine one second on the spacecraft as lasting longer when viewed from Earth as compared to one second as observed on an earth-bound clock i.e. 1....2....3 versus 1.2.3.

The other phenomenon described by relativity theory is that of length contraction. When someone is traveling very fast, again at a velocity approaching the speed of light, length contracts, so that a yardstick moving along at 90% the speed of light, will appear foreshortened as observed by someone stationery on Earth. This follows from the notion of time dilation. Since speed is defined as distance per unit of time, for example, meters per second and time is moving slower, then in order to travel a given distance

---

4   The actual speed of light is 299,792,458 meters/second.
5   As we shall see, it is impossible to move at the speed of light.
6        $t' = t/1-(v^2/c^2)$, where t' = time recorded in the spacecraft moving at a significant percentage of the speed of light; t = time recorded on Earth; v = velocity of the spacecraft; c = speed of light. As the speed of the vehicle approaches the speed of light, then v^2/c^2 approaches one and 1 minus1 = 0. So as the denominator gets smaller and smaller, t' gets bigger and bigger i.e. the time on the spacecraft goes slower and slower. This means one second on the spacecraft lasts longer than once second on Earth i.e. 1...2.... 3 versus 1.2.3... etc.

the distance spanned over a given time period has to be shorter. This way both the astronaut and earthling observe the arrival time at some distant planet as being the same. From the astronaut's perspective she sees herself as moving along in time just as fast as ever. The observer on Earth, however, sees the spacecraft moving slower. In order for the spacecraft to arrive at another planet 'on time' the distance covered must be shorter. Once again the formula describing this phenomenon is given below.[7] If you are having trouble following this don't worry, you are not alone. The two points to remember are that as one moves faster and faster relative to someone on Earth, time moves slower and distance is foreshortened. Neither concept is intuitively evident. After all we live in a world in which time and space appear absolute. Thus, speed not only affects time but also space. Space shrinks the faster one travels. It is important to remember that the astronaut doesn't notice time slowing. It also happens that a space traveler standing in the spaceship is 'thinner', front to back. If she were lying down she would appear to an earth-bound observer to be shorter. The length contraction is always in the direction of motion. The aspect of the object at right angles with the direction of motion is unaffected. Again, this 'thinning' or 'shortening' is not evident to the traveler only to someone on Earth or in, what is called a different, 'inertial frame of reference' (IFR). Captain Kirk riding side-by-side with Spock (who is in another spacecraft moving at the same speed) would not view Kirk as thinner if standing or shorter if lying down. Only someone in a different IFR i.e. moving at a different velocity i.e. accelerating or decelerating, would be aware of such differences. This is why space and time are not absolute, they are different for everyone in a different IFR.[8]

Also, for reasons I won't review here, two beams of light emitted from the center of the spacecraft, one aimed forward and one aimed aft will appear to the astronaut to reach their targets simultaneously. To mission control the beam aimed aft will strike its target first and to an astronaut in a spacecraft catching up to the first craft, the forward directed beam would appear to reach its target first. There is thus a loss of simultaneity at relativistic velocities. Different people see different sequences depending on their individual IFR. Because of this loss of simultaneity, it is possible that cause and effect, the principle of causality, may be confused. One event *A*

---

7        $d' = d \times \sqrt{(1 - v^2/c^2)}$. Here d' is the distance covered i.e. speed times time, times 1 minus velocity of the spacecraft squared divided by the speed of light squared. In this case as the velocity of the vehicle approaches the speed of light $(1 - v^2/c^2)$ goes to zero. Since $(1 - v^2/c^2)$ is now in the numerator, d' become shorter and shorter.

8   If a spacecraft would fly by Earth at a speed approaching *c*, it would appear to be rotated rather than foreshortened for reason I won't give here.

may appear to cause another event *B* in one IFR, whereas in another IFR, *B* may appear to cause *A*. The world of relativity gets very tricky and confusing.

THE FOURTH DIMENSION

In a relativistic world, there is a fourth dimension–time. All points in an Euclidean world can be defined or located by the three-dimensional points x, y and z. Depending on the units of the system and the reference points one uses, a point can be easily located in a three-dimensional world. When one tries to define a point in space, if there is no massive celestial body nearby the three coordinate system, x, y and z works just fine. Without a nearby massive object or, if one is not moving at a relativistic velocity[9] (a significant percentage of the speed of light), space is flat (Euclidean) and, knowing the three Cartesian reference points, x, y and z finding a place in space is relatively easy. However, if an object is passing by a massive object like our Sun then Special Relativity must be utilized when determining positions. One has to account for the fourth dimension, space-time, as well as, the curvature of space induced by the nearby massive celestial body. Consider a tortuous, ill-kempt road with hills, valleys, and many curves, as well as, ruts, potholes and bumps. The coordinates are changing all the time; finding the location of all four wheels at any one moment becomes a complex task.

This is like the problem Einstein faced in 1907 and resolved in 1916 with the General Theory of Relativity. The Field Equation of General Relativity encapsulates his solution.[10] The Field Equation is not easy to understand and the details are not essential for our purposes but, basically, it tells us that large celestial bodies including our Earth distort space. Near any mass the four space-time coordinates, x, y, z and t[11] are always changing, as on the bumpy road described above. Einstein's Field Equation gives the general description of objects moving in space-time. Newton's gravitational equation is a special case of Einstein's Field Equation but does not include the fourth dimension of time.[12]

---

9   Velocity includes both speed and the direction in which an object is moving.
10   Einstein's Field Equation is $\mathbf{G} = (8\pi\,G)/c^4 \times T$, where:
$\mathbf{G}$ = Einstein's curvature tensor; π = 3.1416.
G = Newton's gravitation constant: 5.57259×10^{-8} cm^3 g^{-1} s^{-2}
c^4 = the speed of light to the fourth power.
$\mathbf{T}$ = stress-energy tensor
11   We now have a fourth dimension, time; its symbol is t.
12   Recall that Newton's equation is: $F = GMm/r^2$. F = force of gravity; G = Newton's gravitational constant; *M* and *m* the mass of two bodies, which are gravitationally connected; and r^2 the distance between the two bodies, squared.

A massive body causes time to slow by changing the geometry of space-time near it. A clock on Earth ticks slower than one above Earth, if the relative velocities of the two clocks are the same. Also, light coming from the surface of Earth appears redder while light from high in Earth's stratosphere looks bluer. This is called gravitation red or blue shift. Since space curves in response to mass, it takes longer for an object to move along the surface of the Earth than higher up even though in relativistic terms it is the shortest (geodesic) route. It's somewhat like a plane taking the great circle route to Europe. One must keep in mind that these concepts are not intuitive–we cannot see space-time distorted by mass–we can only see its effects.[13] To the observer in curved space, things look 'straight'. Nonetheless, this effect has been shown, mathematically and observationally, to occur, such as the bending of light around the Sun as observed during a solar eclipse.[14]

A fact that will take on importance in the next two sections is that a space-time interval can be positive, negative or zero. This depends on whether light has enough time to travel between two events *A* and *B*. For example, the Universe is expanding at a very rapid rate–more rapidly at the 'edge' (if there is one) of the Universe. If two objects are moving apart so rapidly that light from, say one star, can never reach another star, then the space-time interval is said to be negative.

One way of looking at the effect of mass on space-time is to use the 'stretched rubber sheet' analogy.

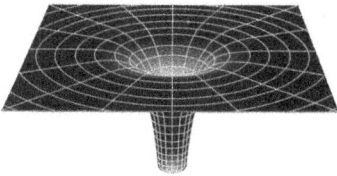

Fig. 9.2. A massive celestial object causing space-time to stretch and curve. [15]

Another way of picturing four dimensions is as below:

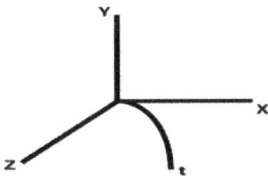

Fig. 9.3. Here is an attempt to show the three Euclidean dimensions and the fourth dimension of time. All are perpendicular.

13   Licker, R. 2001, *On Counter-Intuitive Science*, www.fermentmagazine.org.

14   Seine, C. 2004, *Swiveling Satellites See Earth's Relativistic Wake*, Science, 306:592.

15   Kaufmann, W. J & Freedman, R. A. 1999, *Universe* (New York: W. H. Freeman & Co.) p. 595.

Fig. 9.3. attempts to depict four-dimensional space in a two dimensional graph. This is not, however, visually possible but, if one envisions the four dimensions as all being perpendicular to each other, this would describe relativistic space.

Relativity theory has taken Newton's classical space and transformed it into something we can't really recognize or 'get our mind around' very easily. Relativity takes us from a world in which time and space are absolutes to one where much depends on the observer's relationship to some other observer. How close to a massive body one is as compared to someone else viewing the same event will affect how one sees the sequence of two events. There is no such thing as two events occurring at the same time. Simultaneity is dependent on one's place and pace in space relative to another's place and pace. This creates problems for ethicists because such notions smack of relative or situational morality. Relativity theory chips away at universal absolutes. It is all very unsettling for some.

One concept of relativity not touched on earlier deals with the speed of light, c. Light travels at a finite velocity. This was not always thought to be the case. Early cosmologists believed light traveled instantaneously from point A to point B. It was believed to move at an infinite speed. There was no lag time. It certainly seemed to reach the eye very quickly–too fast to measure. In 1676, Ole Rømer (1644-1720) measured the speed of light by observing Jupiter's moons and noting the time delay related to light reaching Earth from these several Jovian satellites. His estimate was low, around 225,000,000 meters per second but surprisingly accurate considering the technology available then. If he had had access to today's dimensions of the Solar System, his speed of light would have been 298,000,000 meters per second as compared to the present value of 299,792,458 meters per second. Giovanni Cassini (1625-1712) working in Paris with better instrumentation had supplied distance and satellite data that Rømer was able to use in his calculations. Cassini had accurately defined the timing of the Jovian moons' eclipses as they moved around Jupiter. Rømer noted that the timing of these eclipses was slightly off from Cassini's calculations and reasoned that this related to the extra time it took light to travel from Io (Jupiter's innermost moon) to Earth. Knowing the distance to the moons allowed Rømer to estimate the speed of light.

This was one of the first truly 'astronomical' numbers that cosmologists were to accurately determine. The dimensions of the Universe were rapidly expanding. With the findings of Edmund Hubble, in the 1920's, our whole idea of the Universe was very rapidly enlarging.

BLACK HOLES

Newton (1642-1727) believed that light was composed of particles (photons) rather than waves, as Christian Huygens (1629-1695), his Dutch contemporary, had postulated.[16] In 1783, John Michell, (1724-1793) an English clergyman and astronomer, suggested that if light were 'corpuscular', then it could be influenced by Newton's law of gravity.[17] Thus, if a photon has mass, it could be attracted by another mass.[18] In turn, if the mass were great enough, the gravitational force exerted on corpuscles of light radiating from a massive, luminous body (like a very big star) such light would be unable to move outward from this extremely massive body. The light could not escape the gravitational pull of the star and so it would appear to an outside observer as black–emitting no light. Michell called these 'dark stars'. Today, the term black hole is used.

For anything to escape from Earth or any massive body and fly off into space, the object must overcome the gravitational pull of that body. The energy required must be greater than the force of gravity itself. The mathematics behind this is shown below.[19] As an example, for a rocket to escape into space from Earth, its velocity must be 11,200 meters/second (m/s). Michell, aware of the concept of 'escape velocity', conjectured that given a star 5000 times as massive as our Sun but with the same average density, even light would not be able to escape from the surface of such a star. The star, though extremely hot and 'luminous', would appear black.

In 1916, Schwarzschild solved Einstein's Field Equation and in so doing, laid out the mathematical theory explaining black holes. Following this, in 1931, Subrahmanyan Chandrasekhar (1910-1995), while working on stellar evolution, determined that a star with a mass more than 1.4 times our Sun, upon running out of fuel (hydrogen), would collapse, i.e. implode.

---

16   Carroll, B.W. & Ostlie, D.A., 1996, *An Introduction to Modern Astrophysics* (New York: Addison-Wesley Publishing Company). p. 661.
17   Newton's formula, as we have seen, is $F = GMm/r^2$, which is an approximation since it does not include relativistic velocities.
18   It turns out that photons do not have mass but because space is curved around massive bodies, the massless photon will follow the curvature of space.
19   The escape velocity, that is the speed required for an object o leave the gravitational field of a massive body and move out into space is $v = (2MG/r)^{-2}$
Where:
     V = the escape velocity.
     M = mass of the massive object.
     G = gravitational constant of Newton.
     R = the radius of the massive object.

As long as the star is utilizing the energy of hydrogen fusion this prevents it from collapsing under its own gravitational force. Once the 'fuel' is gone, the star implodes. If massive enough, it then becomes a black hole. In 1939, J. Robert Opeenheimer (1902-1967), later the father of the first atomic bomb, using the work of earlier astrophysicists, posited this phenomenon. If the star had the mass of our Sun, it would at first expand into a 'red giant' and then shrink to a very small size–about 1% of its original diameter forming a white dwarf. The white dwarf is very dim with an absolute magnitude of +10 – +15.[20] If the star were more massive than 1.4 times the mass of our Sun (Chandrasekhar's limit) the diameter of the collapsed star, after running out of hydrogen would be about 10 km (6 miles) and very, very dense.[21] These are called neutron stars because, as they collapse, the gravitational force is so great that the atoms (composed of mostly protons and electrons) are crushed together with such force, that the protons and electrons combine to form neutrons. The now 'deceased' star, consists entirely of neutrons[22] and, being very dense and small, tends to spin at enormous speeds, often many rotations per second.[23,24] If the neutron star radiates light or other forms of energy such as gamma or X-rays, they appear like a rapidly spinning lighthouse beacon. These are then called pulsars.

On the other hand, if a star four times more massive than our Sun runs out of hydrogen and collapses, it may form a black hole. It is evident that the kind of celestial body a star ends up as depends on its original mass. A black hole develops when a more massive star dies. This is a catastrophic event characterized by a huge implosion and rebound explosion. During the death of such a star it is a very bright object and appears briefly as a 'new star' (supernova). During its implosion, large amounts of heavy elements (what astronomers call metals)[25] are created. This is the 'star dust' out of which we humans are made. Our Sun, the planets, including Earth, are all progeny of

---

20   Apparent Magnitude is a scale of brightness or luminosity. The smaller the number the brighter the object. A negative number is brighter than a positive one. Magnitude of +6 is much dimmer than −6. A star +6 is just barely visible to the naked eye. Polaris, the North Star, is +2.0. Sirius, our brightest star, is −1.4. The Moon's mean magnitude is −12.7 and the Sun is magnitude −26.7.

21   The formula for this radius is $R_s = 2GM/c^2$. The radius R is equal to two times the gravitational constant times the mass of the star divided by the speed of light squared.

22   An atomic particle slightly more massive than a proton found in all atomic nuclei save hydrogen (though deuterium contains one neutron).

23   Conservation of angular momentum demands that as a spinning object becomes smaller it must spin faster, as with a twirling figure skater who brings his arms closer to his body.

24   This preserves angular momentum.

25   Astronomers call any elements other than hydrogen and helium 'metals'.

this process. Whatever remains of the star may form a black hole, if enough mass remains after the supernova blows up.

A black hole[26] has a huge gravitational field that causes it to evolve one step beyond a neutron star. It is so dense and compact that it virtually disappears into a single point–a so-called singularity. It is so small that it is essentially dimensionless. Its density approaches infinity[27] and its only knowable properties are its mass, electrical charge, rotational velocity, angular momentum and gravity. At a certain radius outside the black hole, everything becomes caught in its gravitational field and is irretrievably drawn into the singularity. This is called the Schwarzschild radius since it is derived from his solution to Einstein's Field Equation. It is also called the 'event horizon' because beyond this point no information about events inside the black hole can be deciphered.[28]

Peculiar things happen at the event horizon. For example, from an outside observer's vantage point, nothing seems to happen at the Schwarzschild's radius (event horizon). In effect, time appears to stop. Recall from relativity theory that the stronger gravity becomes, in a given IFR, the slower time moves. Thus, as one approaches the event horizon where the force of gravity is extremely strong, time dilates to the point that it appears to stop. Once an object enters the event horizon, though this seems to take forever, as viewed by the outside observer, the object will disappear never to be seen again.[29].

Though peering inside the event horizon is impossible, it is mathematically feasible to determine that there is a "singularity" at the center of each black hole. In addition to its infinite density, the singularity's space-time is infinitely curved. Time is wrapped around itself, more will be said of this below.

Do black holes really exist? If they cannot be seen, how would one know they are there or anywhere? It turns out that the evidence for black holes is fairly strong. The commonly used, but oversimplified,[30] method to locate a black hole involves Newton's description of the motion of two celestial bodies revolving around each other (a binary pair). The diameter of the star's orbit (or a star/black hole pair) can be determined observationally. Its period, the time it takes the star to move around its orbit once, can be determined observationally. Using these two parameters one can find the

---

26   American physicist, John A. Wheeler, coined the term black hole in 1968.

27   Density = mass divided by volume. As the volume shrinks the density rises and when the volume is near zero, its density approaches infinity.

28   Density of around 1×10^{17} kg/m^3. A teaspoon of a neutron star on Earth would weigh many, many tons.

29   Stephen Hawking postulated that a black hole could very gradually "evaporate" over billions of years. This is controversial.

30   Oversimplified because it fails to account for relativity theory.

combined mass of the star/black hole pair. The mass of the visible star can be approximated by using its spectroscopic pattern i.e. color. Subtracting the star's mass from the total mass of the two bodies gives the mass of the black hole. If this mass is great enough to be a black hole and no other star is visible, it is a good bet that there is a black hole orbiting the visible star.

Finding the distance to the pair is necessary in order to carry out these calculations.[31] The evidence for black holes increases almost weekly.[32], [33],[34],[35] Knowing that there are black holes and that there are some strange things going on inside the event horizon, we can now look more closely at time and causality.

TIME AND CAUSALITY

Because light travels at a finite speed (300,000,000 m/s), if two events occur at 'different'[36] times and the distance between the two events is great enough and an observer of the two events is situated nearer to one event than the other then it may not be possible for the observer to determine which event occurred first or if one event is the cause of the other.[37] This was touched on briefly earlier.

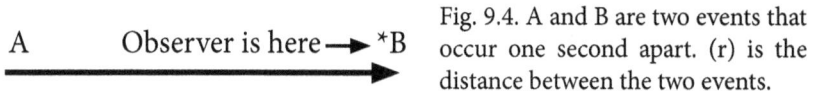

A　　　　　　Observer is here ⟶ *B

Fig. 9.4. A and B are two events that occur one second apart. (r) is the distance between the two events.

Now, if the two events occur one second apart (in the same IFR) A occurring first, the distance between the two events being less than the speed of light multiplied by time (ct) and r is less than 3×10^8 meters (the distance light travels in one second), then the light can travel from A to

31　　　There are a number of ways of determining distance to stars that won't be catalogued here. See Ferguson, K. 1999, *Measuring the Universe* (New York: Walker & Co.).

32　　　Rutledge, R. E., et al. 2000, *A Method for Distinguishing Between Transiently Accreting Neutron stars and Black Holes, in Quiescence.* Astrophysical J., 529:985-996.

33　　　Greiner, J., et al. 2001, *An Unusually Massive Stellar Black Hole in the Galaxy,* Nature, 414:522-525.

34　　　Bailyn, C. 2001, *High-Energy Astrophysics: A New Spin on Black-Hole Mass,* Nature, 414:499-501.

35　　　Genzel, R. 2003, *Near-Infrared Flares from Accreting Gas around the Supermassive Black Hole at the Galactic Center,* Nature, 425:934-937.

36　　　Strictly speaking events don't occur at the same or different times. If the two events are in the same inertial frame of reference, an observer sees them as occurring simultaneously. If they occur in different reference frames, different observers will see them as happening at different times. There is no absolute time in relativity theory.

37　　　Whitrow, G. J. 1972, *The Nature of Time* (New York: Holt, Rinehart & Winston) pp. 117-118.

B before event B occurs in which case the observer * at B will see the two events in proper sequence; A could, in this case, be the cause of B (Situation 1). If, however, r = ct and the distance between A and B is exactly 3 X 10^8 meters and the time is again one second, then the two events will appear to the observer as occurring simultaneously (Situation 2). The events appear to occur simultaneously because they occur one second apart and the light from A takes one second to reach the observer's position at B. On the other hand, if r is greater than ct (>3 X 10^8 meters) then A will appear to occur after B (Situation 3). In this case, the light from A takes longer than one second to reach B and, therefore, event A will appear to occur after event B. In the last two situations, no statement can be made about the sequence of events or the causal relationship between the two events.

These three situations above are somewhat intuitive. According to Einstein and relativity theory nothing travels faster than light and that includes information. Thus, if two events are far enough apart, so that information about their timing, even if in the same IFR, may not be available to an observer if s/he is unable to receive information about the two events in their proper sequence. On Earth this is not usually a problem but in space with its great distances, causality can become confused.

Now, if one includes relativity theory in the mix, things become less intuitive. We know that a clock in a stronger gravitational field (one on the surface of the Earth) moves more slowly than one in a weaker field (say on Mt. Everest).[38] An observer high above the Earth will see a clock on the surface of the Earth moving slower and people aging more slowly as well. Two identical twins, separated at birth with one reared at sea level and the other on the peak of Mt. Everest, will find that the alpine twin is older than his beachcombing clone. One can look at this, as mentioned above, as space being curved more by the stronger gravitational field on the surface of Earth and, thus, taking light (and time) longer to travel through its curved space as compared to light traveling through less curved space at a high altitude.

Note this is the opposite situation for the astronaut moving very fast and the sedentary mission controller discussed earlier. We have seen how the Lorentz transformation equation accounts for this. If the astronaut twin returns to Earth after a period of time she will find herself in the other twin's future, who is now looking and feeling older and maybe less healthy. These phenomena have been verified experimentally. Nonetheless, getting one's

---

38   The difference in times recorded on clocks in two separate gravitational fields is given by $\Delta\tau = \Delta t (1 + (\Phi_B - \Phi_A)/c^2$; where $\Delta\tau$ and Δt are the times shown on the two clocks, F_B- F) are the two differing gravitational fields and c is the speed of light. As can be seen, as the difference in strength of the gravitational fields increases so does the difference in recorded times.

brain around such ideas is difficult. The nineteenth and twentieth centuries brought many such mysterious almost mystical concepts to the fore.

Stephen Hawkins's book, *A Brief History of Time* became a best seller, nothing like Harry Potter but for a non-fiction, theoretical physics book, its success was certainly unexpected. Most people are fascinated by mind-boggling notions that leave them either breathless or befuddled. There are many mysteries concerning the Universe that remain unsolved. Even more mysterious is the question of creation itself. What were the forces that allowed the creation of the Universe? Was there "nothing" before the Big Bang? Was the Universe created out of nothing? Is there a God, in the traditional sense that caused the Universe to be created? Or is there a God of some type beyond the gods we have spoken of in parts I and II? If so, what is IT really like? According to many philosophers, God is the "self-caused cause"–in Aristotle's terms the "unmoved mover". Traditional monotheistic religions tell us that God is eternal–always was and always will be. But was there nothing before God created the Universe? Can something like our Universe create itself? For that matter since God exists outside of time, when did IT create the world?

SELF-CAUSED CAUSE

In 1998, Gott and Li published an article in the Physical Review entitled, *Can the Universe Create Itself?* in which they conclude that, "the laws of physics may allow the Universe to be its own mother." [39] The authors believe that there is no mathematical impediment to a self-created Universe. This section attempts to explain Gott and Li's reasoning for this staggering conclusion.

Aristotle found the problem of first cause so troubling that he sidestepped the issue by positing a Universe extending eternally from the past and eternally into the future with no beginning or end.[40] Although Aristotle believed in the four causes (formal, material, efficient and final) as well as the concept of change, he did not posit a beginning to the material Universe. An eternal, uncreated Universe was attractive to Einstein, as well. He suggested a flat universe, that is, one that is neither expanding nor contracting. Or if it is expanding, it is on a parabolic curve that never entirely flattens out. In other words, Einstein's universe expands forever but at an ever-decreasing rate. To prevent the Universe from collapsing under the force of its own gravity, he postulated a "cosmological constant", which was a force that

---

39   Gott III, J.R., & Li, L. 1998, *Can the Universe Create Itself?* Physical Review D, 58:1-43.

40   Op. cit. Aristotle, 1996.

counteracted the pull of gravity and kept the Universe from imploding.[41] He later called the cosmological constant his biggest blunder though this concept lingers on since the Universe seems now to be expanding while the density of matter in the Universe (and thus the force of gravity) and the nature of dark matter[42] remain unknown. Because of these indeterminate factors we really don't know if the gravitational force in the Universe is great enough to cause the Universe to stop expanding and re-collapse in a "Big Crunch", which then would recycle the Universe with another "Big Bang".

Since the development of the Big Bang theory, there has been ever-increasing evidence that the Universe did, indeed, have a beginning. In 1929, Edwin Hubble published his benchmark paper on the relationship between the distance of nebulae (galaxies) and the speed with which they are receding from Earth.[43] This was the first indication that the Universe was expanding at a remarkably rapid rate. It was this discovery by Hubble that prompted Einstein to claim that his cosmological constant was his greatest miscue. In 1965, Penzias and Wilson, at Bell Laboratories, first detected background microwave radiation (BMR) that turned out to be electromagnetic radiation left over from the Big Bang.[44] Alpher and Herman had earlier calculated that if there had been a Big Bang, the Universe must have been very dense and very hot, which would have left residual electromagnetic radiation throughout the sky.[45] This radiation, though very energetic at the time of the Big Bang, would have, after a few billion years, become less energy dense as the Universe expands.[46] The light from the Big Bang, though blue-shifted[47] initially, would become more and more red-shifted, as the light waves are stretched out, resulting in a BMR such as Penzias and Wilson discovered in 1965. This evidence has made a finite beginning to our Universe a distinct possibility, thus, bringing us back to the question of how the Universe came to be.

---

41   Will, C. M. 1986, *Was Einstein Right?: Putting General Relativity to the Test* (New York: Basic Books) p. 163.

42   Astronomers know there is more matter in the Universe than is observed. Newton's gravitation equation tells us this. The nature of dark matter remains unknown.

43   Hubble, E. 1929, *A Relationship between Distance and Radial Velocity among Extra-Galactic Nebulae*, PNAS, 15. 167-170.

44   Seine. C. 2002, *Microwave Background: Subtle Signals in Ancient Light Promise New View of Cosmos*, Science, 297:2184.

45   Alpher, R.A., & Herman, R. 1948, *Microwave Radiation from the Big Bang*, Nature, 263;z775-778.

46   As the Universe expands, space is created, causing light rays to stretch out and become less energy dense and red-shifted which conserves the total amount of energy in the Universe.

47   High-energy radiation tends to be blue and low energy radiation, red.

Rather than asking the question, "Can something be made out of nothing?" Gott and Li ask, "Can something make itself?" General relativity allows this to be a legitimate question for if a black hole can trap light, it can trap time.[48] If a black hole can bend light upon itself, it can also bend time upon itself. The authors postulate a period in the early Universe when it contained a region of closed timelike curves (CTC).[49] A CTC can be viewed as a trajectory or path of time that is not linear but rather circular and thus turned upon itself, so that time in a CTC does not have a forward direction or arrow, but turns in a circle, such as has been shown mathematically to occur in a black hole as a result of the extreme curvature of space-time resulting from the large mass and gravity of the black hole.

Inside the event horizon of the black hole there exists another horizon, called the Cauchy[50] horizon. Its presence has been mathematically verified. Inside the Cauchy horizon, predictions of motion cannot be made and conditions are such that CTC's may exist within its boundaries. Near to the Cauchy horizon (or sometimes coincident with it) is the 'chronology horizon', which is the actual boundary within which CTC's occur. In this region of space-time, it is possible for objects to move in a time trajectory or path that takes the object back to where it was previously situated in time, thus, making time travel theoretically possible but, more importantly for our purposes, this allows for self-causality.[51] It is to be noted that both the Cauchy and chronology horizons within the event horizon are still outside the black hole's singularity and, therefore, are available for mathematical analysis. Recall that the black hole itself can only be described in terms of its mass, gravity, electrical charge and angular momentum. Outside of the singularity, more can be determined and this allows for mathematical analyses dealing with the concept of self-causality.[52] It would be impossible for any being to survive within the event or Cauchy horizons. The physics of this region would disassemble any body in the region. However, elementary matter could persist, at least until it reaches the black hole's singularity. There are very extreme physical conditions, which develop at the Cauchy

48   Light and time are coupled. Each moves at the same speed.

49   Lobo, F., & Crawford, P. 2002, *Time, Closed Timelike Curves and Causality*, http://www.zamandayolculuk.com/cetinbal/Timecurves.html.

50   Augustine Louis Cauchy (1789-1857): a French mathematician best known for his work on refining calculus and wave theory.

51   Physics Forums, 2005, *What is the Significance of the Cauchy Horizon?* http://www.physicsforums.comarchive/topic/t-52876.

52   Deforms, M. 2001, *Stability and Instability of the Cauchy Horizon for the Spherically Symmetric Einstein-Maxwell-Scalar Field Equation*, Ann. Mathematics, 158:875-925. Deforms uses the Einstein-Maxwell solution to Einstein's Field Equation on which to base his conclusions.

horizon.[53] Light is pulled into the black hole with such force that it becomes blue-shifted, that is, it is compressed into a higher frequency waveform. This causes the light to become much more energetic. As noted earlier, as the star is evolving into a black hole, it implodes causing the matter of the star to explode outward in a rebound fashion. This inflowing blue-shifted light meets the out-flowing matter at the Cauchy horizon. There is a great deal of energy at the Cauchy horizon. As a result of this interaction its density approaches infinity and, at least by one model, there develops what is called 'mass inflation'. In other words, mass is created at the Cauchy horizon out of this tremendous pool of energy.[54] This mass inflation is capable of producing, "a large volume of inflationary matter, little pieces of which resemble the starting piece (of the Universe and) …there is the possibility of forming 'baby universes'…where new pieces of inflating states are formed". If one of these later inflating pieces simply turns out to be the inflating piece that one started out with (at the Big Bang) then the Universe can be its own mother." [55] This is all very counterintuitive and there are arguments on both sides of this debate. Nonetheless, Gott and Li provide mathematical proof for their self-causing Universe.[56] They conclude that we live in an "oscillating Universe", that is, one that goes from Big Bang to Big Crunch[57] The Field Equation underlies all their mathematical speculations. Einstein's General Theory has been verified time and time again and its mathematical consequences deserve serious consideration.

THEORIES OF COSMOGONY

In classifying the several views of creation, there appear to be three options available to the theologian, philosopher and/or cosmologist: (1) a finite Universe created by some power (God?) at some time (in or out of time?) in the past; (2) a Universe existing eternally from the past and

---

53   Brady, P. R., et al. 1992, *Cauchy Horizon Singularity without Mass Inflation*, Physical Review, 97:60-64.

54   This is determined by Einstein's famous formula: $E = mc^2$ in which energy E and mass m are interchangeable.

55   Op. cit. Gott III, J. R., & Li, L. 1998.

56   The mathematical formulations they use will not be reviewed here but is detailed in their paper cited above.

57   Their Universe begins with a Big Bang, expands for several billion years and then, by gravity and other forces, collapses into a Big Crunch which, in turn, re-expands once again, beginning with a Big Bang–doing so indefinitely. But each new Big Bang is the Universe creating itself by closed timelike curves and mass inflation. In their system there need not be a singularity at the center of the Big Bang because the mass expansion simply tunnels back into time via a closed timelike curve.

extending eternally into the future; or (3) a Universe that creates itself and possibly many (even an infinite number) of universes (multiverse). Most people are reasonably comfortable with the idea of God creating the Universe. This concept has a long cultural and literary history and is a tenet of nearly all traditional religions. The Bible and the Qur'an tell us this is how it happened. Such a view also fits with our concept of cause and effect, which seems self-evident to us. All our past experiences argue for a beginning and an end to all natural things. Aristotle said that all sublunary objects are constructible and destructible. All things, living and non-living come into being and, in due course, pass away.

This first (theistic) school of thought, obviously, has a strong religious flavor especially with the strict creationists but there is also a sizeable group of creationists who, though believing in God, accept a role for physical laws in the creation process. In the deistic view, God is the ultimate cause of all things but creation need not have occurred in six days as a result of the creative will of the deity. The Universe could have been set in motion by God but allowed to evolve according to the laws of nature.

The second way of explaining the existence of our Universe was first enunciated by Aristotle in his *Physics* and later espoused by Einstein. Their cosmology gets around the whole issue of causality and, thus, avoids the problems inherent in positing a beginning to the Universe. Aristotle simply denied that the Universe had been created. It existed, in his view, from eternity and will persist eternally into the future. God was the unmoved mover of Aristotle's system but this divine power applied only to movement and change within the Universe rather than to its origins. Many atheists opt for an uncreated, self-moving Universe although the Big Bang theory has cast doubt on the whole idea of an eternal Universe. It appears that the Universe is expanding and recent Supernovae 1A studies seem to confirm this view. The cosmos may not be static, as Einstein once believed but had a finite beginning and though it may expand forever, it started at some point. In other words, it has not always existed.

The third explanation that has been suggested for the existence of the Universe is that it is self-caused. This at first seems to be the least attractive option. This notion goes against common sense and all intuitive images of our world. Reason immediately shouts out, "How can anything create itself?" We know of nothing that can do so. Nothing in our experience suggests such a possibility–the whole idea of self-causality is counterintuitive–many would say even laughable. So how can we determine which is the best theory to explain how the entire Universe came to be? As Robert Nozick puts it, "Why is there something rather than nothing?" [58]

CONCLUSIONS

As noted above, most (at least 70% by recent polls) Americans hold to some type of creationism. This is a God-created Universe. God, in spite of constitutional limitations, pervades our lives in America. Every penny we handle proclaims, "In God we trust". We often say, "Thank God" or "By God" or use more profane statements to emphasize our feelings. There is an ongoing debate about God in schools and religious representation of the Ten Commandments in public buildings or on public grounds. It is not my purpose to debate the propriety of such issues but only to point out the pervasiveness of a deity in our society. There have been many who argue against the existence of God, nonetheless, the idea of God remains strong in the minds of most Americans. Strict creationism would seem to be the most restrictive of all the theories of cosmogony. Fort-five percent of Americans believe in strict creationism. Evolution on the other hand, offers the advantage of scientific research in support of the physical bases for the workings of the world, Both Popes Pius XII and John Paul II have proclaimed the Big Bang theory as not incompatible with Roman Catholic theology.[59] So a God-derived Universe is a widely held view based primarily on Scripture, tradition and faith.

The Aristotelian, atheistic view is also an attractive approach to this problem because it avoids the whole issue of creation and somehow the idea of an eternal Universe has wide appeal. It is the mainstay of atheists for whom an eternal Universe makes more sense than an eternal God. For many theists and deists'[60] God is eternal, so why not make the world eternal? This saves one step in the sequence of causes.

Of the three explanations, self-causality creates the most controversy. It seems far more counterintuitive and it is harder to get an intellectual or emotional grip on such a concept. How can someone or something create itself? On the other hand, the idea of an eternal world is also counterintuitive. The notion of infinity is also counterintuitive. As we have seen, however, many concepts in science are counterintuitive, yet, they have been proven to

58   Nozick, R. 1981, *Philosophical Explanations* (Cambridge, MA: Harvard University Press). Chapter 2.
59   Ibid.
60   Theists believe that God made the world maintains it and has a personal interest in it, whereas the deists see God as creator of the Universe who, then, lets the laws of nature take over its evolution and maintenance.

be valid.[61] The notion of eternity, a subtype of infinity, however, cannot be empirically proven or intuitively grasped. Aristotle's concept of an eternal Universe is no more provable or intuitive than the concept of God or a self-caused Universe.

The reality of black holes has been demonstrated with a high degree of mathematical and observational certitude. The idea of CTC's within a black hole has also withstood the test of mathematical scrutiny, though as of yet, have not been observationally verified. The mathematics of CTC's is based on Einstein's Field Equation, which has withstood the test of time and rigorous empirical science and, therefore, is more intellectually plausible than even the notion of God.

So the question arises: "Which of the three theories of creation is best supported by their various warrants?" The biblical God, though historically, culturally and emotionally attractive, is based solely on faith, the Bible and tradition and is, in the light of strict logic, only magic and myth. One person's myth is another person's sacred doctrine. If one is to objectively evaluate the concept of God, it is no more intuitive and certainly no more empirical than self-causality. God is the self-caused cause of theology and how does this logically differ from a self-caused Universe except that we have some mathematical and physical data to support a self-caused Universe. Similarly, infinite time, that is, eternity, is counterintuitive and logically no more tenable than the concept of God. It is based on philosophical speculation alone. It is a metaphysical concept with only speculative 'reason' for its warrant. Many such philosophical concepts have been shown, over the centuries, to be fallacious. Without some form of empirical verification such 'rational' theories are always suspect–history has shown this to be true over and over again. A self-caused Universe, on the other hand, though non-intuitive and more novel than the other two theories is based on some mathematical and empirical data. The theory of General Relativity, though initially purely a mathematical construct, has been verified in many empirical ways and continues to provide a solid explanation for the macrocosm. If one can overcome the emotional attachment to the first two theories that so many of us learned as children, it may be possible to look more favorably upon self-causality as a viable explanation for the world we live in.

The purpose of this book, as noted before, is not to confirm or deny the existence of God but to reformulate our idea of creation and of God. It is not possible to prove the existence of God but if Thomas Aquinas is right and if God exists, we can in some limited respect come to a definition

---

61   Op. cit. Lisker, R. 2003.

of God based on the world around us.[62] What surfaces from our study of nature does not yield an anthropomorphic God who creates by fiat. Rather, a picture emerges of a deity that works by wonderful, mysterious methods that we are only beginning to understand and may never fully comprehend. God takes on a fuller, more magnificent stature as viewed through the eyes of the scientist and especially the cosmologist. The more our vision of the Universe expands, so will that vision we call God. In the final analysis, the causality utilized by God to create the Universe may not be the causality we have for so long, embraced.

It is crucial to rid ourselves of any kind of AG. The theists are emotionally tied to a loving, personal God. This view of God is comforting. The atheists hate institutional religion almost more than they hate the notion of God. They are repulsed by the apparent irrationality of the theist's God as demonstrated by neo-atheists such a Dawkins. Freethinkers generally find their religious experiences to have been very negative and rebel against all the rigidity and unchristian attitudes and behaviors found in the religions of history.

It is only by developing a new vision of the universal higher power that we can get away from many of these 'hot-button' roadblocks to a realistic definition of God. The key to this is in totally revising our idea of God. We have to find God where IT is–in the world around as wondrous and mystifying as it is. It is nigh impossible to think in other than anthropomorphic terms but if we are to find a meaningful God this is absolutely essential. We must shed concepts like intelligence, rational, personal, providential, caring and the 'mind of God' when defining a proper God. God is nothing like we humans. Thomas Aquinas said this eight hundred years ago but neither he nor we that have followed him have really believed this. It is time to think outside of the anthropomorphic divine 'box'.

In the next chapter we will examine the microscopic world. Relativity deals with the 'big picture' but quantum mechanics explores the atomic and sub-atomic realm. As we shall see, this takes us into territory that few totally understand. Its concepts are even less intuitive and comprehensible than those of relativity theory. We know mathematically and experimentally that quantum theory describes a real domain. Its claims have been verified time and time again. Nonetheless, the concepts it provides are counterintuitive

---

62   Thomas Aquinas, 1948, *The Principles of Nature*, in *An Introduction to the Philosophy of Nature*, trans. R.A. Kocourek (St. Paul, MN.: North Central Publishing Co.). Aquinas says we can know God analogically. God is 'good' and we, as humans, know 'good'. The attribution of good as applied to God and to humans, however, can only be achieved by analogy. Nonetheless, this allows some species of knowledge of God. Nature can, thus, provide a better vision of God.

even more than those of relativity. Because of these quantum 'mysteries' the physical world appears even more mystical and the notion of God becomes more mysterious and awesome as well.

MORE OF THE MYSTICAL, PHYSICAL WORLD

CHAPTER 10

THE QUIZZICAL QUANTUM

Of all the mystical, physical sciences, quantum physics is undoubtedly the most puzzling. It provides more mystifying concepts than even relativity theory. Its many mysteries make it a subject of debate for physicists, philosophers and theologians. Quantum theory brings into question the very idea of certitude as well as the notion of absolutes–concepts that, for many theologians are necessary underpinnings for most religious tenets. The very idea of God may come under attack if quantum theory is as valid as many claim it to be.

Religions are full of mysteries, for example, the Trinity, divinity of Christ, the virgin birth, Christ's Resurrection, the nature of sin, free will, election and predestination, grace, the problem of evil, Heaven and Hell among many other faith-based beliefs. These are but a few of the often widely held but poorly defined concepts that provide the bases for all Christian sects. These are irresolvable issues that baffle the best of religious thinkers and generate a host of contentious, often contrary views. In a way, quantum physics has had a similar history. Einstein, to his dying day, believed that God did not play dice, that is, chance was not part of the workings of the world. Einstein's universe had to be deterministic and common sense could not be ignored in favor of counterintuitive notions as found in quantum theory. Einstein, Niels Bohr (1885-1962) and Werner Heisenberg (1901-1976) carried on a debate over the course of several decades regarding the 'incompleteness' of quantum theory. In Einstein's view, there had to be what he called 'hidden variables' that, in the end, would explain the apparent randomness of this new system–a system that Einstein himself had helped to create. It turns out that both religion and quantum physics are full of many puzzles. The difference between these two disciplines, however, is that quantum mechanics, though as puzzling as theology, provides a path out of its maze of mysteries. Scientists can and have performed experiments that confirm quantum hypotheses. Religion has no such solutions for its disparate dogmas. Based on faith alone, encumbered by the dualism of the supernatural as opposed to the natural world, there is no valid, empirical way to resolve the many disputed doctrines that constitute religion's holy writings that have developed over the centuries. Quantum theory and science in general have only compounded the difficulties inherent in these many theological conundrums. For at least a thousand years, science and religion have battled one another.[1] Roger Bacon,[2] Nicolas Copernicus,[3] Giordano Bruno[4] and Galileo Galilei[5] are but a few of the players in the ongoing struggle between science and religion that continues today with Creationism and evolution, stem cell research etc. The so-called New Atheists, such as Richard Dawkins, Sam Harris and Christopher Hitchens have mounted an intense polemic against the concept of God and religion as an institution.[6] Quantum theory, more than any prior scientific advance, poses the most potentially devastating threat to traditional religion. Copernicus and Galileo questioned biblical concepts concerning the centrality of Earth and humans in God's plan. Religion has survived the heliocentric revolution. Can it surmount the collapse of certitude and absolutes? Victor Stenger in *Quantum Gods* maintains there is no place for the supernatural today.[7]

Paradoxically, quantum theory may provide religion with answers to some of its major theological issues. Authors such as John Polkinghorne[8] and Stuart Kaufman[9] claim God and religion still have a place in the world of modern physics.

If one is to believe Lee Smolin, a battle of sorts, is currently ongoing in physics.[10] String Theory is a mathematical construct that may provide

1   Draper, J. W. 2009, *History of the Conflict Between Religion and Science* (Cambridge, UK: Cambridge University Press).

2   Bacon, R. 1998, *Opus Magnus*, trans. R. Belle (New York: Kesinger).

3   Rosen, E. 1984, *Copernicus and the Scientific Revolution* (Malabar, FL: Robert E. Krieger Publishing).

4   White, M. 2002, *The Pope and the Heretic* (New York: HarperCollins).

5   MacLauchlan, J. 1997, *Galileo Galilei* (London: Oxford University Press).

6   Haught, J. F. 2008, *God and the New Atheism* (Louisville, KY: Westminster John Knox Press).

7   Stenger, V. J. 2009, *Quantum Gods* (Amherst, NY: Prometheus Books).

8   Polkinghorne, J. 2009, *Quantum Physics and Theology: An Unexpected Kinship* (New Haven, CT: Yale University Press).

9   Kaufman, S. 2008, *Reinventing the Sacred: A New View of Science, Reason, and Religion* (New York: Basic Books).

10   Smolin, L. 2006, *The Trouble with Physics: The Rise of String Theory, the Fall of a Science and What Comes Next* (Boston, MA: Houghton Mifflin).

a way to unite the four forces of nature under one system–the so-called General or Grand Unifying Theory. As noted earlier, there are four forces that hold the Universe together, so to speak. These are electromagnetic radiation (light, radio waves, ultraviolet waves, etc.), the strong nuclear force that binds together the nucleus of every atom, the weak force related to radioactive decay and gravity. Physicists have united all but gravity. String theorists claim they have brought gravity into the physical fold. There are, however, problems with String Theory according to Smolin. The main of these difficulties is the lack of experimental evidence to support String Theory. There have been no experiments attempted or even proposed, to empirically establish the real world applicability of String Theory. Smolin suggests that this has led to acrimonious discussions and polarization of String Theorists versus researchers in other fields of physics.

The virtues or vices of String Theory will, in due course, be sorted out, not so with religion. The latter has no tools with which to resolve issues of belief. Faith is faith and it has no ultimate arbiter except the Bible. However, the Scriptures raise more questions than they resolve.[11] Theologians of the various sects have not been able to reach a consensus regarding dozens of theological issues using the Bible or any other faith-based resource. One might even say that theologians over the centuries have been most unchristian, uncharitable, scandalous, slanderous and even murderous in attacking their peers in the name of God. They are their own worst enemies but science may provide some help for religion in its persistent search for 'truth'. Theologians very often claim absolute dogmatic certitude but can rarely, if ever, manage to delineate dogma in a manner acceptable to all Christian combatants. Quantum mechanics, Polkinghorne maintains, can help in the pursuit of religious truth.[12]

QUANTUM MYSTERIES

There are many quantum concepts that are difficult to accept and these usually defy human imagination. Most physicists admit they cannot intuitively comprehend many of its basic notions. Some say that only a handful of physicists really understand this discipline. Quantum phenomena can be defined mathematically and experiments over the past century have established quantum mechanics as a vital facet of physics. Relativity covers the macroscopic world and quantum theory the microscopic realm.

---

11   Erhman, B. D. 2007, *Misquoting Jesus: The Story Behind Who Changed the Bible and Why* (San Francisco: Harper One).

12   Op. cit. Polkinghorne, J. 2007.

Combining these two has turned out to be a difficult task; one yet to be completed.

Three concepts are key to the field of quantum mechanics: the uncertainty principle, particle-wave duality and entanglement. I'll try to briefly and simply outline each as best I can. These are discussed in order to expand our idea of God and in the process, reevaluate the traditional definitions of God as discussed in Part I. My hope is that we might formulate a clearer, more rational concept of God–a definition, which though still mysterious, does justice to God's greatness, while, at the same time, helping to resolves the problem of dualism in theology, beginning with the supernatural/natural dichotomy that appears to be the pivotal dualistic puzzle facing theologians and scientists alike as discussed in chapter 5.

THE UNCERTAINTY PRINCIPLE

In 1927, Werner Heisenberg (1901-1976) demonstrated mathematically that we cannot simultaneously determine both the position and the momentum of an atomic particle.[13] The reason for this uncertainty relates to the effect that the observer has on either the position or momentum of the particle under study. If a researcher looks at a particle using an instrument that employs a photon ('light ray'), in order to determine the particle's position, the photon will affect the momentum of the particle making the exact value of its momentum unknowable On the other hand, if one measures a particle's momentum, its position will be altered making position indeterminate. The smaller the particle under study, the shorter must be the wavelength of the light used to detect position or momentum of the particle. The smaller an object is, the more precise a tool must be in order to study it. For example, one would find that a tape measure is inadequate to measure the size of a bacterium. Using light to measure position or momentum of a very small object, such as an electron, means that if the wavelength of the optic measuring instrument is too long, it is too 'big' to measure a very small object. It would be like a tape measure whose distance markers are one sixteenth of an inch. Such an interval is simply too large to measure a bacterium accurately. A more precise caliper is needed. With a beam of light, the peaks of each wave need to be the same size or smaller than the particle under study. However, the shorter the wavelength, the higher the energy it possesses. This energy will alter the position or momentum

---

13   Ibid, pp. 101-9. The uncertainty principle is stated: $\Delta x \Delta p_x \geq h/4\pi$. The left-sided components are the uncertainties in position and momentum; h is Planck's constant $= 6.626176 \times 10^{-34}$ Js. Momentum is defined mathematically as $p = mv$, where p is the momentum, m is the mass of the moving object and v is its velocity (speed and direction).

of the particle making determination of the other parameter inaccurate. We can check the position and momentum of a locomotive because the light used is so much less energetic and less massive (light has no mass) than the locomotive so that it has little effect on either its position or momentum. The light won't knock the locomotive off its track or slow it down. In the microcosm of atomic particles, however, there is always uncertainty–not an intuitive concept for us who expect predictability in observations of the natural world.

This uncertainty calls into question the whole concept of predictability. Theologians balk at this idea. They see the world as divinely ordered and prefer some degree of determinism in nature–not too much determinism, of course, because this would eliminate the idea of free will, sin, rewards, punishments, Heaven and Hell etc. These are concepts thoroughly etched into the minds of most theologies. Denying absolutes would present a major problem and undermine many of the basic ethical tenets of traditional religion. On the other hand, God does not play dice. According to Einstein, IT has knowledge of and control over all things. God designed the world in a precise way and God is sovereign over all. We've seen that Luther made this an essential element in his theology. To make God's creation a fickle construct would knock the stilts out from under many Christian beliefs.

Gottfried Wilhelm Leibniz (1646-1716), philosopher and mathematician, claimed that God had made this the 'best of all possible worlds'.[14] If God is omniscient, omnipotent and perfect in all ways, so must be ITs handiwork. Such a God cannot tolerate indeterminism. To be knowable implies that the world, like its maker, is orderly and rational. This is the classic MG as discussed in chapter 2. Thus, quantum physics presents problems for the theist. Once again, science is at loggerheads with religion. Though the Pope has accepted evolution as consistent with Scripture, to my knowledge he has not made a statement regarding quantum theory. Stephen Hawking makes mention of an encounter he had with the Pope at a Vatican conference several years ago. The Pope suggested that cosmologists should not inquire into the Big Bang itself. Their research ought to be limited to events after this initial creative act since creation, including the Big Bang is the business of only God and theologians. Because much of Big Bang theory deals with quantum and relativity concepts, it may be that this gives us some insight into the Church's attitude toward the new physics. In a way, the Pope may have a point. It is known, for example, that the laws of physics, as currently understood, do not apply to the first fraction of a second after

---

14   A concept lampooned by Blaise Pascal in *Candide*.

the Big Bang.[15] Maybe this is when God's creative work took place. Who is to say? At any rate, these quantum questions raise theological issues that stir endless debates. Did God have a 'hand' [16] in creation and, if so, how big is God's 'hand'? Is a divine 'hand' always at work in nature? Does God play dice or is ITs role only as an observer of a random, counterintuitive, mystical world that is forever beyond our understanding and maybe even the comprehension of the divine 'intellect'? Can we countenance a God who is not omniscient and omnipotent? These are difficult questions for the majority of people who look for a benevolent, all-perfect divine father who they hope will guide them through this earthly veil of tears. There is already too much uncertainty in our lives and now we are told that the very foundations of our Universe rest 'firmly' on quicksand!

Some would say that Heisenberg's uncertainty principle only applies to the microscopic and not macroscopic world and therefore need not concern theologians or more specifically ethicists. However, our macroscopic world begins in the microscopic realm. Human consciousness, reason, decision-making and ultimately ethics are based on the workings of the brain. The brain in turn is a complex network of atoms, molecules, nerve cells (neurons), interconnections (synapses), electrical and chemical reactions that are microscopic in scope and this is where Heisenberg's uncertainty principle functions. If there is a soul, as theologians believe, it must interact with this neuro-chemical microcosm. The soul cannot bypass nerves, chemicals and electrical impulses. It does not act directly on the brain or muscles.

Not only the physical world but also our biological and psychological worlds are uncertain. Human behavior cannot be predicted with absolute certitude. We live in a probabilistic Universe. Behaviors can be predicted in a given population, however, what an individual will do in any given situation cannot be determined with certainty. Human behavior very often follows irrational patterns, making decisions that are not based on measured reason. Ariely's *Predictably Irrational* [17] describes many of these behaviors as relate to the economy, however, such irrationality extends to all aspects of human life. What we do depends on many factors that are often unconscious, seemingly random and irrational.

---

15   Planck's time is 1 X 10^{-43} second after the Big Bang begins; that's a decimal point with 42 zeros and a 1 after it. The laws of physics as we know them do not apply during this brief period of time. A very brief time during which God may have done ITs creative thing.
16   A 'hand' in creation is another one of those forbidden divine anthropomorphisms–sorry once again about this mental lapse!
17   Ariely, D. 2010, *Predictably Irrational: The Hidden Forces That Shape Our Decisions* (New York: Harper).

Moralists generally opt for ethical absolutes. The fact is that ethics is constantly changing. Slavery was acceptable into the nineteenth century. Even the Bible speaks of slavery in amoral terms.[18] Women were denied the vote. Early on they were economic inferiors to their husbands (and probably still are in many situations). Being 'drawn and quartered' was an acceptable form of capital punishment in the United Kingdom until 1814.[19] Most European countries now consider capital punishment unacceptable. Burning at the stake was allowed by both Catholic and Protestant theologians. It was once a mortal sin for Catholics to eat meat on Fridays. Dying with this sin on one's soul meant Hell fire for all eternity. I often wonder what has happened to all these Friday meat-eaters? Are they still burning in Hell or have they received a reprieve? Eternal suffering in Hell is the punishment meted out to both murderers and masturbators–this hardly seems fair especially since I was never a murderer though was a ....! Most Jews and Christians consider the Ten Commandments as the standard of morality. Initially, the Jews believed the Decalogue applied only to the treatment of fellow Jews. For gentiles anything including murder and rape was allowed. Joshua killed everyone in Jericho save Rehab, a prostitute, and her family (Joshua 6:24). Even the commandment, "Thou shalt not kill" is not absolute. Self-defense, capital punishment, wartime killing and abortion are all legal and considered moral by many. In 2007, 55% favored Roe v. Wade, 43% opposed it and 2% were undecided.[20] Michael Servetus was put to death by Calvin and Giordano Bruno was dispatched by the Catholic Church–both for their views on the Trinity. Isaac Newton hid his views regarding the Trinity for fear he would suffer a similar fate. Today we have the Unitarians and Bishop John Spong (a retired Episcopal bishop) who deny the Trinity and go untouched. Now we have relativity, the uncertainty principle and probability theory all telling us things are not absolute.

MORE UNCERTAINTY

There is not always a defined cause and effect relationship evident in the Lilliputian atomic world studied by physicists. Events may and often do occur randomly. One example of this is found in what is called 'tunneling'. This phenomenon is called tunneling because it is as if an atomic particle

---

18   Genesis 20:14: "Then Abimelech brought sheep and cattle and male and female slaves and gave them to Abraham, and he returned Sarah his wife to him."

19   Drawn and quartered involved, first hanging until nearly dead, then disembowelment, genital excision for men and finally amputation of arms and legs. Nobles were beheaded as a more humane method of punishment.

20   ABC news and Washington Post poll.

that needs to jump over an energy 'fence' in order to get on the other side of this 'fence' actually tunnels under it without using the energy it takes to jump over. A particle, such as an electron, therefore, may appear in places that it is not supposed to be, at least according to classic Newtonian physics. For an electron to move from a lower energy level, for example, in one orbit around the nucleus of an atom to a higher energy level farther away from the nucleus, requires additional energy. At times, however, an electron or other particle will show up where it isn't supposed to be because the energy for the move has not been supplied to the particle. Erwin Schrödinger (1887-1961) in 1927 developed an equation that describes the probability that a particle will be detected in one of several positions at any given moment. This is referred to as his 'wavefunction' even though it is not a true wave but rather a probability pattern that describes where a particle might be found at any given time, depending on when one looks for the particle. Schrödinger's wavefunction explains why a particle may be detected in places that it shouldn't be if there were only Newtonian physics running the Universe. It is Schrödinger's equation that describes particle tunneling.

The same thing is seen in radioactive decay where there is a specific half-life for any given radioactive elementary isotope.[21] A half-life, you will recall, is the time it takes for half of a given amount of an element, say, uranium 238, to decay to uranium 235. This happens at a very precise rate but when it comes to an individual atom, it may or may not decay at that rate. As a whole, however, a lump of uranium 238 will follow the predicted rate of decay.[22] Why individual isotopes don't decay smoothly is unknown. The uncertainty principle describes, at least mathematically, all sorts of microscopic events that are not seen in the macroscopic world. After Newton had defined the law of universal gravity and his laws of inertia, the Universe appeared to be deterministic. Everything seemed to happen in a very defined and predictable way.

As a result of Newtonian physics, Pierre Simon Laplace (1749-1827) developed an absolutely deterministic worldview. Everything, including the behavior of humans, seemed etched in stone. If one knew a set of values surrounding an event that occurs in the present, one could theoretically completely describe its past history and predict its future course. However, with the uncertainty principle, things took on a cloak of unpredictability. No one, possibly even God (and some theologians support this view), could

---

21   A radioactive elementary isotope is an atom that will lose one or more neutrons over time thus converting into a lighter form of the same element. U238 will decay to U235 having lost three neutrons in the process. Elements can also decay into other elements. Uranium eventually is converted into lead, for example.
22   Uranium 238 has a half-life of 4.46 billion years.

exactly forecast future events. The Universe was now random, not precisely predictable. This was all very disturbing to many. Einstein was particularly distressed by this prospect and let it get in the way of his accepting quantum theory even though he was one of the founders of quantum theory.

ENTANGLEMENT AND THE EINSTEIN-PODOLSKY-ROSEN PARADOX

Einstein was not philosophically content with the uncertainty of quantum theory and when he was at Princeton in 1935, after fleeing the Nazi threat, he set out to prove the Copenhagen group (Bohr and Heisenberg) wrong. Einstein collaborated with Podolsky and Rosen to show that the relationship between two particles or photons was not uncertain. They began with 'thought experiments'[23] to prove their point. Aristotle, Thomas Aquinas and many other philosophers have held firmly to the concept of 'cause and effect'–nothing could cause itself. The principle of cause and effect has been a time honored one. All of this went by the wayside, at least for the subatomic world, when Niels Bohr and Werner Heisenberg along with Max Planck and others enunciated quantum mechanics. Nonetheless, Einstein was determined to prove these physicists wrong. In their 1935 paper Einstein, Podolsky and Rosen (EPR) proposed that quantum theory had to be 'incomplete' and that there must be 'hidden variables' to explain the 'non-locality' of particles or photons. Non-locality means that particles and photons behave in entirely random disconnected ways. By 'incomplete' EPR meant that there are 'hidden variables,' which if known, would explain uncertainties without the need for quantum concepts. EPR conceded that both position and momentum could not be measured simultaneously in the same particle yet, if two particles were originally connected (entangled), had complementary spins (one clockwise and the other counterclockwise so that their total momentum equaled zero) and they were subsequently separated but maintained this momentum relationship, then in such a particle pair one could measure the position of one particle *A* and know the position of the other particle *B* without measuring *B* directly and likewise one could measure the momentum of particle *B* and then know the momentum of particle *A*. The two particles were thus 'locally' connected even if widely separated. This way one could determine the position and momentum of the

---

23   Giordano Bruno first proposed 'thought experiments' in the 16th century. Bruno, the 'heretic' discussed earlier, was not inclined to mathematical proofs as had been Ptolemy and Copernicus so he resorted to 'thought experiments' that he believed accomplished the same thing, that is, provided a proof for any given proposition he intended to establish without employing mathematics.

two particles and thus could deny Heisenberg's principle of uncertainty. At the same time, this EPR system did not require communication between the two particles and so did not posit communication at speeds faster than that of light, as quantum theory demands. This 'thought experiment' provided measurement of position in one particle and momentum in the other paired particle and thus the observer did not disturb the whole system but mathematically could derive both position and momentum with certainty.

Quantum theory holds that observing the position of a particle disrupts the particle enough to preclude measurement of its momentum. The EPR 'thought experiment' avoids this pitfall by indirectly determining position and momentum off of the opposite particle of the pair. The problem with EPR's solution is that quantum theory states that a particle measured one time has a fifty-fifty chance of spinning one way and a fifty-fifty chance of spinning the opposite way. Its spin is uncertain until observed. Thus, a particle may be found to spin clockwise when first measured but it could be spinning counterclockwise on the next observation. Its paired particle would always spin in the appropriate (opposite) direction as though the one particle is signaling to its partner particle, "Hey, I'm spinning this way so you spin the other way". And with the next measurement, "Hey, now I'm spinning the other way so get with it and spin the opposite way". If one particle A is observed in order to determine position or momentum of the other particle B, fine, but then when one looks at B to determine A's position or momentum there's a fifty-fifty chance its spin and momentum will have changed leaving uncertainty about its paired particle's spin, position and momentum.

To add to the uncertainty and befuddlement, some physicists posit 'ghost' particles or photons. There are two 'ghosts' for each particle: 'ghosts' A_1 and A_2 and B_1 and B_2. When the one 'ghost' is made 'real' by being observed (it isn't really there until the experiment is conducted according to quantum theory) and assuming 'ghost' A_1 was materialized by a toss of the coin (fifty-fifty chance) then the other 'ghost' B_2 would materialize with the opposite spin. The other two 'ghosts' would remain unreal and nonexistent. This is all very counterintuitive but experiments have proven the Copenhagen group right and EPR wrong.

Recall that the communication between particles A and B in quantum physics occurs instantaneously, that is, at super-luminal speeds–faster than the speed of light–though nothing is supposed to move faster than the speed of light according to relativity theory. As noted, this phenomenon is called 'entanglement'.[24] It is not known how two paired particles like electrons can communicate instantaneously even if separated by many millions of miles.

---

24   Op. cit. Aczel, A. D. 2001.

This is another one of these mystical, physical events that defy understanding but I believe tell us something about the 'real' God for whom I am searching.

It is not the mysteries of the Trinity, Incarnation or Resurrection that we should be puzzling over when trying to understand God but rather the mysteries of the world around us that are not only more mysterious but also more interesting. These are puzzles that we can establish as real through empirical science and which in the end are inscrutable–findings that can make our lives more rational and congenial.

WAVE-PARTICLE DUALITY

The nature of light has long puzzled philosophers and scientists alike.[25] Isaac Newton (1642-1727) viewed light as corpuscular (little packets), while Christian Huygens (1629-1695) believed light to be in a waveform. In 1802, Thomas Young demonstrated that light was a wave using a 'double slit' experiment. When light is beamed through two narrow slits onto an observing screen as shown in Fig. 10.1. it can be shown to be a waveform.

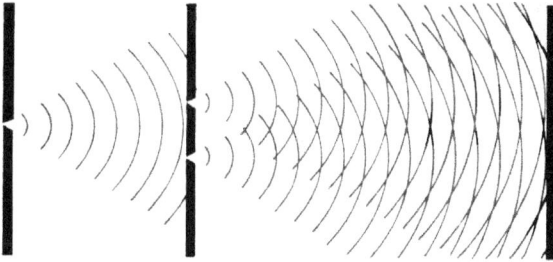

Figure 10.1. Thomas Young's two-slit waveform experiment.

This results in an interference pattern as shown in Fig. 10.2.

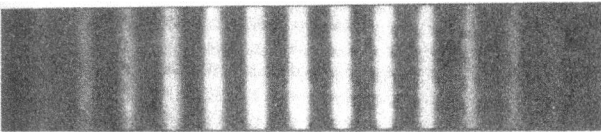

Figure. 10.2. Two slit fringe pattern.

The light waves will be out of sync because they take different paths to the screen. Some wave-peaks will reinforce waves from the other beam of light coming through the second slit creating light lines; some light waves will

25   Park, D. 1997, *The Fire Within the Eye: A Historical Essay on the Nature and Meaning of Light* (Princeton, NJ: Princeton University Press).

interfere with waves from the other slit which accounts for the dark lines. A light-dark 'fringe' pattern is thus formed.

That light travels as waves rather than particles became physical 'gospel' until the twentieth century when Max Planck found light to be corpuscular. Now instead of light waves, physicists spoke of photons (packets of light). If only one slit is used it was noted that the pattern seen was of a particulate nature (multiple dots of light appeared on the observing screen), indicating that light came in particles rather than waves in which case the characteristic light-dark interference pattern should not develop even if two slits are used.

The situation was to become more complicated, however when Louis de Broglie (1892-1987), who had been studying waveforms, became a quantum enthusiast. It was during his doctoral studies in 1923 that he stumbled onto the notion of a universal duality of waves and particles. He was a musician, aware of harmonic theory and the unity of waves and particles like a musical string with waves superimposed on it. He saw Bohr's model of the atom as an example of this duality. Electrons were, in his view, like particles whizzing around the atom's nucleus but at the same time the atom's electron shell or 'cloud' was vibrating vigorously. In fact, he extended this concept to all bodies. Every material object was both a wave and a particle he claimed. Broglie expressed this relationship using Planck's constant. The momentum of a particle times its wavelength is equal to Planck's constant. Momentum is mass times velocity, so this contains the particulate aspect while at the same time the body also possessed a waveform.[26] Like Einstein's $E = mc^2$, matter and energy are the same thing just in different forms. So particles and waves are the same, just in two different forms. By Planck's formula, it turns out that mass and wavelength are inversely related. Thus, a large body like that of a human has a very small waveform but a large mass. Because our mass is so large, the body's waveform is virtually imperceptible. Because light particles (photons) have essentially zero mass, its waveform is its most prominent feature, i.e. little mass, big waves.

In the latter half of the twentieth century, other traditional particles like electrons, neutrons and atoms were studied for their waveforms and all were found to possess both a waveform and mass (and since they are all moving, also momentum). The bigger the momentum (mass time velocity)

---

26   Planck had formulated the quantum in terms of energy and wave frequency: E = hn, where *E* is the energy of a particle, *h* is Planck's constant, 6.626 X10^{-34} jeules and *n* (Greek nu) is the wave frequency (so many peaks per second). This is equivalent to Broglie's equation p = h/l, where *p* is the momentum, *h* Planck's constant and *l* the wavelength. Since frequency and wavelength are inversely related, Planck's constant is divided by the wavelength.

the shorter the wavelength. This duality is well established experimentally and indicates that all energy forms and all objects in nature are both waves and bodies at the same time. We don't think of ourselves as waves but that's because we are too big a body to perceive our waveform using the five senses. Again this is all very counterintuitive stuff. How can an object be a particle and a wave at the same time?

But wait, wait, there's more mystery. The two-slit experiment clearly shows that light comes in waves. The one slit experiment shows that light comes in packets. However, things become much more complicated if one sends only a single photon at a time through the two slits. It turns out in doing this, that over time the interferences fringe pattern shown in Fig. 10.2 will gradually develop. So even though the photons are not passing through the two slits at the same time, they seem to have a memory that will allow for 'retroactive' interference and thus the occurrence of fringes even though classical physics requires two overlapping waves as seen in Fig. 10.1. In 1979, John Wheeler showed that even if the experimenter delayed the decision about a one slit versus a two slit experiment until after a photon had passed through a single slit and then opened the second slit later, the pattern seen could be changed. So if a photon was sent through one slit and then later a second photon was sent through the other slit the pattern that develops changes after the fact as though the photons have memories! It's all very 'weird' as my grandchildren would say.

We know that any thing traveling at the speed of light does so timelessly. Thus, a photon passing through one slit does so 'out of time', so to speak. The second photon passing through the other slit later is also 'timeless'. It may be that the two photons don't have memories but both pass 'timelessly' through the two slits and thus can form a fringe pattern after the fact even if they go through the two slits at different times according to our 'in time' perspective. Strange business, indeed!

This wave-particle duality is obviously another one of the mysteries of physics–a mystery we can't visualize but can empirically confirm. This duality is one more awesome aspect of nature to be marveled at and pondered. These are more 'divine' mysteries if you will.

A FEW OTHER THINGS TO PONDER

Not long ago I was walking along a wharf in San Diego looking down at ocean waves rolling onto the beach. By checking the seaweed floating in the water, it was obvious that the waves move in with rhythmic regularity but the water and many things suspended in the water don't move much at all. There is something moving the water up and down in a typical waveform but what is this something? We would say it is energy, mostly supplied by wind blowing over the ocean water from hundreds of mile west of San Diego. But again, just what is this energy that moves through the water making waves without pushing the water forward very much? It's not electrical energy. It's wind energy, as we now know because this form of energy is being harnessed to generate electrical energy. But what is wind energy? Well the Sun's radiant heat and the motion of the Earth cause it. But when you get right down to it, we can describe wind energy or any other form of energy but can't really intuit it. Electricity is said to be electrons moving along copper wires. But what moves the electrons–an electrical potential–but what exactly is electrical potential? After watching the waves with their mesmerizing qualities and pondering these mysteries for some time, I gave up the pursuit of energy and followed my wife, son, David, and daughter-in-law, Paki, back home.

The nerve cells (neurons) transmit electrical energy via moving ions like K^+, Ca^{++} or Na^+ but what is the energy that moves these ions? We know that negatively charged particles attract positively charged ones but why? We speak of electromagnetic waves such as light waves but how are electricity and magnetism connected. James Clark Maxwell described this relationship mathematically 150 years ago but do his formulae really tell us what electromagnetic energy is?

We are all familiar with Einstein's famous equation, $E = mc^2$. This tells us that energy is equal to the mass of an object times the speed of light squared. So mass and energy are interchangeable. We all know this. The first atomic bombs worked this way. Uranium was converted into energy and the most destructive weapon ever made came into being. We all think we know what mass is. It's something hard and tangible. And we all know what energy is; it moves things. But the fact is that atoms that make up 'hard, tangible' objects are mostly empty space. And as we've just seen, energy isn't so easy to understand at its core. Even more puzzling, I think, is, how do we imagine, intuit or think of mass being converted into energy and vice versa? The energy-mass duality may be just as puzzling as the particle-wave duality. Or how can two electrons communicate instantaneously even if millions of miles apart (entanglement). Our world is full of these mysteries that we take for granted just because they are familiar, everyday concepts.

The physical concepts discussed in this and the last chapter are novel and may excite our imagination but there are many other aspects of nature that are commonplace phenomena that if viewed with a new 'eye', not accepting them as we did as children, take on new and puzzling aspects. I believe these puzzles can give us a novel and expanded view of God.

CHAPTER 11

NEO-NATURALISM

THE CHANGING 'FACE' OF GOD

We now turn to Neo-Naturalism and its God. Neo-Naturalism is an approach to the divine that attempts to avoid all the pitfalls of the Gods we have discussed in earlier chapters. It redefines God utilizing nature, including relativity and quantum theory as discussed in chapters 9 and 10 but it also includes some of the simple mysteries of the world around us. At the same time, the Neo-Natural God allows room for the unknown, the mysterious and the spiritual (though not the supernatural). Neo-Naturalism will not meet the needs of all and will certainly raise the ire of some, nonetheless, it offers a view of God that provides for both the rational and animal aspects of human nature. Hopefully it may meet the emotional, psychological and spiritual needs of some traditionally religious souls while providing for the rational requirements of the agnostics and atheists of the world.

Science has been a threat to religion for centuries. Any system that undermines the supernatural world is seen as a direct attack on traditional religions. Plato and Aristotle were considered the 'enemy' at one time until Augustine and later Aquinas 'Christianized' them. With the Enlightenment and its offspring, Deism, science again threatened the theistic God. Leibniz saw Newton's new physics as hacking away at the underpinnings of Christian theology.[1] Newton's laws of motion allowed material bodies to continue moving on their own thus eliminating the need for a supernatural force to maintain the movement of stars and planets. Celestial bodies, following Plato had been viewed as divine or at least as semi-divine angels and Newton now made such supernatural beings superfluous.

John Locke (1632-1704) suggested (though did not unequivocally claim) that matter might be capable of thought–another blow to the supernatural.[2] The soul, angels, God and other spirits were all under siege.

---

1 Stewart, M. 2006, *The Courtier and the Heretic, Leibniz, Spinoza, and the Fate of God in the Modern World* (New York: W. W. Norton & Co.), p. 274.

2 Locke, J. 2007, *An Enquiry Concerning Human Understanding* (Kindle edition).

The Enlightenment also chipped away at the notion of free will. If natural laws ran the Universe as the deists maintained, then did Adam really freely sin by eating that notorious apple?[3] If he didn't sin, then there was no Fall, no Original Sin, no need for salvation or Christ's death on the cross. Under this scenario Christianity was doomed.

Religions and their theologies have evolved over the eons. Animism was gradually transformed into the primitive polytheism and mythology of the Fertile Crescent, Egypt and ancient Greece. Spirits dwelling in trees, streams and all natural things became the gods of the sky, earth, seas, Sun and Moon. These gods were essentially big, strong humans with all the virtues and vices inherent in human nature. With Jewish, Christian and Islamic monotheism, God 'matured' into an infinitely powerful, all-knowing and eternal divinity while retaining some human features along with these newly acquired metaphysical qualities. Monotheism, however, maintained elements of polytheism in the Trinity, Christ's mother, Mary, as almost divine, and the saints who held sway over virtually every aspect of our lives much like the Greek gods. There was, as well, a hint of pantheism with an omnipresent God dwelling in every cubic centimeter of the Universe. The monotheistic God was transcendent and providential–metaphysical and anthropomorphic. This God is likewise the mystical deity of ancient anchoritic monks, Teresa of Avila, Meister Eckhart, Thomas Merton and mystics of all faiths. Karen Armstrong and others believe the only way to know God may be through mystical union with the divine.[4] Accordingly, God cannot be plumbed by reason (*logos*) but only through the mystical experience of God (*mythos*).

The evolution of a Christian monotheistic concept of God came about through the early Church Fathers, the pronouncements of the Nicene and other Church Councils, as well as through the writings of Augustine, Aquinas, Luther, Calvin and many others over the centuries. Karen Armstrong suggests that religion and its tenets have continued to evolve in order to meet the needs of twentieth century believers.[5] John Shelby Spong maintains that we must move beyond the traditional theistic view of God to Post-Theism.[6] Many religious souls would violently disagree with this notion. After all, God is God, absolute and immutable. To think of redefining

---

3   The Bible doesn't explicitly say it was an apple. It might have been one of those strange cumquats.
4   Ibid. Armstrong, K. 1993, Chapter 7.
5   Armstrong, K. 2000, *The Future of God in Christianity in the 21st Century*, ed. D. A. Brown (New York: Crossroads Publishing).
6   Spong, J. S. 2002, *A New Christianity for a New World: Why Traditional Faith is Dying & How a New Faith is Being Born* (San Francisco: HarperOne).

God in any way is anathema, unthinkable and blatantly heretical. Yet there is convincing evidence that the concept of God has changed over time.[7] In spite of the changing 'face' of God, IT has retained many mixed facets making for a God full of contradictions. And though Armstrong and others are indeed right in that a rational awareness of God is not possible as currently defined by the various religions, I believe a rational definition of God based on the Universe as viewed through science can make the 'real' God known to us. Science provides a God that can be approached through reason, never to be fully understood yet available as more than a conflicted theological concept. *Logos* and *mythos* can be complementary in helping us penetrate the divine essence. But to know God as presently defined is impossible because IT is replete with logical inconsistencies that by their very nature defy rational elucidation.

Neo-Naturalism is a system that attempts to redefine God with a view to developing a truly reasoned understanding of God–as far as currently possible. This definition of God is based on the mysteries of nature as found primarily, though not exclusively, in relativity and quantum theory. It utilizes the established mysteries of nature that can potentially fill us with the awe, spiritual feelings and even the mystical sense associated with traditional religions.

The mystical experience is not the sole property of religion. Studies in recent years have demonstrated scientifically that a variety of activities including mediation, yoga, physical exercise, contemplating a mantra etc. are associated with spiritual states. When I peered through my eight inch Schmidt-Cassegraine telescope, viewing myriad celestial objects not visible to the naked eye, I never failed to experience a sense of awe, amazement and spirituality. There are such awe-inspiring wonders everywhere in the Universe! Very few of us have not been captivated by a beautiful picture, new baby or the sight of a loved one. Couples who are united in love when married, filled with joy over a delightful child or (and I think this is the most spiritual of all) when two people have grown old together in love, do indeed find these the times when God comes to them. This is spirituality that cannot be expressed to anyone other than one's partner and then only by a look, a touch, a smile or a belly laugh over something only you and s/he understand. When I am with a patient who is suffering both physically and emotionally and s/he and I become connected as patient and doctor and there is a sense that I care about his or her needs and want to help by listening or by prescribing some helpful medicine; this is a spiritual moment. I believe firmly that these same feelings can be found in the God of Neo-Naturalism.

---

7   [4] Op. cit. Armstrong, K. 1993.

Naturalism is a dirty word for many theists. It smacks of materialism and is seen as atheistic and utterly without spiritual elements, leaving no room for God. But God as imagined by present day religious adherents is mired in a morass of logical inconsistencies and though this traditional God may meet a variety of human needs IT cannot provide for the intellectual fulfillment many seek in their God. Neo-Naturalism can provide for both *logos* and *mythos*. It eliminates the mind-body dualism and the dilemmas found in this and all the dualisms that characterize traditional religions. Neo-Naturalism moves nature beyond the purely mechanical and materialistic realm–it captures the beauty, mystery and spirituality found in the world around us.

Religion has brought community, solace and security to billions over the centuries. Since prehistory men and women have found mysteries, morals, symbolism and satisfaction in myths, monuments, sacred writings and the majesty of liturgy and prayer. Institutional religion has and continues to provide charity for many in need. Before governments were structured well enough to care for those impoverished by sickness, war or famine, the churches did what they could to relieve the woes of souls that suffered from these many misfortunes. The role of deacons in the early Roman Church was to care for the needy. Even today many unfortunates worldwide benefit from the ministrations of dedicated people of faith. Untold millions benefit from the emotional, psychological, material and spiritual help they derive from religion. Religion continues to prosper in the United States and many Third Word countries. It is evident that religion, especially Fundamentalism, is on the upswing. At the same time, church attendance in western countries is on the decline. Evident, too, is the increasing polarization of theological views. People seem to embrace their beliefs with ever increasing stubbornness. The twenty-seven percent or so of 'dyed in the wool' U.S. fundamentalists will not, any time soon, change their minds about the answers religion supplies for the many puzzling mysteries that face them. For these souls traditional beliefs meet all their emotional and intellectual needs. Nonetheless, we must move forward. Religion has and continues to evolve.

Having explored the nature of God and our world in the previous chapters, it is time to define God, as best we can and in the process find out what this higher power is and is not. We seek to discover a rational God that is both emotionally and intellectually satisfying, at least for those who strive to understand the Universe as fully as possible. This search mandates that we accept the God we find even if IT is not made in our image and likeness and even if IT doesn't meet all the human needs we would like IT to meet. This process requires humility of the kind most of us have never before been willing to embrace. Most religions put us humans at the center of the

Universe as God's special creations. According to many, God has made the Universe as our playground. In Genesis we are to have dominion over all the Earth and its creatures:

> Then God said, "Let us make man in our image, in our likeness, so that they may rule over the fish in the sea and the birds in the sky, over the livestock and all the wild animals and over all the creatures that move along the ground (Genesis 1:26).

We would like to believe that *Homo sapiens* is center stage. However, one need only look to the far reaches of the Universe to realize that we are but an infinitesimally tiny part of the Universe. We can no longer be arrogant about who we are and where we fit into creation. We must approach the Universe as humble humans with Earth as a miniscule speck in the cosmos. What happens here on Earth is of little consequence to any but us humans. If there were a God as traditionally defined, IT would be taken up with an infinite array of cosmic issues, much too busy to provide any but a chance glance at this little world we live on. As much as we would like to be *numero uno*, we simply are not top dog.

GOD IS NOT SIMPLE

If God is a supernatural spirit, IT is simple–no working parts–as we've already said. This idea of God as simple goes back to Greek philosophy. What we have seen of the metaphysical God (MG) and supernatural beings makes it difficult to maintain God as a simple spirit. In fact, it is hard to posit a spirit or supernatural being of any sort. There are just too many problems with these Problem Gods. To summarize:

1. A spirit is transcendent, that is, it belongs to other than a physical domain.
2. Such a God, by definition, may be omnipotent and omniscient and able to do anything we want IT to do, except IT cannot logically interact with any of ITs physical creations and still be infinite.
3. An infinite God has no boundaries and thus cannot make contact with other beings. Relationships require contact points.
4. Also, a spirit cannot be infinite. It does not exist in space or time. Infinity can only apply to physical objects.
5. We can construct a God that has all the attributes we want in a God but the 'real' God doesn't have to be any of the things we want IT to have. There is no logical requirement that IT be made in our

image and likeness and, in fact, logically IT can't be so. Such a God is purely speculative and can be nothing more than mythical. IT has no more reality than Santa Claus or the Tooth Fairy. The traditional God meets our emotional needs but not our rational, intellectual needs.

6. An anthropomorphic God (AG) made in our image and likeness cannot be spiritual, infinite or metaphysical. IT cannot be omnipotent and omniscient. IT, therefore, cannot have created and maintained the Universe.

7. God as spiritual cannot be personal and providential. Spirits cannot interact with physical beings. There is no solution for the body-mind duality problem.

8. We only receive information through our five senses. We cannot, therefore, know or interact with spirits because they cannot be sensed.

9. A MG as a simple spirit offers no explanations for how a spirit can perform any tasks on or in a physical world. Everything IT does must be magical, unexplained and thus irrational.

10. There are no possible rational or intellectually comprehensible descriptions of a MG. The infinite is not knowable.

11. A MG cannot be all-powerful because power, force and momentum only apply to material bodies. Power is an anthropomorphic term.

12. To say that a divine spirit can do anything we'd like IT to do is meaningless.

All these objections to God as a simple spirit follow from what has been discussed in earlier chapters. And more objections could undoubtedly be listed. The point is that a supernatural spirit cannot fit the job description required of the God many desire. Neither can an AG. The gods of the Bible, Qur'an and mythology are a result of imaginative wishful thinking. IT may meet our emotional but never our rational needs. In fact, the supernatural as a domain is woefully inadequate in explaining any of the mysteries facing us today. To use the supernatural as an explanation for rational beings fails to meet any standard for truth. I think the supernatural world has to go. This is an unsettling notion but in order to better understand our world including ourselves, I see no alternative. As young people say today, "Get real". Thus, the Neo-Natural God is not a spirit or supernatural.

THE UNIVERSE IS NOT SIMPLE

God is not simple and neither is the Universe. There is no doubt that the Universe is very complex and this complexity begins with subatomic particles and extends to the farthest reaches of the visible and invisible Universe.[8] We can neither imagine a nanometer (one billionth of a meter) nor 13.7 billion light years (the best estimate of the age and size of the Universe). Since the Big Bang, 13.7 billion years have elapsed. Our Earth is so massive (6×10^{24} kilograms[9]–6 with 24 zeros after it); a figure that is impossible for any human to grasp. The Earth pales in comparison to the mass of the Sun, estimated to be 2×10^{30} kilograms (2 with 30 zeros after it). We have looked at these figures earlier. The point is that God has to be equal to all these incomprehensible concepts. God is only definable by this immense Universe of ours.

When people talk about something being infinite there is no way this can have any meaning for us. A mathematician may provide some measure of meaning for the infinite but even this is beyond our comprehension. As mentioned before, many mathematicians have gone mad over the notion of the infinite.[10]

The Universe is not only huge but it is unimaginably diverse. Stars come in many flavors. There are very massive white, hot stars and relatively small and cool red stars. Our Sun on the surface is 'only' about 6000° Kelvin and this is considered 'cool' in stellar terms. There are white dwarf and brown dwarf stars and, as noted, neutron stars. Then there are protostars and dying stars such as red giants (which our Sun will become in 3 or 4 billion years. Some stars repeatedly swell up to become novae and others blow up into supernovae. There are different kinds of supernovae, the most interesting currently is the Supernova 1A (SN 1A), which has a specific luminosity (brightness) allowing astronomers to measure their distance and thus estimate the size of the Universe and whether it is expanding or not. Presently, it seems the Universe is expanding and will continue to do so forever. Might we ask what 'forever' means!

We've already seen that planets come in several sizes and types. Mars, Earth, Venus and Mercury are primarily iron, nickel and silicon. Jupiter, Saturn, Neptune and Uranus are mostly hydrogen and helium with an iron-nickel-silicon core. Then there are moons of all sorts. Some like our Moon are relatively inactive, others like Jupiter's Io have volcanoes spewing out noxious gases. Europa has a water-ice surface. One could go on cataloguing the marvels of the heavens for days.

Then there is the microcosm of atoms, molecules and subatomic particles–the quantum world with all its incomprehensible mysteries

---

8   Dark matter and dark energy make up well over half of the Universe and we have yet to identify these portions of the Universe.
9   A kilogram is 2.2 pounds.
10   Op. cit. Aczel, A. D. 2001.

as discussed in Chapter 10. We've seen electrons that spin in a perfectly coordinated dance (entanglement) even though separated by millions of miles. Some particles, such as electrons, can be in two places at one time, light rays are both waves and particles and there are virtual particles that turn into real particles for no reason and pop out of existence just as quickly and mysteriously. There are fields of energy throughout the Universe that are unobserved until some of their energy appears out of nowhere. And I have talked about 'ghost' particles that aren't real until we look for them.

As we have seen, there are four fundamental forms of energy in the Universe that keep the Universe interacting properly. There are photons, gluons, neutral Z and charge W particles and presumably gravitons to hold everything together. Then there are a host of particles including electrons, protons, neutrons quarks, bosons and their antiparticles such as positrons that are positively charged twins of electrons. These and many, many more micro- and macro- objects that make up and keep the Universe running and in the process boggle the mind. One finds it hard enough to memorize their names, not to mention what they are, what they do and how they do it.

The biological microcosm has its own array of mysterious molecules that make life possible and give us blue or brown eyes, straight or curly hair and thousands of other characteristics. DNA tells every living thing how to build, keep itself going and inform the next generation about its makeup. DNA has a four 'letter' alphabet: A, T, G and C with which it writes the great biological novel. Reading the DNA code with its puny alphabet, we can identify mental illness, diagnose and treat diseases, map the movement of ancient peoples, determine when they started moving and where they came from. We can find our ancestors and relatives including fathers and mothers, brothers and sisters. It is possible to figure out what causes some diseases and whether we have passed them on to our children. And of course, we can find and convict criminals using DNA.

Biology and medicine tell us how the body works, why it heals and what causes diseases ranging from diabetes to Dengue Fever (a tropical viral disease with bleeding tendencies that has made its way into the United States recently). Medical school consists largely of memorizing anatomical parts, normal and pathological anatomy and physiology, signs and symptoms of diseases and how to treat them. The process is grueling. The world of medicine, like all other disciplines in science, is very, very complex. There are few simple answers. Positing a soul or praying to a spirit doesn't explain or cure any disease. Double-blind studies to determine the benefits of prayer have yielded negative results. To explain these results one is told that God doesn't like being tested or that ITs ways are unfathomable. These explanations are unhelpful at best. If we are to find a rational God to better understand our world, a God that stirs our emotions, fills us with awe and gives us solace, IT cannot be a spirit and IT can neither be simple nor provide simple answers. The world and God are too intricate to provide easy answers that meet the thinking person's needs.

THE SOUL IS NOT SIMPLE

Genesis tells a simple story about the beginning of the world and the creation of all earthly creatures–simple and incredible. Bible stories are helpful for children or others who like easy solutions. Myths have been shown to be useful in some populations such as the young and fundamentalists. Faith makes for easy answers. Many fervent faithful 'just know' in their heart of hearts that what the Bible tells them is infallibly true. For the creationist, Genesis says it all. But as we saw in an earlier chapter, how we got here is not so simple. We didn't just pop into existence over six days. It took billions of years for the millions of species that have been and are now roaming Earth to evolve. In fact, if Noah were to pack into the ark even one pair of each species, it would have taken many hundreds, maybe thousands of years to build such a large vessel and thousands of people to care for all these creatures even for only forty days–an impossible task. We don't know exactly how many species there are on Earth but estimates run into the millions. There are probably a million or more insects alone. At any rate, Creationism is an explanation that fails the test of rational analysis. Evolution, on the other hand, provides a scientifically sound system for the development of all species.

Plato posited a simple soul because in order for the human soul to be immortal it could have no 'working parts'. A simple, undivided soul, Plato claimed, would be immortal and he believed there was an afterlife, although Hades, the Greek hell, was not a fiery place as is the Christian Hell. Also, the Elysian Fields, the Greek version of heaven, though a pleasant place was not like the Christian Heaven. A soul composed of component parts is necessarily corruptible, mortal and thus was unacceptable to Plato. Christian theology essentially adopted this scheme of the soul. The same is true for the Christian God. IT has to be simple in order to be immortal and eternal.

Our complex world requires complex, verifiable explications. The Neo-Natural God has to be complex. Only science is up to the task. Mathematics can help but religion, philosophy, mythology and mysticism provide only half-truths, half-solutions and often misleading answers. Religion has created divisions and driven us farther from the truth–often it is part of the problem rather than part of the solution. On the other hand, religion has also fostered good science as noted in chapter 3. Currently, the major religious obstructionists are Jewish, Christian and Islamic fundamentalists.

NEO-NATURAL SOLUTIONS

After Francis Crick and James Watson, along with Rosalind Franklin, worked out the structure of DNA, Crick moved on to study brain function. Crick's book, *The Astonishing Hypothesis,* is subtitled *The Scientific Search for the Soul* and in it he attempts to describe the manifold functions of the brain especially as relates to vision.[11] He readily admits that research in the field is far from complete. The brain is a very complicated organ. It contains trillions of nerve cells (neurons) and even more nerve-to-nerve connections (synapses). The more interconnections between neurons, the more sophisticated are its operations. The brain is capable of millions of tasks including sensation, muscle function, emotional responses, social, sexual and intellectual activities and yes, consciousness. It can monitor and moderate behaviors, remember a manifold number of facts, integrate information, make judgments, initiate ethical behavior, imagine real and fanciful beings, recognize faces, vertical and horizontal lines, estimate the passing of time, see, hear, taste, feel and smell–a seemingly endless array of activities. The list goes on and on and neuroscience is daily finding more and more about the brain and its many mysteries.

It is an easy thing to attribute all these functions to the soul but it is unquestioned that the brain has focal and synaptic connections that can explain many of the above listed activities. We know things happen in the brain that control emotions, store data and make the muscles work. To simply claim it is the soul that accounts for all these activities says nothing, while brain localizations and interactions tell us a great deal about our conscious and unconscious selves. Neuroscience has predictive and practical value as does any science worthy of its name. By definition a science, including neuroscience, must give us explanations that are scientifically meaningful; practical and predictable otherwise it is only a pseudoscience. Positing a soul offers nothing of value except a sense of being 'right' or a feeling of security in a world that is often confusing and conflicted.

The scientific literature is replete with brain research. We know the memory is largely located in the hippocampus, emotions in the limbic system and speech in the (usually left) temporal lobe and there are literally thousands of journal articles that tell us about the localization of various brain functions. More interesting perhaps has been the complex interactions

---

11   Op. cit. Crick, F. 1994.

that connect various parts of the brain and code for very intricate and sophisticated activities, including even self-awareness.

Figures 11.1 and 11.2[12] show the major parts of the brain. The front of the brain (frontal lobe) controls higher functions including reason, awareness and conscious control of behaviors. The prefrontal lobe (the front of the frontal lobe) appears to be most involved in these processes. The parietal lobe deals with muscle movements and sensation. There are certain parts of the parietal lobe that control motion and feeling in specific parts of the body. The occipital lobe (back of the brain) is the visual area. A lesion in this region can cause blindness even if the eyes are functioning normally. The cerebral cortex (gray matter) provides conscious awareness of what is going on in and around us. The hypothalamus connects the brain to the various hormone-producing glands involved in metabolism, sexual activity and fight/flight responses. The cerebellum coordinates many activities including the smooth motion of the arms and legs as well as coordinated speech. The thalamus connects the parietal lobe to the muscles and is often affected in strokes. The pons and medulla manage breathing and heart contractions. The amygdala, fornix, and mammillary bodies are part of the limbic system that is involved in emotional responses. And the olfactory area is where we recognize smells.

The functions listed above have been known for some time but recent research has brought to light many new and revealing brain activities. The hippocampal areas of the brain shrink (atrophy) in patients with Alzheimer's disease which makes sense because memory loss is a major feature of this disorder. Recent studies have provided more details about how the hippocampus works. Apparently, the brain can make 'maps' of our environment and certain cells (place cells) are involved in this task.[13] In addition, there are several different types of cells in the hippocampus that are involved in orienting a person during varying environmental conditions. For example, we may drive home different ways and there may be new buildings along the way. All these variables are accounted for in the hippocampus and allow us to make it home in spite of these novel alterations. Loss of these cells can account for Alzheimer's patients getting lost on the way home. The soul would have nothing to do with such functions or malfunctions. The traditional explanation given by theologians is that the soul mediates its function through the brain. If the brain is damaged the brain can't do its work of mediation. This seems implausible and redundant. Besides we have

12   Netter, F. H. 1972, *The CIBA Collection of Medical Illustrations*, (Summit, NJ: CIBA Publishing).
13   Leutgab, S., et al. 2005, *Independent Codes for Spatial and Episodic Memory in Hippocampal Neuronal Ensembles*, Science 309:619. . This study was done using mice.

already seen that a spirit like the soul has no way of connecting with the material brain–the same old 'body-mind' dualism problem.

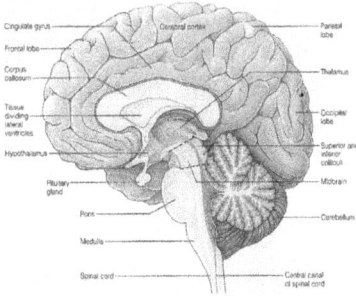

Fig. 11.1 A section cut through the center of the brain from front to back showing major areas of the brain.

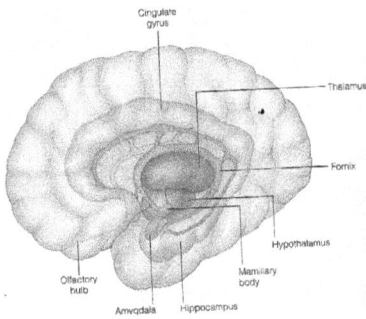

Figure 11.2. View of the left side of the brain showing some surface and internal structures.

Similar but distinct images are kept separate in our mind by a specific area of the hippocampus–the dentate gyrus and CA3 region.[14] This allows us to remain properly oriented even when we could be confused by related but separate surroundings. There are myriads of such potentially confusing situations that the brain manages to keep straight preventing disorientation when a less sophisticated brain would fail us. These and many other tasks are performed by our brain and can do so without any help from a spiritual soul.

As noted, emotions arise from the limbic system. This, however, is not a conscious area of the brain. The prefrontal lobe is associated with consciousness and in a study using magnetic resonance imaging (MRI) in humans, it was found that fear was associated with a shift in brain activity from the ventromedial i.e. lower, inner aspect of the prefrontal cortex to the periaquiductal area (around a spinal fluid duct).[15] This shift in activity was correlated with increasing dread and decreasing confidence that the person could avoid a perceived danger. Fear is undoubtedly a complex emotional response but this study helps to localize certain aspects of fear to specific brain regions, again without involvement by a soul.

14   Leutgab, S. 2008, *Detailed Differences*, Science, 319:1623-4.
15   Mobbs, D., et al. 2007, *When Fear is Near*, Science, 317:1079-83.

If there is a soul, how does it induce a fight or flight responses when epinephrine (adrenalin) seems to do this on its own? Can a material thing affect a spiritual entity and vice versa? Does the soul cause the release of epinephrine and if so, how? The soul seems superfluous in face of brain and hormonal activity. The brain does quite well on its own, it would seem. We know that stimulating certain areas of the brain will induce conscious awareness of specific brain activities. For example, electrical activation of the occipital cortex will elicit a visual image just as if the eyes were seeing the actual object. It is the electrical impulse that causes the image. The soul does nothing unless the electricity stirs the soul but then we are back to the question of how the immaterial soul can be affected by a material electrical shock.

The brain can tell time, or at least it can estimate the passage of time. We can generally tell what time of day it is; how long before I get to my daughter's house or even when it is time to wake up. Every night I set the alarm for 6:45 knowing that I don't have to get out of bed until 7:20. Rarely do I miss waking near that time. How the brain marks time is being elucidated through neuroscience. It turns out that the hypothalamus is our twenty-four hour timepiece but for shorter intervals of time such as milliseconds, minutes or hours there is no one localized area of the brain keeping time.[16] Rather, networks of neurons scattered throughout the brain including the prefrontal lobe, posterior parietal cortex and hippocampal memory areas gauge shorter time intervals. A patient with a prefrontal brain tumor will consistently underestimate short periods of time such as a few seconds. Time seems to pass quicker for these persons. Determining one color involves the V4 area of the visual (occipital) cortex but estimating how long the color remains visible involves several cortical areas–prefrontal, parietal and basal ganglion (a deeper area of the brain). Identifying color, motion or shapes is also fairly localized in the brain.

There are parts of the brain that control social activity.[17] The medial (inner) prefrontal lobe seems to be active when people make judgments about another person's mental status i.e. "thinking about other people thinking" as one author puts it. The temporo-parietal junction (border between the temporal and parietal lobes) also may be involved in assessing another person's mental states. There is evidence that feeling excluded from a social situation is mediated by the same areas in which we perceive physical pain. A sense of social loss appears to be centered in the anterior cingulate cortex–the more the sense of loss, the greater the activity in this area of the

16   Bhattacharjee, Y. 2006, *A Timely Debate about the Brain*, Science, 311:596-8.
17   Blakemore, S. J. 2006, *How Does the Brain Deal with the Social World?* Science. 314:60-1.

brain[18]. The prefrontal cortex is also involved in social loss, however, here the less the sense of loss the more the activity–just the opposite of the anterior cingulate region of the brain. These areas have been associated with physical pain as well. Attempts at localizing gender and racial biases have been made though definitive results are pending. These same authors, Eisenberger et al., had earlier demonstrated that the same neurochemicals involved in physical pain are active in psychological distress. Endorphins alleviate pain and their absence aggravates it, opiates reduce both physical and emotional anguish. Oxytocin, a hormone released from the pituitary gland, is known to enhance maternal feelings for a child. When a baby is newly born and its face is all scrunched up every woman that sees the baby will say, "Oh, how cute". A man just roles his eyes and says nothing, knowing if he tells the mother what he really thinks of the baby, it will produce an angry outburst or a flood of tears. Men just don't have enough oxytocin to see beauty in a newborn! Our souls have nothing to do with baby beauty.

Brain imaging, usually using MRI, have shown regional brain activity in a variety of emotional states; including a response to breathlessness, craving for chocolate, winning the lottery, a pleasurable response to a pretty face, musical ecstasy, sympathy for other humans, and male sexual arousal. The cingulate gyrus has two distinct 'emotion' zone's. The anterior (forward) gyrus elaborates negative feelings whereas the posterior (back of the cingulate) mediates positive responses. The central portion of the cingulate integrates or combines emotions with cognition, that is, awareness of environmental circumstances. Stressful tasks activate this area as well, sadness is associated with the cingulate and several other deeper areas of the brain. Feelings of grief and intense loneliness also show imaging activation in these regions. Both the perception of physical pain and social isolation provide survival value and support–Darwinian mechanisms that play a role in survival responses.

In Antiquity and the Middle Ages a frequent medical diagnosis was that of 'love sickness' now classified as a 'grief reaction', which can lead to full-blown depression. Now we have a definite physical localization and chemical basis for this disorder. We also know that antidepressants mediate their effects in part through the cingulate gyrus. Related feelings such as love, playfulness and friendship are all connected with the cingulate. There are many such networks in the brain that are now known to initiate and/or mediate a host of psychological and/or physiological changes. As with so many scientific discoveries, we are continuing to fill 'gaps' in our knowledge of the brain and there is less need for a spiritual soul to cover these 'gaps'. The

---

18   Panksepp, J. 2003, *The Pain of Social Loss*, Science, 302:237-9.

trend is evident, in time there will be fewer 'gaps' and the soul will be less needed.

ETHICS AND THE BRAIN

Neuroscience has identified areas of the brain involved in ethical decisions. This is basic to our understanding of morality and it is no longer valid to say scientists are unconcerned with or unable to study moral behaviors. They, in general, have been aware of these issues and are even more so today.

FAIRNESS

For a long time humans were thought to be the only creatures that exhibited 'reciprocal fairness'. Self-interest is often at odds with fairness towards others. The urge to be fair with those that are fair with you appears to be controlled by the right dorsolateral (upper outer) prefrontal cortex.[19] The left side of the brain appears not to be involved in fairness responses. The right side of the brain is also responsible for musical and mathematical skills and a stroke on the right side may cause personality changes. I've seen patients with right-sided lesions become more irritable although others are more benign in their relationships. These post-stroke changes may be related to effects of the stroke on the fairness centers.

There are also localized areas of the brain that deal with distributive justice. This ethical function is concerned with how individuals and societies distribute benefits and burdens in a just or moral manner.[20] Using MRI, it has been found that the putamen determines how to fairly distribute goods and services while a related part of the brain, the insula, encodes for inequities and the caudate/septal subgenual region provides for both efficiency and inequity. All these areas are deep structures in the brain. Such results suggest that one's awareness of rights and duties are intuitive responses related to an emotional feeling of fairness. Whether there is an inborn deontological (theory of rights and duties) ethic remains to be seen. These neurological findings suggest that ethical behaviors are mediated by the brain and not necessarily by a soul. They also support the contention that religion is not the only source for ethical standards. Parents and societal norms are also part

---

19   Koch, D., et al. 2006, *Diminishing Reciprocal Fairness by Disrupting the Right Prefrontal Cortex*, Science, 314: 829-32.
20   Hsu, M., et al. 2008, *The Right and the Good: Distributive Justice and Neural Encoding of Equality and Efficacy*, Science, 320:1092-5.

of ethical development but there seems to be some innate ethical standards with which we are born.

Recent sociobiological studies indicate that we humans possess altruistic propensities that relate to Darwinian survival instincts.[21] We tend to be most altruistic toward close family and friends but at times this behavior extends even to strangers. Much of altruism develops as a result of parenting and other environmental factors but there are also evolutionary influences that play a role in altruism of both lower animals and humans. Chimpanzees demonstrate altruism.

As mentioned, reproductive altruism is mediated through the hormone oxytocin. Obviously, there is a natural selective advantage for the mother to care for her offspring. No 'altruism gene' has been found but it is likely that there are multiple genes involved in altruism. Even children are altruistic toward their siblings at a time when they may not have been exposed to altruistic behaviors which also suggests a genetic basis for altruism. In any event, sociobiologists maintain that altruism, because of its natural selective survival benefit, has to be in some degree 'hard-wired' in the genes and not just mediated by religious influences or parental modeling. We have ample evidence to support a biological basis for altruism without enlisting an altruistic soul. It has also been shown that serotonin, a neurohormone involved in depression and anger, modulates behavioral responses to unfairness.[22] It is known that violent criminals have lower levels of serotonin, which correlates with the higher incidence of depression, anger and violent acting out found in this population.

MYSTICISM AND THE BRAIN

Mysticism and awareness of the presence of God through mystical experiences have long been of interest to theologians and psychologists. In recent years, studies have surfaced that indicate mysticism is not the sole property of religious believers. Research indicates that the mystical experience and the sense of God arising out of such encounters are associated with activity in specific areas of the brain[23] Neurotheology is the term applied to the study of brain function during spiritual experiences. Andrew Newberg and Eugene D'Aquili at the University of Pennsylvania have been studying

21   Barber, N. 2004, *Kindness in a Cruel World: The Evolution of Altruism* (Amherst, NY: Prometheus Books).

22   Crockett, M. J. 2008, *Serotonin Modulates Behavioral Responses to Unfairness*, Science, 320:1739.

23   Horgan, J. 2003., *Rational Mysticism* (New York:Mariner Books) pp. 73-90.

the physiology of mysticism for several decades. *The Mystical Mind*[24] and *Why God Won't Go Away*[25] present the results of imaging studies performed on volunteers including Catholic nuns and Buddhist monks. During contemplative prayer and Tibetan meditation the majority of subjects demonstrate increased neural activity in the prefrontal cortex and decreased function in the posterior superior parietal lobe. Their first studies involved only three nuns and eight monks. In a subsequent review article the changes in cognition, sensory perception, affect, hormonal and autonomic nervous system responses during meditative states were summarized.[26] As with all brain operations, meditation is a very complicated process. Though much has been learned about spiritual experiences, many of the neurological sequences involved in mystical encounters remain ill-defined.

As was noted at the beginning of this section, the brain is not simple. In our attempt to understand human consciousness, meditation research may provide one of the most productive areas of study. Newberg and Iversen included five studies in their review and in addition to pulse, blood pressure, hormonal and immunological studies, functional neuro-imagining were obtained on meditating subjects. These studies used computer tomography, single photon emission computed tomography (SPECT), positron emission tomography (PET) and functional magnetic resonance (fMRI). All these tests offer somewhat different advantages and disadvantages when studying the brain.

It has long been known that meditation, no matter what type, lowers blood pressure, pulse, perspiration and increases skin temperature–all part of the relaxation response. Meditation of any kind, including progressive relaxation, transcendental meditation, yoga, prayer such as saying the rosary, reading, listening to quiet music or a meditative recording and focusing on a mantra all induce relaxation-type physiology. Being listened to, comforted, emotionally supported, touched (appropriately) and sexual activity all result in positive physiological changes.

Some of these experiences are 'top down', that is, they begin cognitively and physiological changes follow. Others are 'bottom up', beginning with various activities such as dancing, running or other exercises, playing an instrument, singing or sexual intercourse and then are followed

24   Newberg, A. & D'Aquili, E. 1999, *The Mystical Mind* (Minneapolis, MN: Fortress Press).
25   Newberg, A., D'Aquili, E. & Rause, V. 2001, *Why God Won't Go Away* (New York: Ballantine Books). D; Aquili is now deceased.
26   Newberg, A., & Iversen, J. 2003, *The neural basis of the complex mental task of meditation: neurotransmitter and neurochemical considerations*, Medical Hypotheses, 61:282-991.

by the relaxation response. All these alter physiology and secondarily induce mystical brain activity. Many parts of the brain and multiple neurohormones or neurotransmitters (that excite a series of nerve cells) have been implicated in the meditative state. Neurotransmitters include glutamate, serotonin, melatonin, gamma amino butyric acid (GABA) and others. Areas of the brain affected are the right and left prefrontal cortices, the anterior nucleus of the hypothalamus, right and left thalamic reticular nuclei, hippocampus, right and left amygdala (limbic system) and, as we have seen, several other areas.

Realizing this material is complicated and the neuroanatomy and physiology unfamiliar to many readers, I mention only a few of the chemicals and brain areas involved in meditation in order to emphasize the bodily aspects that explain what is often considered functions of the soul. These data make the notion of a supernatural soul increasingly superfluous. This brief overview helps to make the point that consciousness, meditation and a host of other brain activities can be explained by other than traditional religious concepts. Both the macrocosm (Universe) and the microcosm (human beings) are unimaginably intricate creations and simple answers such as a spiritual soul or a supernatural God don't provide meaningful, descriptive or practical explanations for these many human activities.

The supernatural world was invented at a time when we looked for answers to questions that puzzled primitive and ancient peoples who were without the tools of modern science. We know more about the world today than two or three thousand years ago and it is only reasonable to revise our definition of God utilizing new scientific information. It is time for a new divine paradigm. If one is satisfied with easy answers and doesn't want to be bothered with the reality as illuminated by present day science or if one is content with a magical God as currently defined by traditional religions, then the age-old theology of the Ancients and Medievals may be enough and s/he can be satisfied with these views. If it works don't fix it. However, if such beliefs are not adequate to meet one's intellectual and emotional needs and if a person is willing to put in the time and trouble to find better (though still incomplete) solutions, then this book may help the reader in fulfilling such an awesome task. As I mentioned at the beginning, the notions the nuns and priest provided me as a child were adequate for a long time but over the years, I have felt a need for better answers that are more emotionally and intellectually meaningful. It seemed to me that it was time to move beyond religious mythology and ancient ideas. We live in a vibrant, busy world full of novel ideas that are filled with promise for astonishing insights beyond any imagined in past centuries and I want to be part of this information explosion. There is so much to learn and so little time and energy to learn it.

But rewards are found in the very effort one expends to find a meaningful God. It is, in a sense, like climbing Mt. Everest only better. There is a great view at the top but there are even more mystifying vistas and still more wonderful worlds beyond to conquer.

REDUCTIONISM

Reductionism is the school of thought that believes the Universe, including humans can be reduced to and thus explained by physical or chemical means alone.[27] This implies that human phenomena such as emotions and thoughts are to be ultimately explained by interactions of fundamental particles such as electrons, protons, atoms and molecules. A dictionary definition of reductionism is that it is an attempt or tendency to explain a complex set of facts, entities, phenomena, or structures by another, simpler set. For many scientists the Universe is eternal and uncreated–it just is. The Universe is all there is and one need not look further. The physical, mechanical workings of the world are all there is and there is nothing more that need be enlisted to explain all phenomena. There are, however, scientists that believe there is a place for God in the workings of the world including Haught,[28] Kaufmann,[29] and Polkinghorne.[30] Kauffman maintains that a reductionist view can only explain happenings and not meanings, morals or values. He holds that:

> If no natural law suffices to describe the evolution of the biosphere, of technological evolution, of human history, what replaces it? In its place is a wondrous, radical creativity without a supernatural Creator. Look out your window at the life teeming about you.

The world is full of mysteries. It may be that there is no divine agency at work in this world but until we explain everything on a purely reductionist basis there is room for some kind of divinity. Maybe atoms and laws can explain everything but why then do we see such grandeur all about us? Why do we look for anything more? Our intuition and imagination cry out for more than nuts and bolts. The workings of the world and especially

---

27   Stenger, V. J. 2009,*Quantum Gods: Creation, Chaos, and the Search for Consciousness* (Amherst, NY, Prometheus Books).

28   Haught, J. F. 2008, *God After Darwin: A Theology of Evolution* (New York: Perseus Books).

29   Kauffman, S. A. 2008, *Reinventing the Sacred* (New York: Basic Books).

30   Polkinghorne, J. *Quantum Physics and Theology: An Unexpected Kinship* (New Haven, CT. & London: Yale University Press).

the human body are more than just a machine. There is much more than just automatic, mechanical happenings behind the mystical, physical Universes and I would suggest this is the Neo-Natural God. In the next chapter we shall investigate more thoroughly what kind of entity this God or higher power might be and how one can define the Neo-Natural God.

CHAPTER 12

THE NEO-NATURAL GOD

A DIVINE HISTORY

We don't know when the notion of religion or God began. The idea of some type of higher power or God probably dates to at least 300,000 B.C.E. and possibly earlier. The Neanderthals (*Homo neanderthalensis*) began burying their dead about this time and soon after included tools and other artifacts, suggesting that they believed in an afterlife. The *Homo sapiens'* concept of God dates to at least 45,000 B.C.E. and probably much earlier. Archeological evidence from cave art in France and elsewhere supports this belief and it is likely that a human divine archetype extends back much further.

Religion as we know it appears to have come from proto-Indo-European sources. This form of religion led to both Vedic mythology and proto-Indo-Iranian religion that was the basis of early Mesopotamian religions. The first written accounts of these religions are provided by the Sumerians, dating to around 3000 B.C.E. Ancient Babylonian, Egyptian, Greek and Roman polytheistic sects followed.

The first recorded monotheism appeared around 1400 B.C.E. during the reign of the Egyptian pharaoh, Akhenaton. This was short lived as the idea was met with general resistance by noblewo/men and commoner alike. However, beginning around 600 B.C.E. there emerges the first persistent monotheisms, which included Zoroastrianism, Mithraism and, of course Judaism followed by Christianity and Islam.

Judaism may have been initially polytheistic though some modern Jewish scholars would dispute this. Nonetheless, it is probably not a coincidence that monotheistic Zoroastrianism emerged in the sixth century B.C.E. about the same time that the Jews were freed from Babylonian captivity in the mid sixth century B.C.E. The Jews are said to have been in Babylon from 582 B.C.E. to 538 B.C.E. The Old Testament records several instances of Jewish polytheism as opposed to adoration of Yahweh as the one and only true God. The story of the golden calf is a typical example of Jewish apostasy in the early history of the Jews:

> 1 When the people saw that Moses was so long in coming down from the mountain, they gathered around Aaron and said, "Come, make us gods (1 Exodus 32).

Not infrequently, the sufferings that the Jews endured were blamed on their failure to accept Yahweh as the one true God. It is also known that the Canaanites, who were polytheists, influenced Jewish heretical beliefs early on.

Many Greeks may have been monotheists as well.[1] Plato posited the "Good" as the ultimate Form. This was later adopted by Augustine in his attempt to Christianize Greek philosophy. Aristotle also portrayed God as the 'Unmoved Mover'. Though not a creative power, this was Aristotle's ultimate divinity. For that matter, the Egyptian Ra was the Sun God and held authority over all other gods. The same was true for Zeus (the Roman Jupiter). There was a 'top divine dog' in most religions. Baal played this role in Babylonian theology and Enlil was at one point the supreme deity for the Sumerians.

The progression from animism to polytheism to monotheism was a gradual process. Similarly the evolution from an anthropomorphic to a metaphysical God and finally a hybrid AG?MG also took time. For the Mesopotamians there was always 'something' that preceded the world. The God of Genesis was the first true creative God. Prior to this, the supreme deity was the organizer of the original uncreated chaos. The unmoved world was eternal for Aristotle and his 'Unmoved mover' put it in motion. Atoms were uncreated primary elements according to Democritus and the other atomists. However, the Jews, at least after the Babylonia captivity, professed that God created the world out of nothing. There was no primordial chaos as had been the case previously. Notwithstanding this, the original monotheistic God was largely anthropomorphic. Only over time did IT take on the character of a truly metaphysical being. The Gnostic God was probably the first truly metaphysical and fully transcendent being. For the Gnostics everything that was accomplished, including creation, was done through a semi-divine mediatrix, Sophia. It was with the Gnostics that we find the first infinite, eternal, omnipotent, omniscient, all-perfect and totally aloof higher power. This God may have been the last fully metaphysical deity.

---

1   Vex, P. 1988, *Did the Greeks Believe in Their Myths?: An Essay on the Constitutive Imagination*, trans. P. Wissing (Chicago: University of Chicago Press).

Once Christianity flowered, God became a hybrid–part anthropomorphic and part metaphysical. God had to be both transcendent and imminent in order to meet all the psychological and intellectual needs of both the faithful and theologians even though these two characteristics are incompatible.

As with everything, religion is an evolving entity. Along this line, Cumont notes:

> The ancient beliefs of the Persians had been forcibly subjected in Babylon to the influence of a theology that was based on the science of the day and the majority of the gods of Iran had been likened to the stars worshiped in the valley of the Euphrates.[2]

This has been true of all ages. In any speculative endeavor, whether philosophical, religious or poetic, we can do no better than what the current state of scientific knowledge allows us. Everything else can only be based on reason, intuition, feelings, wishes and wants and all of these are fallible. However, as our database grows, we are able to develop better hypotheses, discover actual laws and define more rational and workable paradigms. As sophisticated as we are today, new facts continually emerge and enhance our thinking. This leads to intellectual progress–to a better more practical and productive society–a world that improves life for all of us. Today's science is tomorrow's religion.[3] This is not a new idea. Paul Carus expressed this notion over 100 years ago:

> We must investigate the religious problem and replace the old errors, with their dualistic superstitions, by sound and scientifically correct views [4]

At the beginning of this book the claim was made that everyone except for an occasional psychotic, knows that there is a 'higher power' in this Universe of ours. It is evident that none of us is at the top of the cosmic heap. Even atheists must face this reality. The question of a divinity, God or higher power in the final analysis boils down to how one defines this ultimate entity. For the many reasons given above, God as traditionally defined is not logically acceptable. God cannot be a spirit and rule the physical world nor can God be like humans and oversee the supernatural realm. IT cannot be metaphysical in this physical world.

2   Cumont, J. 1903, *The Mysteries of the Mithra* (Kindle Edition) Location 1258.
3   This is a cogent quote from my wife, Rachel.
4   Carus, P. 1900, *The History of the Devil and the Idea of Evil* (Kindle Edition) p. 404.

Polytheism is just another form of anthropomorphism and the transcendent God is another type of MG. Could God be pantheistic or panentheistic as Spinoza suggested? This might be a possibility but then we are faced with the problem of differentiating between God and the Universe. If God is the Universe, then we are all pieces of God. Moreover, how can we be free and truly individual if we are part of the deity? Also, wouldn't we know that we are little bits of God? God after all is omniscient. God, in any of ITs aspects (though God as a spirit can't have different aspects or parts) would still be omniscient. In reading Spinoza's *Ethics*, it is immediately evident that his pantheistic God is highly metaphysical and thus extremely speculative and essentially unknowable by humans.

We also know from quantum mechanics that the world is not deterministic. Many atheists would say that the Universe is but one big machine and that is all there is. Yet, from the foregoing, it appears the world is not simply a massive automaton. Heisenberg's uncertainty principle tells us that the Universe is full of chance happenings. All behaviors, including human acts, can only be predicted on the basis of probability theory. There are no absolute certainties, all animals, human or otherwise, make irrational decisions. Laplace's billiard ball Universe is passé. The Ancients spoke of Fortune or Fate as the goddess that dealt us a chancy life scenario. What happens to each of us in the course of our lives is, indeed, fickle and fortuitous. Obviously we have some say-so over what life brings us but much of life is beyond our control. The world is a combination of decisions we make and the daunting consequences that follow. Rachel and I have been married nearly fifty years; however, what brought us together was a combination of lucky circumstances. Each of our lives might have turned out much differently. This is true for most of us. Very little is set in stone at birth. This is part of the mystery of life.

There are many mysterious events in the cosmos. Any object large or small may be both a particle and a wave simultaneously. One particle can be in two places at the same time. Electron pairs can mysteriously communicate instantaneously even if separated by millions of miles. Space curves, time slows, yardsticks shrink, causality may be questioned and people age at different rates. All these are counterintuitive notions but all have been demonstrated scientifically. We live in a very puzzling world. Where does God fit into this mystical, physical and chancy world of ours?

Neo-Naturalism is a hybrid theology. Traditional religion claims a mysterious, supernatural world and a God who created it. Atheism espouses a purely mechanical, deterministic world without a God. Religion offers a hybrid God, part human and part metaphysical and spiritual. Neo-Naturalism provides a God or higher power that is in some way bound to the Universe but is at the same time not of the Universe. The Neo-Natural God may be defined as a cosmic force, to use Santayana's phrase. However, IT has to be more than a 'force'. IT must be the universal principle that explains all the wonders and counterintuitive aspects we have examined and gives us hints about a God that is more puzzling yet more exciting and interesting than any yet defined. And along with this newly defined novel and fascinating God we get one that is logically consistent and scientifically knowable. We don't have to worry about whether IT had a virgin mother or rose from the dead–all of which are really meaningless in terms of our daily lives–but rather we can fuss over why this 'divine' world of ours is the way it is and as an added bonus, receive practical benefits that flow from science and make our lives better and more bountiful. What a theological deal!

Paul Tillich views God as not possessing 'being' in the same sense the Universe does. As humans, we have 'being' but not so with God or the higher power. Tillich sees God as the basis of 'being', IT provides the underpinnings for 'being' as we know it. God transcends 'being', this would be another example of God's non-anthropomorphism. If we imagine God as having 'being' in the same respect that ITs creatures have 'being', we are guilty once again of viewing God as we view ourselves. To do so is to put God in the same class or category that includes the set or class of all creatures including us humans. To do this leaves God bound to human ideas and concepts. We are using our Euclidian world to define God; this is not possible. God is to be defined within the realms of relativity and quantum theory or whatever scientific paradigm best fits with our current understanding of the Universe at any given time in the future. It may be that String Theory will provide the best divine definition in the twenty-second century–who is to say?

Deifying natural objects is nothing new. There have been Sun and Moon worshipers as well as cults associated with glades, rivers, groves and any number of natural places and phenomena. Zoroastrianism and its religious offspring, Mithraism[5] deified the four elements of Empedocles: fire, air, water and earth. They also considered the four winds and four seasons to be divine. Plato, Aristotle and Augustine viewed the stars as divine or semi-divine. Nature has always captured the imagination of humans and what we could not understand we deified. All things mysterious and seemingly magical were held in awe. Could it be that our monotheistic deity is simply a personification of all these mystical, physical phenomena? Freud thought so.

---

5   Zoroastrianism and Mithraism as outgrowths of the proto-Indo-Iranian religions ultimately evolved into Judaism and Christianity. They were both monotheisms with Zoroaster and Mithras as the prototypes of Christ. Many of their religious tenets were similar to those of Judaism and Christianity. Mithra, for example, was also born on December 25th, died, was resurrected and will come for a final judgment.

Today, however, we are confronted by mystical, physical happenings that are truly baffling, counterintuitive and which confound our earthbound imaginations. Nonetheless, all these awesome, at times eerie events are empirically demonstrated to be actual, factual realities. I am not suggesting that we deify these physical phenomena, though they seem divine at times. Rather, the mysteries of the physical world provide clues to how one might view the Neo-Natural God. They give us a glimpse of the divine–a window into ITs nature. It is crucial that we not define this God in any anthropomorphic or metaphysical way. This will only pull us back into the logical maelstrom we find ourselves in when trying to define God using these conventional theological concepts. Employing the mystical, physical Universe to lead us to a better understanding of God does not guarantee that we will succeed in developing a fully intuitive concept of God. The likelihood is that this will never happen. However, it will provide a better vision of the divine–one that is still awesome, wondrous and worthy of worship.

We have seen in outline what the Neo-Natural God is not. What are the positive aspects of the Neo-Natural God:

1. IT is defined and known through Nature.
2. IT is intricately connected to Nature.
3. IT cannot be thought of as outside Nature.
4. IT provides the basis for Nature and 'being' itself.
5. The mysteries of the Universe are the only divine mysteries.
6. As our knowledge of the Universe expands so will our knowledge of God.
7. God takes care of us through Nature and its laws.
8. God and thus Nature are probabilistic.
9. Ethics is defined by human nature and our position in society.
10. God provides us with free will and thus we are responsible for our behaviors.
11. God is defined by Nature, its laws and mysteries.

This definition tells us a lot about God but leaves many unknowns. The fact is that, as theologians have told us for centuries, we cannot know God perfectly. Nonetheless this description of the Neo-Natural God provides a rational and meaningful deity.

In addition, this God can fulfill our religious and spiritual needs and allow us to maintain the role of religion that is so integral to the lives of many billions of humans. Religion or spirituality cannot be dismissed as intellectually barren as the neo-atheists suggest. The human need for spiritual experiences and community are too deeply imbedded in human nature to deny wholesale. A redefined Neo-natural God overcomes the objections the atheists and neo-atheists raise to undermine the value and virtue of religion.

Tillich does believe in a personal God and I think this idea is no longer tenable if one is to properly define God in light of modern science. Nonetheless, nature has ways of taking care of its creatures. This is what evolution by natural selection is all about. This is why we have evolved feelings of fairness, altruism and caring. When we are empathic this helps us as well as others. We try to take care of ourselves as well as others because this makes the world better. This system may be as personal and providential if not more so than is the world of traditional religion because we are asked to take care of each other in times of need. In fact, religion is part of this personal and providential process but not the only part. God works through each of us to help each other.

There are many unanswered questions about the Universe that need to be resolved and there is room within this mystical, physical, neo-naturalistic world for some kind of divine force or power but none like any of which we have yet conceived. This higher power will have to be associated with or underlie all the complexities of the Universe including the many counterintuitive phenomena discussed above. IT cannot be magical, supernatural, metaphysical or anthropomorphic. Such a deity is too constrained and conflicted for the world of quanta and relativity. If the deity 'takes care' of us humans, IT does so through Darwinian selective forces, physical laws and the pure milk of human kindness. Nonetheless, we are being taken care of–we have developed and survived as a species for at least 200,000 years. We see evil in the world because we are forever adapting to an ever-changing environment. This is the way of the world. Religion is one resource we humans have used for centuries to provide succor and security within our local and global societies. We cannot influence the neo-natural God through prayer but rather through our family, friends and neighbors. Nonetheless, there are forces at play that allow us to not only survive but also enjoy life. This kind of providence is not to the liking of many religious faithful but this is the reality of our uncertain Universe. If nothing else, this world of ours is full of beauty and majesty that shouts for something more than electrons, energy, universal laws and billiard balls. Even if there is no God of traditional religion, no personal, providential and loving AG, still we as humans can look for a universal 'something' through which we can connect and with which we may explain the mysteries and wonders of Carl Sagan's *Cosmos*. We need a God we can reach out to, if only emotionally and spiritually, in order to satisfy certain basic human needs. Such a God can provide us with the awe and aesthetics we find in the cosmos. To offer nothing more than an uncaused, mechanical but eternal material Universe as the materialistic atheists do, seems just as, if not more counterintuitive, than any of the mystical, physical phenomena we have discussed.

Quantum and relativity theories have shown us that the world is not simply mechanical, ours is not a deterministic world. Even the very idea of matter or a material world is obsolete. The world of physics can no longer be thought of as fixed, firm and predictable. Things pop in and out of existence all the time. Fred Hoyle may have been right in suggesting that matter is continuously being created to fill the expanding Universe. We know space is being created continuously. Something must be created at the same time to fill this space. Are these self-created entities? Certain particles don't exist until some conscious being begins to study them. Do we create these particles just by looking for them? What force underlies this creative activity? It certainly is not any of the forces as defined by Newton. Might we not call this force or power the Neo-Natural higher power or divinity?

If there is any point I would like to leave with you, the reader, it is that the higher power whatever IT may be is nothing like anything we have encountered heretofore. IT must be some incomprehensible infrastructure that gives being to the Universe. IT must be as mysterious as the macro- and microcosm IT supports and IT is nothing like *Homo sapiens*. The higher power is intrinsically bound to this mystical, physical world that continues to stir our imagination and motivate us to search for new and daunting discoveries every day. We are on an exciting journey of discovery. Discovering God is part of this journey.

BIBLIOGRAPHY

Abel, T., et al. 2002, *The Formation of the First Star in the Universe*, Science, 295:93-98.

Aczel, A. D. 2001, *The Mystery of the Aleph* (New York: Washington Square Press).

Alpher, R. A., & Herman, R. 1948, *Microwave Radiation from the Big Bang*, Nature, 263; z775-778.

Ambrose, S. 2001, *Paleolithic Technology and Human Evolution*, Science, 291:1748-1753.

Argyle, M. 2000, *Psychology and Religion: An Introduction* (New York: Routledge).

Aristotle, 1984, *On the Soul, The Complete Works of Aristotle*, 402^{a}1-5 (Princeton, NJ: Princeton University Press).

Baba, H., et al. 2003, Homo erectus *Caldarium from the Pleistocene of Java*, Science, 299:1384-88.

Bacon, F. 1998, *Opus Magnus*, trans. R. Belle (New York: Kesinger).

Bailyn, C. 2001, *High-Energy Astrophysics: A New Spin on Black-Hole Mass*, Nature, 414:499-501.

Bains, S., et al. 2000, *Termination of Global Warmth at the Palaeocene/Eocene Boundary through Productivity Feedback*, Nature, 407:171-174.

Ball, P. 1999, *The Self-Made Tapestry Pattern Formation in Nature* (New York: Oxford University Press).

Ball, P. 2004, *Artificial Cells Take Shape*, Nature, 6 December 2004 (Online News).

Balter, M. 1999, *Restorers Reveal 28,000-Year-Old Artworks*, Science, 283:1835.

Balter, M. 2004, *Dressed for Success: Neanderthal Culture Wins Respect*, Science, 306:40-41.

Barber, N. 2004, *Kindness in a Cruel World* (Amherst, NY: Prometheus Books).

Bard, E. 2001, *Extending the Calibrated Radiocarbon Record*, Science, 292:2443-44.

Barnsky, A. D., et al. 2004, *Assessing the Causes of Late Pleistocene Extinctions on the Continents*, Science, 306:70-75.

Bartlett, R. 2008, *The Natural and Supernatural in the Middle Ages* (New York: Cambridge University Press).

Bauval, R., & Gilbert, A. 1994, *The Orion Mystery* (New York: Three Rivers Press).

Berra, T. 1990, *Evolution and the Myth of Creationism* (Stanford, CA: Stanford University Press).

Bertranpetit, J. 2000, *Genome, Diversity, and Origins: The Y-chromosome as a Storyteller*, PNAS, 97:6927-6929.

Bethe, M. 1996, *Darwin's Black Box: The Biochemical Challenge to Evolution* (New York: Simon & Schuster).

Biology Analysis Group, 2004, *A Draft Sequence for the Genome of the Domesticated Silkworm* (Bombyxmore), Science, 306:1937-1940.

Boccaccio, G. *Decameron: Second tale of the first day.* (New York: W. W. Norton).

Boethius, 1962, *The Consolation of Philosophy*, trans. R. H. Green (Indianapolis, IN, Bobbs-Merrill).

Brady, P. R., et al. 1992, *Cauchy Horizon Singularity without Mass Inflation*, Physical Review, 97:60-64.

Brasier, M., & Anticline, J. 2004, *Decoding the Ediacaran Enigma*, Science, 305:1115-1117.

Broom, D. M. 2004, *The Evolution of Morality and Religion* (Kindle Edition).

Brown, P., et al. 2004, *A New Small-Bodied Hominim from the Late Pleistocene of Flores, Indonesia*, Nature, 431:1055-1061.

Buckle, R. van, et al. 2004, *The Building Blocks of Planets within the "Terrestrial Region" of Protoplanetary Discs*, Nature, 432:479-482.

Buser, R. 2000, *The Formation and the Early Evolution of the Milky Way Galaxy*, Science, 287:69-74.

Cahill, T. 1996, *How the Irish Saved Civilization* (New York: Anchor Books).

Caponigri, A. R. 1963, *A History of Western Philosophy: Philosophy from the Renaissance to the Romantic Age* (Notre Dame, IN: University of Notre Dame Press).

Carpenter, E. 1996, *The Origins of Pagan and Christian Beliefs* (London: Senate Random House).

Carroll, B.W., & Ostlie, D.A. 1996, *An Introduction to Modern Astrophysics* (New York: Addison-Wesley Publishing Company).

Castleden, R. 1987, *The Stonehenge People* (New York: Routledge & Kean Paul).

Cavelli-Sfoza, L. L., et al. 1988, *Reconstruction of Human Evolution: Bringing Together Genetic, Archeological, and Linguistic Data*, PNAS, 85:6002-6.

Cela-Conde, C. J., & Ayala, F .J. 2003, *Genera of the Human Lineage*, PNAS, 100:7684-89.

Chou, H. H., et al. 2002, *Inactivation of CMP-N-acetylneuraminic acid Hydroxylase Occurred Prior to Brain Expansion During Human Evolution*, PNAS, 99:11736-41.

Conroy, G. C., et al. 1998, *Endocranial Capacity in an Early Hominid Cranium From Sterkfontein, South Africa*, Science, 280:1730-31.

Copleston, F. 1957, *A History of Philosophy*, vol. II (Westminster, MD: Newman Press).

Crick, F. 1994, *The Astonishing Hypothesis: The Scientific Search for the Soul* (New York: Simon & Schuster).

Crockett, M. J. 2008, *Serotonin Modulates Behavioral Responses to Unfairness*, Science, 320:1739.

Crowe, M. J. 1990, *Theories of the World from Antiquity to the Copernican Revolution* (New York: Dover).

Dante Alighieri, 1950, *The Divine Comedy, Purgatories,* Canto XXXII. (New York: Random House, Modern Library).

Darwin, C. 1979, *Origin of Species* (New York: Hilliard Wang).

Davies, P. 1993, *The Mind of God* (New York: Simon & Schuster).

Davis, P. 1983, *God and the New Physics* (New York: Simon & Schuster).

Dawkins, R. 2008, *The God Delusion* (New York: Mainer Gooks).

De Chardin, P. T. 1950, *The Phenomenon of Man*, trans. B. Wall (New York: Harper & Row).

Deforms, M. 2001, *Stability and Instability of the Cauchy Horizon for the Spherically Symmetric Einstein-Maxwell-Scalar Field Equation*, Ann. Mathematics, 158:875-925.

Denham, T. P., et al. 2003, *Origins of Agriculture at Kuku Swamp in the Highlands of New Guinea*, Science, 301:189-93.

Dennett, D.C. 2007, *Breaking the Spell: Religion as a Natural Phenomenon* (New York: Penguin).

Dick, S. J. 1982, *Plurality of Worlds: The Origins of the Extraterrestrial Life Debate from Democritus to Kant* (Cambridge, UK: Cambridge University Press).

Doolittle, R. F. 1983, *Probability and the Origins of Life,* in *Scientists Confront Creationism,* ed. L.R. Godfrey (New York: W.W. Norton & Co.).

Draper, J. W. 2007, *History of the Conflict Between Religion and Science* (Charleston, NC: Nab Press).

Duggen, C. 1994, *A Concise History of Italy* (Cambridge, UK: Cambridge University Press).

Durant, W. 1957, *The Reformation* (New York: Simon & Schuster).

Ebert, D. 1998, *Experimental Evolution of Parasites,* Science, 282:1432-35.

Eggers, D., et al. 2005, *Hubble Space Telescope Observations of Star-Forming Regions in NGC 3994/3995,* Astronomical J. 129:136-48.

Ehrman, B. D. 2005, *Misquoting Jesus: The Story Behind Who Changed the Bible and Why* (San Francisco: HarperOne).

Erasmus, D. 1993, *The Praise of Folly and Letters to Marten Van Door,* trans. B. Raise (London: Penguin).

Feuerbach, L. 1989, *The Essence of Christianity* (Buffalo, NY: Prometheus).

Flynn, G. J., et al. 2003, *Chemical and Mineralogical Analysis of an Extraterrestrial Particle in Aerogel,* Lunar and Planetary Science, 35:18-22.

Foley, R. 1998, *The Context of Human Genetic Evolution,* Genome Research, 8:339-47.

Garber, J. J. 2008, *Harmony in Healing: The Theoretical Basis of Ancient and Medieval Medicine* (New Brunswick, NJ: Transaction Publishers).

Genteel, R. 2003, *Near-Infrared Flares from Accreting Gas around the Supermassive Black Hole at the Galactic Center,* Nature, 425:934-37.

Gibbons, A. 1998, *Which of Our Genes Makes Us Human?* Science, 281:1432-34.

Gibbons, A. 2002, *In Search of the First Hominids*, Science, 295:1214-19.

Gibbons, J. C. 2009, *The Faith of Our Fathers* (Charlotte, NC: Tan Publishing).

Godfrey, L.R. 1983, *Creationism and Gaps in the Fossil Record*, in *Scientists Confront Creationism*, ed. L. Godfrey (New York: W. W. Norton & Co.).

Goren-Unbar, N., et al. 2004, *Evidence of Hominim Control of Fire at Gusher Benot Ya'aqov, Israel*, Science, 304:725-27.

Gott III, J. R., & Li, L. 1998, *Can the Universe Create Itself?* Physical Review, 58:1-43.

Gould, S. J. 1999, *Rocks of Ages: Science and Religion in the Fullness of Life* (Library of Contemporary Thought) (New York, Ballantine Books).

Grant, E. 1996, *Planets, Stars and Orbs: The Medieval Cosmos, 1200-1687* (New York: Cambridge University Press).

Grant, P. R., & Grant, B. R. 2002, *Unpredictable Evolution in a 30-Year Study of Darwin's Finches*, Science, 296:707-11.

Grant, R. 2006, *Storm* (Eugene, OR: Wipe & Stock Publishers).

Greiner, J., et al. 2001, *An Unusually Massive Stellar Black Hole in the Galaxy*, Nature, 414:522-25.

Hamer, D. 2005, *The God Gene: How Faith is Hardwired into Our Genes* (New York: Anchor Books).

Hanegraaff, H. 1998, *The Face That Demonstrates the Farce of Evolution* (Nashville, TN: World Publishing).

Harold, F. B., & Eve, R. A. (Eds.) 1995, *Cult, Archaeology and Creationism: Understanding Pseudoscientific Beliefs about the Past* (Iowa City, IA: University of Iowa Press)

Harris, Sam, 2006, *Letter to a Christian Nation* (New York: Alfred A. Knopf).

Haught, J. F. 2008, *God and the New Atheism* (Louisville, KY: Westminster John Knox Press).

Hesiod, 1953, *Theogeny* (New York: MacMillan).

Hitchens, C. 2007, *God is Not Great* (New York: Hachette Book Group).

Holden, C. 1997, *Archeology: Tooling Around–Dates Show Early Siberian Settlement*, Science, 275:1268-70.

Holden, C. 2001, *Oldest Human DNA Reveals Aussie Oddity*, Science, 291:230-31.

Hogan, J. 2003. *Rational Mysticism* (New York: Mariner Books).

Hubble, E. 1929, *A Relationship between Distance and Radial Velocity among Extra-Galactic Nebulae*, PNAS, 15. 167-70.

Huey, R. B., et al, 2000, *Rapid Evolution of a Geographic Cline in Size in an Introduced Fly*, Science, 287:308-9.

Hume, D. 2010, *Dialogues Concerning Natural Religion* (Kindle Book).

Hutton, N. 1968, *The Evidence of Evolution* (New York: American Heritage Publishing).

Huxley, T. 2001, *Man's Place in Nature* (New York: Modern Library).

Irenaeus, 1992, *St. Irenaeus of Lyons: Against the Heresies* (Malwah, NJ: Paulist Press).

James, W. 1902, *Varieties of Religious Experience* (New York: Modern Library).

Kaufman, S. 2008, *Reinventing the Sacred: A New View of Science, Reason, and Religion* (New York: Basic Books).

Kay, R. F., et al. 1998, *The Hypoglossal Canal and the Origin of Human Vocal Behavior*, PNAS, 95:5417-19.

Kerr, R. A. 2004, *Evidence of Huge Deadly Impact Found Off Australian Coast?* Science, 304:941-42.

Kierkegaard, S. 1973, *The Concept of Dread*, trans. W. Lowry (Princeton, NJ: Princeton University Press).

Kieth, M. S., & Anderson, G. M. 1963, *Radiocarbon Dating: Fictitious Results with Mollusk Shells*, Science, (August 16, 1963).

Kimball, C. 2002, *When Religion Become Evil: Five Warning Signs* (San Francisco, CA: Harper).

Kitagawa, H., & van der Plight, J. 1998, *Atmospheric Radiocarbon Calibration to 45 yr B.P.: Later Glacial Fluctuations and Cosmogony Isotope Production*, Science, 279:1187-90.

Klein, R. G., & Edgar, B. 2002, *The Dawn of Human Culture* (New York: Hahn, Wiley & Sons).

Klicka, J., & Akin, R. M. 1998, *Pleistocene Speciation and the Mitochondrial DNA Clock*, Science, 282:1955-59.

Knoll, A. H., & Carroll, S. B. 1999, *Early Animal Evolution: Emerging Views from Comparative Biology and Geology*, Science, 284:2129-37.

Knoll, A. H., et al. 2004, *A New Period for the Geological Time Scale*, Science, 305:621-22.

Kramer, S. N. 1959, *History Begins at Sumer* (Garden City, NY: Doubleday).

Kuhn, S., et al. 2001, *Ornaments of the Earliest Upper Paleolithic: New Insights from the Levant*, PNAS, 98:7641-46.

Leakey, M. G., et al. 1998, *New Specimens and Confirmation of an Early Age for* Australopithecus anamnesis, Nature 393:62-66.

Lehn, J-M. 2002, *Toward Self-Organization and Complex Matter*, Science; 295:2400-03.

Lewis-W. D. 2002, *The Mind in the Cave: Consciousness and the Origin of Art* (London: Thames & Hudson).

Li, L., & Lindquist, S. 2000, *Creating a Protein-Based Element of Inheritance*, Science, 287:661-4.

Licker, R. 2001, *On Counter-Intuitive Science*, www.fermentmagazine.org.

Lister, A. M., & Sher, A.V. 2001, *The Origin and Evolution of the Woolly Mammoth*, Science, 294:1094-97.

Lobo, F., & Crawford, P. 2002, *Time, Closed Timelike Curves and Causality*, http://www.zamandayolculuk.com/cetinbal/Timecurves.html.

Lorentz, H. A. 2009, *Einstein's Theory of Relativity: A Concise Statement* (Whitefish, MT: Kissinger Publishing).

Lowie, R. H. 1952, *Primitive Religion* (New York: Liveright).

Lucretius, 1951, *On the Nature of Things.* (Baltimore, MD: Penguin).

Lyell, C. 1997, *Principles of Geology* (London: Penguin).

MacArthur, J. 2001, *The Battle for the Beginning: The Bible on Creation and the Fall of Adam* (www.ThomasNelson.com: W Publishing Group).

MacLauchlan, J. 1997, *Galileo Galilei* (London: Oxford University Press).

Manuel, F. E. 1974, *The Religion of Isaac Newton*: The Fremantle Lecture 1973 (New York: Oxford-Clarendon).

Marti, M., et al. 2004, *Targeting Malaria Virulence and Remodeling Proteins to the Host Erythrocytes*, Science, 306:1939-33.

Mayer, H. E. 1988, *The Crusades*, 2nd Edit. (New York: Oxford University Press).

McEvoy, J. 2000, *Robert Grosseteste* (New York: Oxford University Press).

Mundil, R., et al. 2004, *Age and Timing of the Permian Mass Extinctions: U/Pb Dating of Closed-System Zircons*, Science, 305:1760-62.

Newberg, A., & Iveersen, J . 2003, *The neural basis of the complex mental task of meditation: neurotransmitter and neurochemical considerations*, Medical Hypotheses, 61:282-91.

Newberg, A., D'Aquili, E. & Rause, V. 2001, *Why God Won't Go Away* (New York: Ballantine Books).

Newberg, A. & D'Aquili, E. 1999, *The Mystical Mind* (Minneapolis, MN.: Fortress Press)

Newberg, A. 2009, *How God Changes Your Brain: Breakthrough Findings from a Leading Neuroscientist* (New York: Ballantine).

Nozick, R. 1981, *Philosophical Explanations* (Cambridge, MA: Bellican, Harvard University Press).

Ovchinnikov, I. V., et al., 2000, *Molecular Analysis of Neanderthal DNA from the Northern Caucasus*, Nature, 404:400-03.

Paine, T. 2003, *Common Sense, Rights of Man and Other Essential Writings of Thomas Paine* (New York: Signet Classics).

Paley, W. 2006, *Natural Theology* (New York: Oxford University Press).

Pals, D. L. 1996, *Seven Theories of Religion* (New York: Oxford University Press).

Patterson, J. W. 1984, *Thermodynamics and Evolution* in *Scientists Confront Creationism*, ed. L. Godfrey (New York: W.W. Norton & Co.).

Peters, E. 1988 *Inquisition* (Berkeley, CA.: University of California Press).

Physics Forums, 2005, *What is the Significance of the Cauchy Horizon?* http://www.physicsforums.comarchive/topic/t-52876.

Plato 1977, *Timaeus and Crito* (London: Penguin Books).

Plato, 1945, *The Republic* (New York: Oxford University Press).

Plato, 1981, *Apology*, in *Plato: Five Dialogues*, trans. G. M. A. Grube (Indianapolis, IN: Hackett).

Polkinghorne, J. 2009, *Quantum Physics and Theology: An Unexpected Kinship* (New Haven, CT: Yale University Press).

Raup, C. M. 1983, *The Geological and Paleontological Arguments of Creationism*, in. *Scientists Confront Creationism*, ed. L. Godfrey (New York: W. W. Norton & Co.).

Rink, W. J., et al. 2004, *Confirmation of Near 400 ka Age for the Yabrudian Industry at Tabun Cave, Israel*, J. of Archeological Science, 31:15-20.

Rosen, E. 1984, *Copernicus and the Scientific Revolution* (Malabar, FL: Robert E. Krieger Publishing).

Rudolph, K. 1977, *Gnosis: The Nature and History of Gnosticism*, Trans. R. M. Wilson (San Francisco: Harper).

Rumpke, N. A. 1966, *Prolegomena to a Study of Cataclysmal Sedimentation*, Quarterly of the Creation Research Society, 3:16-37.

Rutledge, R. E., et al. 2000, *A Method for Distinguishing Between Transiently Accreting Neutron Stars and Black Holes in Quiescence*. Astrophysical J., 529:985-96.

Salzburg, S. L., et al. 2001, *Microbial Genes in the Human Genome: Lateral Transfer or Gene Loss?* Science, 292:1903-6.

Seine, C. 2004, *Swiveling Satellites See Earth's Relativistic Wake*, Science, 306:592.

Seine. C. 2002, *Microwave Background: Subtle Signals in Ancient Light Promise New View of Cosmos*, Science, 297:2184.

Serene, P. C. 1999, *The Evolution of Dinosaurs*, Science, 284:2137-47.

Smith, D. J., et al. 2004, *Mapping the Antigenic and Genetic Evolution of Influenza Virus*, Science, 305:371-76.

Smith, F. H., et al. 1999, *Direct Radiocarbon Dating for India G_1 and Velika Pecina Late Pleistocene Hominid Remains*, PNAS, 96:12281-86.

Smolin, L. 2006, *The Trouble with Physics: The Rise of String Theory, the Fall of Science, and What Comes Next*. (Boston, MA: Houghton Mifflin).

Spence, L. 1990, *Ancient Egyptian Myths and Legends* (New York: Dover).

Sponheimer, M., & Lee-Thorp, J. A. 1999, *Isotopic Evidence for the Diet of an Early Hominid*, Australopithecus africanus, Science, 283:369-70.

St. Augustine, 2010, *On Grace and Free Will* (Cambridge, UK: Cambridge University Press).

Staff, 1971, Australopithecus: *A Long-Armed, Short-Legged Knuckle-Walker*, Science News, 100:347.

Stenger, V. J. 2009, *Quantum Gods: Creation, Chaos, and the Search for Cosmic Consciousness* (Amherst, NY: Prometheus Books).

Swisher, C. C., et al. 1999, *Cretaceous Age for the Feathered Dinosaur of Liaoning, China*, Nature, 400:58-61.

Thomas, L. E. & Cooper, P. E. *Mystical Experiences: An Exploratory Study*, Journal for the Scientific Study of Religion, 1978, 17(4): 433-37.

Tinkaus, E., et al. 2003, *An Early Modern Human from the Pester cu Oases, Romania*, PNAS, 100:11231-36.

Tippett, K. 2007, *Speaking of Faith* (London: Viking).

Trinkets, E. 1997, *Appendicular Robusticity and the Paleobiology of Modern Human Emergence*, PNAS, 4:13367-73.

Valladas, H., et al. 1987, *Thermoluminescence Dates for the Neanderthal Burial Sites at Kebara in Israel*, Nature, 330:159-60.

Valladas, H., et al. 2001, *Paleolithic Paintings: Evolution of Prehistoric Cave Art*, Nature, 413:479.

Verdi, G., et al. 2004, *Flint Mining in Prehistory Recorded by* in-situ-*Produced Cosmogony* ^{10}Be, PNAS, 101:7880-84.

Voltaire, 1966, *Candide* (New York: Norton & Co.).

Wade, N. 2007, *Before the Dawn: Recovering the Lost History of Our Ancestors* (New York: Penguin).

Ward, P. D., & Brownlee, D. 2000, *Rare Earth: Why Complex Life is Uncommon in the Universe* (New York: Copernicus Books).

Wells, S. 2002, *The Journey of Man* (New York: Random House).

Wells, S. 2007, *Deep Ancestry: Inside the Genographic Project* (Washington, DC: National Geographic).

White, M. 2002, *The Pope and the Heretic* (New York: HarperCollins).

Wiens, R.C., 2002, *Radiometric Dating: A Christian Perspective.* http://www. Talkorigins.org/faqs/dating.html.

Will, C. M. 1986, *Was Einstein Right?: Putting General Relativity to the Test* (New York: Basic Books).

Williams, E. J. B., & Hurst, L. D. *Proteins of Linked Genes Evolve at Similar Rates,* Nature, 407:900-07.

Yan, H. 2004, *Nucleic Acid Nanotechnology,* Science, 306:2048-49.

Yan, H., et al. 2003, *DNA-Templated Self-Assembly of Protein Arrays and Highly Conductive Nanowires,* Science, 301:1882-84.

Yan, H., et al. 2004,*Building Programmable Jigsaw Puzzles with RNA,* Science, 306:2068-70.

INDEX

guilt and shame 42

H

Hades 26, 63, 74
Harris, Sam 13, 39, 70, 152, 180, 226
Hawking, Stephen 167, 170, 183
Hegelian
  dialectic 30
Heisenberg
  uncertainty princi;e 14
Heisenberg, Werner 179, 182
Hell 11, 22, 26, 57, 61, 72, 73, 76, 77, 79, 99, 101, 124, 130, 137, 138, 142, 179, 183, 185
Henry VIII 64, 67
heresies 50, 52
Hermes 26, 143
Hinduism 126
Hindus 26, 70
hippocampus 203, 204, 210
Hitchens, Christopher 13, 180, 227
Holy Orders 45
Holy Spirit 78, 82
Homo erectus 112, 221
Hubble, Edwin 112, 164, 171, 225, 227
Humanae vitae 49
Humanism 32, 33
Hus, John 62, 63, 64
Huygens, Christian
  light as waves 165
hypothalamus 205, 210
hypothesis
  null 110
  predictions using 110

I

idealism 72
immanent 28
immorality
  among atheists 60, 62, 99, 100
Inertial frame of reference 167, 168, 169
infinite 16, 19, 20, 21, 22, 23, 24, 25, 28, 30, 31, 32, 71, 78, 126, 130, 136, 138, 148, 149, 150, 158, 164, 167, 174, 176, 197, 198, 199, 214
infinity 20
Inquisition 12, 48, 56, 57, 58, 59, 60, 67, 230
  Spanish 58
Intelligent design 68, 83, 84, 86, 87, 99, 101, 116
interactionism 71

O

P

symbolism 41, 43, 45, 196

T

Tanchelm 53
Ten Commandments 42, 175, 185
Tertullian 50
theologians 12, 14, 16, 22, 27, 30, 31, 32, 38, 49, 50, 54, 64, 65, 72, 74, 77, 78, 79, 82, 83,
    128, 132, 133, 134, 135, 139, 140, 142, 143, 144, 145, 179, 181, 182, 183, 184, 185,
    203, 208, 215
Theology
  natural 24
Tombaugh, Clyde 110
transubstantiation 45, 53, 62, 65
Triassic period 105
trilobites 105
Trinity 12, 27, 59, 65, 76, 119, 179, 185, 194
two-slit waveform 189

U

Uncertainty Principle 14, 182
uniformitarionism 105
Unitarian 12
Universe 13, 14, 16, 17, 19, 20, 24, 25, 28, 29, 30, 31, 32, 34, 35, 37, 48, 77, 78, 81, 82, 86,
    92, 94, 99, 101, 102, 111, 118, 119, 130, 131, 138, 142, 143, 144, 147, 149, 150, 151,
    152, 158, 159, 164, 168, 170, 171, 172, 173, 174, 175, 176, 177, 181, 184, 194, 195,
    196, 197, 198, 199, 200, 210, 211, 215, 216, 217, 218, 219, 220, 221, 226, 233
Usher, James 48

V

Valla, Lorenzo 64
Vatican
  Observatory 46
Venice 55, 56, 59
Venus 26, 199
VMAT2
  God gene 81
void 30
Voltaire 51, 66, 232

W

Wheeler, John 167, 191
white dwarf. 166
woman apostles 49
Wycliffe, John 62, 63, 64

www.ingramcontent.com/pod-product-compliance
Lightning Source LLC
Chambersburg PA
CBHW070346090426
42733CB00009B/1308